America's Four R  S0-AXS-313
The More or Less United States

By: Stanley Yavneh Klos
ISBN: 978-0-9752627-1-9

In this powerful, historical work, Stanley Yavneh Klos unfolds the complex 15-year U.S. Founding period, revealing, for the first time, four distinctly different United American Republics. This is history on a splendid scale -- a book about the not quite unified American Colonies and States that would eventually form a fourth republic, with only 11 states, the *United States of America: We The People.*

The More or Less United States is about human nature, ambition checking ambition, hyper-inflation, the dissolution of the U.S. *Constitution of 1777* government, the 13-year development of a U.S. Head of State, treaties, loans, and the far-reaching consequences of war won in 1784 for U.S. Independence. Above all, *America's Four Republics: The More or Less United States* is a fascinating, often surprising, story of one of the most important political founding periods in human history.

Washington? Get in Line: *"The Articles of Confederation not only formed our nation," says Stanley Klos, author of President Who? Forgotten Founders, "it was used to preserve it ... "The Presidents were the ones who held it together," says Klos, "even though our first government was a miserable failure."* - **Cover Story, U.S. News and World Report**

Chopping Down History: *"One of the declared objectives of our Constitution states, 'in order to form a more perfect union,' Mr. Klos said. "What does that say? We already had a union. We're not talking about a lie here," he continued. "George Washington was first president under the Constitution of 1787. We're talking about a half-truth."* -- **The New York Times**

"I am fortunate to have had such a high-minded opponent in this last race. Some of the tactics that you resisted are truly deplorable and represent just the sort of campaigning which so often serves to cause the American people to dislike politics and distrust politicians. I am proud to know you and glad you are a fellow West Virginian. Diogenes with a lighted lamp in broad daylight, worked the street of Athens "looking for a man" I have found one: Stan Klos." - ***Robert C. Byrd***, **U.S. Senator**

Stanley Yavneh Klos is an author, independent scholar, adjunct professor, entrepreneur, and former Italian Basketball Association player. His education includes a BA in American Studies, BS in Zoology, MA in Rhetorical Theory & Historic Public Address (all from Idaho State University) and a Ph.D. Candidacy in Communications and Marketing from Penn State. Klos also attended St. Peter's College. In 1983, upon the discovery of 18th-century Philadelphia shipping records in his attic, Klos began to research and exhibit primary source documents.

Stan has authored numerous publications while assembling rare primary source collections that have headlined a plethora of special exhibits at universities, national historic sites, libraries, and museums. Recent exhibits include the *Louisiana Bicentennial Celebration* at the state capitol, *America's Four Republics: The More or Less United States* at the Annapolis Continental Congress Festival, and *John F. Kennedy: A Wounded Nation* at the Old US Mint in New Orleans.

Stan has keynoted numerous special events including the Franklin D. Roosevelt American Heritage Center Museum's grand opening and the 2003 re-entombment of First Lady Martha & President Samuel Huntington. His work has appeared in hundreds of print and digital publications including History Channel's *Brad Meltzer's Decoded, The Declaration of Independence*, U.S. News & World Report 2006 cover story, *"Washington? Get In Line"* & the Discovery Channel's *"Unsolved History: Plots To Kill Lincoln."* He has authored five books, *President Who? Forgotten Founders; The Rise of the U.S. Presidency and the Forgotten Capitols*; *Happy Birthdays USA, Economic Home Runs*, and *America's Four Republics: The More or Less United States*.

Naomi Yavneh Klos became the first full-time Director of the University Honors Program at Loyola University New Orleans in 2011, after serving as the Associate Dean of the Honors College at the University of South Florida. A Professor of Languages and Cultures, she is the author of numerous articles on gender and spirituality in the representation of both the virginal and the maternal body in Renaissance Italy, as well as three award-winning essay collections on gender in the early modern world. She is currently completing a book, *Flights of Angels*.

A former president of the Society for the Study of Early Modern Women and founding director of the Council of Undergraduate Research's Arts & Humanities division, she is chair of the AJCU Honors Consortium and a member of the Board of Directors of the National Collegiate Honors Council. Dr. Yavneh Klos received her A.B. from Princeton University and her M.A. and Ph.D. degrees from the University of California, Berkeley, all in Comparative Literature with an emphasis in Italian Renaissance Studies. She lives with her husband, Stanley Klos, and five of their twelve children in New Orleans, Louisiana.

Acknowledgements

The second edition of this book was prepared especially for the Washington's Birthday Celebration (WBCA), a month-long event held each February in Laredo, the seat of Webb County in south Texas, which celebrates the birthday of George Washington. It is the largest celebration of its kind in the United States with approximately 400,000 attendees annually. Through the efforts of Toni L. Ruiz, our non-partisan *America's Four United Republics* exhibit of rare historic documents will be displayed at the Villa Antigua Border Heritage Museum January 21 – February 24, 2015. Mrs. Ruiz has also organized numerous events around the WBCA celebration ranging from a Texas A&M University student debate on *Who was the First President?* to a performance of the *Happy Birthdays USA* skit by middle school students. The media release for the month long festivities can be found in the appendix of this book. Thank you, Toni L. Ruiz for your hard work and inspiring this second edition.

Dr. Naomi Yavneh Klos worked diligently on the editing, keeping the work on message, and serving as the scholarly advisor required for the completion of this book. Seth Kaller, always helpful, is credited with changing the book's title from *America's Four United Republics* to its current form. The Northwest Territorial Mint did the medallion illustrations, and artist William Browning painted the *Forgotten U.S. Capitols* oil on canvas. On the academic front, special thanks are due Dr. Kenneth Bowling, Co-editor of George Washington University's *First Federal First Federal Congress Project*, who suggested expanding the research on the Continental Congress, Congress of the Confederation, and United States in Congress Assembled nomenclature; Dr. William Ewald, Professor of Law, University of Pennsylvania, for his lecture at our Annapolis *America's Four United Republics* exhibit that opened my eyes to Edmund Randolph's herculean work on framing the *Constitution of 1787*; historian Dr. Glenn Grasso for suggesting that the book contrast the respective duties of the presidents of the Continental Congress and United States in Congress Assembled; and Rodney A. Ross, Leif Durley, and their Supervisors at the Center for Legislative Archives at the U.S. National Archives who provided key primary sources necessary to complete this work.

Finally, a second thank you is extending to Dr. Bowling for his the time he spent with me explaining *Article the First* and its framing in the *Bill of Rights*. His counsel was invaluable and had I sought it in the first edition, the last chapter of this book would not have had to be re-written.

By: Stanley Yavneh Klos

Published By:

Historic.us
Palm Harbor, Florida 34683
Second Edition
ISBN: 978-0-9752627-1-9

"Time stands still; it is we who pass all too quickly through it."
- Louis A. Klos, Ph. D.

To Raphael & Kuni Yavneh in thanks for Naomi.

Historic.us is a non-profit corporation dedicated to challenging the public to view history critically through the lens of primary sources. The mission is to develop, through Historic.us exhibits, a respect for truth, the critical intelligence to seek it and a willingness to query pre-conceived notions and biases. We seek to awaken a public mastermind that recognizes the importance of incorporating primary sources into its understanding of the historic record.

Palm Harbor, Florida 34683

Edited by: Dr. Naomi Yavneh Klos

Medallion and Artwork Design by:
William Browning, Northwest Territorial Mint & Stanley Y. Klos

ISBN: 978-0-9752627-1-9

TABLE OF CONTENTS

INTRODUCTION
TAVERN TO TAVERN

*Delegates from the United Colonies of America first caucused
at the City Tavern in Philadelphia on September 1, 1774*

The transformation of the United States of America from thirteen British colonies into the current republic was a complex political process that spanned nearly 15 years. To describe this progression, many governmental institutions -- the United States Department of State, for example, and the Smithsonian Institute, divide the U.S. Republic's founding into two governmental components: the *Continental Congress,* first, and then the current U.S. tripartite system, composed of *The United States House of Representatives and Senate in Congress Assembled (U.S. Congress), The President of the United States of America, United States Supreme Court.*[1] Some historians have been more thorough and expanded this dichotomy by dividing the Continental Congress Era into three different phases: the *First Continental Congress,* The *Second Continental Con*gress, and the *Congress of the Confederation.*[2] Other historians use the term found in the Articles of Confederation, the *United States in*

---

[1] See, for example, Department of State, *Common Core Document of the United States of America* ... *"In 1783 the Continental Congress voted to establish a federal city, and the specific site was chosen by President George Washington in 1790."* Washington D.C., 2012 http://www.state.gov/j/drl/rls/179780.htm and Smithsonian Institute, Traveling exhibit: *A Glorious Burden, The American Presidency, "John Hanson was the First President of The Continental Congress,"* http://americanhistory.si.edu/presidency/home.html.

[2] See, for example, Kenneth R. Bowling," 'A Tub to the Whale': the Founding Fathers and Adoption of the Federal Bill of Rights." *Journal of the Early Republic* 8 (Fall 1988), 225

Congress Assembled,[3] rather than the *Congress of the Confederation,* for the March 1st, 1781, to March 3rd, 1789, U.S. Founding period.

In addition to the challenges posed by the diversity of the nomenclature used to described the stages of the U.S. Republic, even casual readers about this period are besieged by conflicting, dates, evidence, and facts in works (ranging from peer-reviewed scholarly essays to Wikipedia articles) that cloud fundamental issues such as discerning the true date of U.S. Independence[4] or identifying the first U.S. "Head of State"[5] or even determining what body of law was the first U.S. Constitution.[6] The U.S. Founding convolution is ubiquitously apparent in everything from school text books to Library of Congress exhibits.[7] Even the U.S. Supreme Court, in its opinions, does not recognize the lawful difference between the "Continental Congress" and the Articles of Confederation's "United States in Congress Assembled."[8] These and other U.S. Founding misunderstandings stem from the failure of scholars and politicians alike to examine properly the primary source record in order to establish a sound political timeline, framework and nomenclature for the early United American Republics that eventually formed the current Republic of the United States of America

This volume's mission is to produce a timeline, framework, and nomenclature, *drawn from primary sources,* for the four distinct republics that eventually formed the United States of America. The book's sixth chapter is dedicated to answering commonly asked United States founding questions. The final chapter discusses the

---

[3] For example, Stanley L. Klos, *President Who? Forgotten Founders.* Carnegie, PA: Estoric.com, 2004, 127.

[4] Examples include White House, *"Our Government,"* http://www.whitehouse.gov/our-government and US Department of State, *"Federal Holidays July 4, 1776,"* http://exchanges.state.gov/englishteaching/resources-et/celebrate/federal-holidays.html

[5] See, again, the Smithsonian Institute's traveling exhibit: *"A Glorious Burden, The American Presidency,"* referenced above.

[6] Robert Goldwin, for example, argues "the Articles were not a true constitution but a self-described treaty of alliance among the states." *James Madison's "Sagacious, Powerful, and Combining Mind"* Library of Congress, 2012. http://www.loc.gov/loc/madison/goldwin-paper.html.

[7] See, for example, Alan Brinkley, who declares, "The first elections under the Constitution took place in the early months of 1789. Almost all of the newly elected congressman and senators had favored ratification...." New York: McGraw Hill, 2007, p. 168 and Library of Congress *Creating the United States Exhibit*: *"Confederation Congress Elects Its First President John Hanson"* Charles Thomson to George Washington, November 5, 1781 letter, Manuscript.

[8] *"Appreciation of the Continental Congress's incapacity to deal with this class of cases was intensified by the so called Marbois incident of May 1784 ..."* Sosa v. Alvarez-Machain 542 US 692. Supreme Court of the U.S., 2004, p. 22.

possible political sabotage of *Article the First,* the first and only amendment in the 1789 *Bill of Rights,* which was not ratified by the United States.

TAVERN TO TAVERN

On October 6th, 1788, renovations commenced on the U.S. Capitol building. These renovations had been approved by the 8th United States in Congress Assembled (USCA) to build-out a floorplan designed to accommodate the new government structure called for in the U.S. Constitution of 1787. On October 8th, 1788, Congress moved the Seat of Government from the capitol building to Fraunces Tavern. Congress was able to form quorums on October 9th and 10th but the 9th USCA failed to form the quorum necessary to convene the last Confederation Congress on November 3, 1788. Nevertheless, USCA Secretary Charles Thomson and other federal officials continued to conduct the nation's business in Fraunces Tavern until March 4th, 1789, when the new government of the United States commenced in the newly renovated capitol building that was renamed "Federal Hall." The confederation republic thus faded away in a building similar to where the Continental Congress first caucused in 1774, a former British Colonial tavern.

CHAPTER I
AMERICA'S FOUR REPUBLICS:

The More or Less United States
September 5, 1774 to March 4, 1789

Before identifying the key junctures in the evolution of the United States and its republics, it is imperative that we define the term "republic*"* in its 18th-Century American context. One of the most important works on the classification of political systems during the 18th-Century was Baron de Montesquieu's work; *The Spirit of Laws* (1748). Montesquieu defined three kinds of government: republican, monarchical, and despotic. Regarding a confederation republic he averred:

> This form of government is a convention by which several smaller states agree to become members of a larger one, which they intend to form. It is a kind of assemblage of societies that constitute a new one, capable of increasing, by means of new associations, till they arrive to such a degree of power as to be able to provide for the security of the united body.[9]

From the inception of the United Colonies of America in 1774 to the Revolutionary War's concluding *Definitive Treaty of Peace* ratified in 1784, the 13 Original Colonies and States formed three distinct confederation republics that fulfilled Montesquieu's requisite of forming "new associations ... to such a degree of power

---

[9] Charles de Secondat Baron de Montesquieu, *De l'esprit des lois*. Translated and cited in Alexander Hamilton, "Federalist IX: The Utility of the Union as a Safeguard against Domestic Faction and Insurrection", *Independent Journal*, New York: November 21, 1787.

as to be able to provide for the security of the united body." According, then, to the *philosophe*'s definition, the *First United American Republic* commenced with the colonial formation of an association titled, *The Continental Congress of the United Colonies of North America.*

Alexander Hamilton, in his Federalist letter of November 1787 in which he quotes Montesquieu, goes further in defining "confederate republic" writing:

> The definition of a confederate republic seems simply to be "an assemblage of societies," or an association of two or more states into one state. The extent, modifications, and objects of the federal authority are mere matters of discretion. So long as the separate organization of the members be not abolished; so long as it exists, by a constitutional necessity, for local purposes; though it should be in perfect subordination to the general authority of the union, it would still be, in fact and in theory, an association of states, or a confederacy. The proposed Constitution, so far from implying an abolition of the State governments, makes them constituent parts of the national sovereignty, by allowing them a direct representation in the Senate, and leaves in their possession certain exclusive and very important portions of sovereign power. This fully corresponds, in every rational import of the terms, with the idea of a federal government.

In Hamilton's terms, then, a "confederacy" relies not just on a union of states under some form of federal authority, but likewise the retention by each of these states of their own governmental authorities, both subordinate to and "constituent parts of...national sovereignty."

Finally, in 1788, United States in Congress Assembled Delegate James Madison in Federalist No XXXIX defined the word "republic," placing clear emphasis on the derivation of its power from the people:

> ... we may define a republic to be, or at least may bestow that name on, a government which derives all its powers directly or indirectly from the great body of the people, and is administered by persons holding their offices during pleasure, for a limited period, or during good behavior. It is essential to such a government that it be derived from the great body of the society, not from an inconsiderable proportion, or a favored class of it; otherwise a handful of tyrannical nobles, exercising their oppressions by a delegation of their powers, might aspire to the rank of republicans, and claim for their government the honorable title of republic. It is sufficient for such a government that the persons administering it be appointed, either directly or

indirectly, by the people; and that they hold their appointments by either of the tenures just specified ...[10]

Reflecting upon these definitions of a republic by Montesquieu, Hamilton and Madison, this book puts forth the proposition that there were three distinct republics that led to the current government, a fourth republic, of the United States of America. Each Republic is so delineated because it marks a divergent stage in the evolution of the United States; the names designated to each period are derived from the republic's founding resolution or constitution, as follows:

- **First United American Republic:** *United Colonies of North America: Thirteen British Colonies United in Congress* [11] was founded by 12 colonies[12] on September 5th, 1774, and expired on July 1st, 1776, with the enactment of the *Resolution for Independency*. The republic was governed by a British Colonial Continental Congress[13] which, by 1775 provided for the security of its members with the formation of a Continental Army, the creation of a post office, the election of foreign ministers, and the issuing of its own currency. Peyton Randolph[14] and George Washington[15] served, respectively, as the national republic's first President and Commander-in-Chief;

- **Second United American Republic:** *The United States of America:*[16] *Thirteen Independent States United in Congress*[17] was founded by 12 colonies[18] with the passage of the *Resolution for Independency* on July 2nd,

---

[10] James Madison, "Federalist XXXIX: Conformity of the Plan to Republican Principles." *Independent Journal*, New York: January 16, 1788.

[11] The name, the *United Colonies of North America*, was not adopted by the Continental Congress until the passage of the *Declaration Setting Forth the Causes and Necessity of Their Taking up Arms*. Although the republic was named the *United Colonies of North America* on July 6th, 1775 in this resolution, the word *"North"* would be dropped in various legislative references by early 1776.

[12] Georgia sent no delegates.

[13] The name "Continental Congress" was formally adopted by the Delegates with the enactment of the *Articles of Association* on October 20, 1774. The 1774 Congress is commonly referred to as the *First Continental Congress*.

[14] Peyton Randolph was elected President of the Colonial Continental Congress on September 5th, 1774, which convened at Carpenters' Hall in Philadelphia.

[15] George Washington was issued his Commander-in-Chief Commission of the Colonial Continental Army on June 19th, 1775 with the *"commission to continue in force, until revoked by this, or a future Congress."*

[16] The name, *United States of America* was formally adopted by US Continental Congress by the enactment of the *Declaration of Independence* on July 4, 1776.

[17] The term *"Free and Independent States"* was formally adopted by Second Continental Congress in Richard Henry Lee's Resolution for Independency passed on July 2, 1776.

[18] New York did not approved independence from Great Britain until July 9, 1776.

1776 and expired on March 1st, 1781, with the enactment of the Articles of Confederation. The republic was governed by a United States Continental Congress. [19] John Hancock[20] and George Washington served, respectively, as the republic's first President and Commander-in-Chief;

- **Third United American Republic:** *The United States of America: A Not Quite Perpetual Union* [21] was founded by 13 States[22] with the Articles of Confederation's[23] enactment on March 1st, 1781, and expired on March 3rd, 1789. The republic was governed through the United States in Congress Assembled. Samuel Huntington[24] and George Washington served, respectively, as the Republic's first President and Commander-in-Chief;

- **Fourth United American Republic:** *The United States of America: We the People*[25] was formed by 11 states[26] with the *United States Constitution of 1787's* enactment on March 4th, 1789. The current republic is governed by *The United States House of Representatives and Senate in Congress Assembled (Bicameral Congress), The President of the United States of America (U.S. President), United States Supreme Court (U.S. Supreme Court)*, with the nomenclature all espoused in the *Constitution of 1787.*[27] For the purpose of this book the U.S. House of Representatives and Senate in Congress Assembled is abbreviated to the *U.S. Bicameral Congress.* George Washington served as both the Republic's first President and its Commander-in-Chief.

---

[19] The U.S. Continental Congress is also known as the Second Continental Congress.

[20] John Hancock was elected President of the Second Continental Congress on May 25, 1775. He remained the presiding officer of Congress until his resignation on October 29, 1777.

[21] The term *"The Perpetual Union"* was formally adopted by Congress in the *Articles of Confederation* on November 15, 1777 and ratified by all 13 States on March 1, 1781.

[22] Although formulated by Congress on November 15, 1777, the Articles of Confederation required unanimous ratification by all 13 states before they could be enacted. By February 1st, 1779 12 states had ratified the Constitution of 1777. Maryland delayed its adoption by over two years, ratifying on February 2, 1781.

[23] Articles of Confederation, March 1, 1781. *JCC, 1774-1789.*

[24] Samuel Huntington was elected President of the US Continental Congress on September 29, 1779. After the enactment of the Articles of Confederation on March 1, 1781, Samuel Huntington called to order and presided over the new Articles of Confederation Congress on March 2, 1781, as USCA President.

[25] The term *"We the People"* was formally adopted by the Philadelphia Convention on September 17, 1787 in the preamble to the current U.S. Constitution and ratified by the eleven States forming the new republic by the summer of 1788.

[26] The States of North Carolina (11/21/1789) and Rhode Island (5/29/1790) did not ratify the *Constitution of 1787* until after the government was formed in New York on March 4, 1789.

[27] Constitution of the United States, Charters of Freedom, National Archives, http://www.archives.gov/exhibits/charters/constitution.html

Having distinguished the four republics and their governing bodies, we will now examine them one by one to discover how the classifications and nomenclature might delineate a generally accepted framework for the U.S. Founding period.

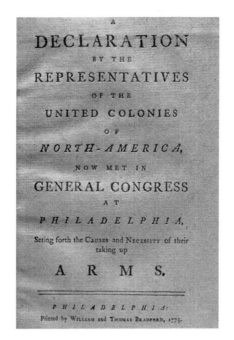

Continental Army 1775 Massachusetts Company Enlistment Oath to the United Colonies of America and his General Washington with A United Colonies of North America Declaration "Setting forth the Causes and Necessity of their taking up Arms."[28]

---

[28] Continental Army Company Oath Broadside, Boston, 1775. Photo printed with thanks to the Library of Congress, Rare Book and Special Collections Division, Printed Ephemera Collection; Portfolio 40, Folder 40.

CHAPTER II
THE FIRST UNITED AMERICAN REPUBLIC

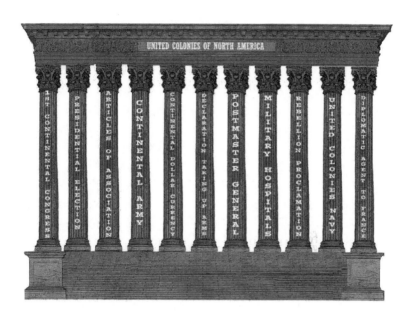

UNITED COLONIES OF NORTH AMERICA
THIRTEEN BRITISH COLONIES UNITED IN CONGRESS
SEPTEMBER 5TH, 1774 TO JULY 1ST, 1776

The United States Congress can trace its origins back to September 1st, 1774, at Philadelphia's City Tavern,[29] located on Second Street, just north of Walnut Street. Although City Tavern did not host a quorum of colonies, the pub was the site of the first caucus of congressional delegates and the decision was made, with from 25 to 30 delegates present, that the members would wait until September 5th, for the additional representatives to arrive before formally commencing the new colonial assembly. Delegate Robert Treat Paine recorded in his diary on September 1, 1774:

---

[29] A reconstruction of the City Tavern is located at 138 South 2nd Street, at the intersection of Walnut Streets in Philadelphia, Pennsylvania. The original City Tavern was constructed in 1773 and was partially destroyed by fire on March 22, 1834. The original structure was demolished in 1854 and was reconstructed in 1976 for the United States Bicentennial Celebration.

"6 o'Clock the Members of the Congress that were in Town met at City Tavern & adjourned to Monday next."[30]

On the same day, Delegate Samuel Ward wrote in his diary:

The Delegates from N. Jersies & two from Province of N York arrived, conversed with many Delegates & at Evening had a Meeting at the New Tavern & took a List of those present, in all twenty five.[31]

Silas Deane wrote to his wife, Elizabeth Deane after the meeting:

The Delegates from Virginia, Maryland, the Lower Counties, & New York, are not arrived. We spent this Day in visiting Those that are in Town, & find them in high Spirits particularly the Gentlemen from the Jersies, and South Carolina. In the Evening We met to the Number of about Thirty drank a Dish of Coffee together talked over a few preliminaries, & agreed to wait for the Gentlemen not arrived until Monday Next, before We proceeded to Business.[32]

On September 5th, 1774, the deputies representing eleven colonies assembled at 10 am at the tavern. Delegate James Duane reports:

The Members of the Congress met at Smith's [Sic City] Tavern. The Speaker of the Pennsylvania Assembly having offerd the Congress the use of the State house; & the Carpenters the use of their Hall,[33] It was agreed to take a View of each. We proceeded to the Carpenter's hall. Mr. Lynch proposed the Question whether as that was in all respects Suitable it ought not to be fixed upon without further Enquiry. I observed that if the State house was equally convenient it ought to be preferred being a provincial & the Carpenter's Hall a private House. And besides as it was tenderd by the Speaker it seemed to be a piece of respect which was due to him, at least to enquire whether the State House was not equally convenient. The Question was however called for; & a great Majority fixed upon the Carpenters Hall.[34]

Delegate John Adams provided this account of the Delegates selection of Carpenters' Hall in his letter to Charles Francis Adams:

---

[30] Robert Treat Paine's Diary, September 1, 1774, Smith, Paul H., et al., eds. Letters of Delegates to Congress, 1774-1789. 25 volumes, Washington, D.C.: Library of Congress, 1976-2000).
[31] Ibid, Samuel Ward's Diary, September 1, 1774.
[32] Ibid, Silas Deane to Elizabeth Deane on September 1, 1774.
[33] Carpenters' Hall is located in the Center City Philadelphia. The two-story red brick building was completed in 1773 and set back off Chestnut Street with the address of 320. The building is on the National Register of Historic Places & part of Independence National Historical Park.
[34] Ibid, James Duane Diary September 5th, 1774.

Monday. At ten the delegates all met at the City Tavern, and walked to the Carpenters' Hall, where they took a view of the room, and of the chamber where is an excellent library; there is also a long entry where gentlemen may walk, and a convenient chamber opposite to the library. The general cry was that this was a good room, and the question was put, whether we were satisfied with this room? And it passed in the affirmative. A very few were for the negative, and they were chiefly from Pennsylvania and New York. [35]

In 1774, the population of the 13 colonies that would eventually form the United States now surpassed two million inhabitants with no "continental" newspaper or magazine. Consequently, the Delegates were nearly all unknown to each other; most had never even heard the names of their new colleagues. There were, however, several exceptions. John and Samuel Adams were Boston leaders identified with deep-seated opposition to Great Britain and known all over the colonies. Virginia Militia Colonel George Washington had achieved colonial celebrity through his service with British regulars during the French and Indian War. Peyton Randolph was known as the judicious Virginia House of Burgesses' Speaker and the Colonial Virginia attorney general who had struck down Lt. Governor Dinwiddie's Pistole Land Tax in a London hearing before the British Lords of Trade.[36] Patrick Henry was known as an eloquent orator gaining colonial favor from his memorable opposition to the Stamp Act in 1765. There were other delegates who were men of some influence in their colonies, but the new congress had little knowledge of their character. It was a new beginning.

The American Colonial conference convened at Carpenters' Hall on September 5th, 1774 reviewing, first, the credentials of the representatives and then electing Peyton Randolph of Virginia as their presiding officer or President.[37] The members also elected a secretary, Charles Thomson of Pennsylvania, to maintain a record of the proceedings. Secretary Thomson would serve in this capacity for fourteen years and six months in the First, Second and Third United American Republics.

After the elections, the members turned to establishing the rules of the new colonial body. It was not until the following day that the debate concluded and the

---

[35] John Adams and Charles Francis Adams, *The Works of John Adams, Second President of the United States*, Boston: Little, Brown, and Company, 1865, p 365.
[36] Governor Robert Dinwiddie letter to Peyton Randolph, October 23, 1754. Printed in John C. Fitzpatrick, editor, *The Writings of George Washington from the Original Manuscript Sources, 1745-1799.*
[37] The word President in 1774 meant *"to preside."*

members voted against forming a committee to further consider rules of order. Instead they enacted the following resolutions on September 6th, 1774, to conduct colonial business:

Resolved, That in determining Questions in this Congress, each Colony or Province shall have one vote.—The Congress not being possessed of, or at present able to procure proper materials for ascertaining the importance of each Colony. Resolved, That no person shall speak more than twice on the same point without leave of the Congress. Resolved, That no Question shall be determined the day on which it is agitated and debated, if any one of the Colonies desire the determination to be postponed to another day. Resolved, That the Doors be kept shut during the time of business, and that the Members consider themselves under the strongest obligations of honour to keep the proceedings secret, until the majority shall direct them to be made publick. Resolved, unanimously, That a Committee be appointed to state the Rights of the Colonies in general, the several instances in which these rights are violated or infringed, and the means most proper to be pursued for obtaining a restoration of them.[38]

The proceedings of this body were deemed private and this *"pledge of secrecy"* would remain the rule in the successive confederation republics. Secrecy would also be vowed by delegates thirteen years later during the Philadelphia Convention that framed the U.S. Constitution of 1787. Consequently, the debate to determine the name of this new association is not a matter of public record. Historians, accordingly, are relegated to reviewing delegate letters and colonial resolutions to determine the origin of the name of the association that would go on to enact and direct united colonial measures.

The colonies had individually passed 12 different resolutions naming the Philadelphia gathering and its membership in various different forms:

New Hampshire ... General Congress; **Massachusetts** ... meeting of Committees from the several Colonies; **Rhode Island** ... general congress of representatives; **Connecticut** ... Congress of commissioners; **New York** ... Congress at Philadelphia; **New Jersey** ... general Congress of deputies; **Pennsylvania**... Colony Committees; **Maryland** ... General Congress of deputies from the Colonies; **Virginia** ... General Congress; **South Carolina** ... deputies to a general Congress; **Delaware** ... general continental congress;[39] **North Carolina** ... general Congress.[40]

---

[38] *JCC, 1774-1789,* September 6, 1774
[39] *Ibid.*
[40] *JCC, 1774-1789,* September 14, 1774

It would be Delaware's term, a *Continental Congress* that was formally adopted on October 20, 1774, in a resolution known as the *Articles of Association*. The Articles of Association implemented a British trade boycott[41]; the naming of the colonial congress in the *Articles of Association* can be found in the resolution's first paragraph:

We, his majesty's most loyal subjects, the delegates of the several colonies of New-Hampshire, Massachusetts-Bay, Rhode-Island, Connecticut, New-York, New-Jersey, Pennsylvania, the three lower counties of Newcastle, Kent and Sussex on Delaware, Maryland, Virginia, North-Carolina, and South-Carolina, deputed to represent them in a **Continental Congress**, held in the city of Philadelphia, on the 5th day of September, 1774. [42]

The name was primarily chosen to distinguish this congress from the many other congresses being held throughout the Colonies at that time. The terms "Colonies of America," "United Colonies," and "Colonies of North America" were all used in 1774 delegate letters, colonial newspapers, and colonial congressional journals. George Washington's June 19th, 1775, Commander-in-Chief Commission, for example, uses the term "United Colonies," followed by the names of the 13 members of the Continental Congress. The name, the *United Colonies of America*, was not introduced as part of a First Continental Congress resolution until Thomas Jefferson's 1775 Declaration *Setting Forth the Causes and Necessity of Their Taking Up Arms.*

We the representatives of the United Colonies of America now sitting in General Congress, to all nations send greeting of setting forth the causes and necessity of their taking up arms.[43]

Jefferson's Declaration was edited and approved on July 6th, 1775, with the addition of the word "North" to designate the republic the "United Colonies of North

---

[41] The colonies believed that Great Britain would redress their grievances, enumerated in the *Articles of Association*, after they imposed economic sanctions. On December 1, 1774 the colonial boycott became active and trade with England fell sharply. The British Parliament and King George III responded by enacting on March 30, 1775 the New England Restraining Act which sanctioned the northeastern American colonies: (1) Effective July 1, 1775, New England trade was to be limited to England and the British West Indies; trade with other nations was prohibited. (2) Effective July 20, 1775, New England ships were barred from the North Atlantic fisheries. This measure improved the colonial Canadian alliance and damaged New England economy.
[42] Articles of Association, *JCC, 1774-1789*, October 20, 1774.
[43] *Ibid.*, July 6, 1775

America." [44] Ten days later, the Continental Congress issued George Washington's Commander-in-Chief Commission omitting "of North America" and referring to the republic only as "United Colonies:"

... And you are to regulate your conduct in every respect by the rules and discipline of war, (as herewith given you,) and punctually to observe and follow such orders and directions, from time to time, as you shall receive from this, or a future Congress of these United Colonies, or committee of Congress. This commission to continue in force, until revoked by this, or a future Congress.

On July 21st, 1775, Benjamin Franklin would, in *Article I* of an Articles of Confederation draft, also utilize the word "north":

The Name of this Confederacy shall henceforth be the United Colonies of North America.[45]

It would not be until January 1776 that the Continental Congress, as well as the colonies themselves, would drop the word "North," referring instead to the Continental Association as the "United Colonies of America:"

Resolved, By this Assembly, That Roger Sherman, Oliver Wolcott, Samuel Huntington, Titus Hosmer, and William Williams, Esqrs. be, and they are hereby appointed Delegates to represent this Colony at the General Congress of the United Colonies of America.[46]

As can be seen, the aforesaid First Continental Congress' resolutions, rules, and various other acts clearly formed "a body of laws" among the colonies, thus establishing the *First United American Republic: The United Colonies of North America -- Thirteen British Colonies United in Congress.* The United Colonies Continental Congress, the new republic's governing association, convened from September 5th, 1774, to July 1st, 1776, passing resolutions, laws and acts necessary to conduct a war to win independence from the British Empire. Although independence was not declared until July 2nd, 1776, the United Colonies Continental Congress (U.C. Continental Congress) acted as a quasi-central government for the 13

---

[44] Jefferson, Jefferson writes: *1775. June 23. Congress appointed a committee to prepare a Declaration to be published by Genl. Washington on his arrival at the camp before Boston, to wit, J. Rutledge, W. Livingston, Dr. Franklin, Mr. Jay, and Mr. Johnson.* Thomas Jefferson., Manuscript letter, Library of Congress.
[45] *JCC, 1774-1789*, July 21, 1775
[46] *JCC, 1774-1789*, January 16, 1776.

Colonies, meeting the definition of a confederation republic as evidenced by a review of key United Colonies Continental Congress legislative milestones recorded in the Journals of the Continental Congress:

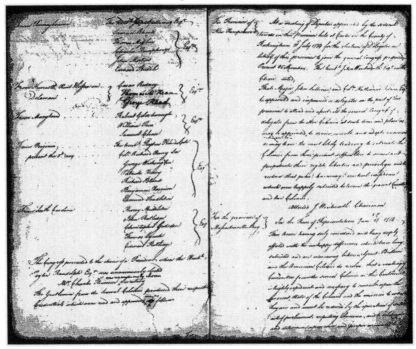

Original Journal of Congress manuscript open to September 5th, 1774, recording the convening of the First Continental Congress, delegates in attendance, the elections of Peyton Randolph, President and Charles Thomson, Secretary marking the establishment of the First United American Republic: The United Colonies of North America. -- Image courtesy of the National Archives of the United States.

- September 5th, 1774: a Colonial assembly convenes at Carpenters' Hall in Philadelphia and elects Peyton Randolph, President, and Charles Thomson, Secretary;
- September 17th, 1774: assembly endorses Suffolk Resolves from Massachusetts;
- September 27th, 1774: assembly adopts a nonimportation agreement;
- September 30th, 1774: assembly resolves to halt exports to Great Britain, Ireland, and the West Indies effective September 10th, 1775;
- October 14th, 1774: assembly resolves and adopts declaration of grievances and rights;

- October 20th, 1774: assembly approves the Articles of Association and names itself a "Continental Congress;"
- October 21st, 1774; Congress approves an address to the people of Great Britain and one to the inhabitants of the colonies;
- October 22nd, 1774: Congress agrees to reconvene on May 10th, 1775, *"unless the redress of grievances, which we have desired, be obtained before that time."* Congress elects Henry Middleton of South Carolina, President;
- October 26th, 1774: Congress approves an *Address to the King* and a *Letter to the People of Quebec* and dissolves itself;
- Colonial Continental Congress measures provoked British Regulars to march out of Boston, attempting the capture of hidden military supplies. In early expeditions, the British were not opposed, found nothing, and returned to Boston. On April 19th, 1775, however, shots were fired during the British advancement on Lexington and Concord, launching the first military engagement of the Revolutionary War;
- May 10th, 1775: Congress re-convenes at the Pennsylvania State House; reelects Peyton Randolph, President and Charles Thomson, Secretary. Ethan Allen and Benedict Arnold seize Fort Ticonderoga;
- May 24th, 1775: Congress elects John Hancock president;
- June 10th, 1775: Congress resolves to establish the Continental Army;
- June 15th, 1775: the Colonial Continental Congress appoints George Washington as Commander-in-Chief of the Continental Army;
- June 17th, 1775: the Battle of Breed's Hill forces the retreat of Minutemen;
- June 22nd, 1775: Congress commissions eight Brigadier Generals;
- June 23rd, 1775: the Colonial Continental Congress resolves that "a sum not exceeding two millions of Spanish milled dollars be emitted by the Congress in bills of Credit, for the defense of America in the following form:
    - 49,000 bills of 8 dollars each ... $392,000
    - 49,000 do. of 7 dollars each ... $343,000
    - 49,000 do. of 6 dollars each ... $294,000
    - 49,000 do. of 5 dollars each ... $245,000
    - 49,000 do. of 4 dollars each ... $196,000
    - 49,000 do. of 3 dollars each ... $147,000
    - 49,000 do. of 2 dollars each ... $98,000
    - 49,000 do. of 1 dollars each ... $49,000
    - 11,800 do. of 20 dollars each ... $236,000;
- July 6th, 1775: the Colonial Continental Congress approves a *United Colonies of North America Declaration ... Setting Forth the Causes and Necessity of Their Taking Up Arms* against Great Britain;
- July 21st, 1775: the Colonial Continental Congress considers Benjamin Franklin's *Articles of Confederation* as a possible constitution for the United Colonies of North America;
- July 26th, 1775: Congress appoints Benjamin Franklin as postmaster general for one year;

- July 27th, 1775: Congress resolves to establish Military Hospitals;
- July 29th, 1775: the U.S. Continental Congress *Resolved, That Michael Hillegas, and George Clymer, Esqrs. be, and they are hereby appointed, joint treasurers of the United Colonies;*[47]
- August 23rd, 1775: King George III proclaims that the colonies are in state of rebellion;
- November 13th, 1775: Major General Richard Montgomery occupies Montreal Canada;
- November 28th, 1775: Congress adopts *"Rules for the Regulation of the Navy of the United Colonies;"*
- December 31st, 1775: General Montgomery is killed in the Battle for Quebec City and American troops retreat from Canada;
- March 2nd, 1776:Congressional Committee of Secret Correspondence appoints Silas Deane agent to France to transact business *"commercial and political;"*
- March 17th, 1776: The Continental Army led by General Washington forces the British to evacuate Boston;
- April 1st, 1775: Congress establishes the United Colonies Treasury Office;
- April 6th, 1775: Congress opens the trade of the United Colonies *"to any parts of the world which are not under the dominion"* of the King George III.

The above acts -- including passing resolutions, establishing an army and a navy, appointing a Commander-in-Chief and a postmaster, and creating currency --and numerous others are primary source evidence that the Colonial Continental Congress established the First United American Republic. This republic, the United Colonies of North America, first attempted to negotiate for its colonial autonomy within the British Empire and, when unsuccessful, waged a war for independence against Great Britain. As we have seen, although the first caucus of 25-30 colonial deputies was held on September 1st, 1774, at City Tavern, the delegates did not formally convene its association until September 5, 1774, at Carpenter's Hall. This later date, therefore, marks the beginning of *The First American Republic: United Colonies of North America.* This "new form of government," as defined by Baron de Montesquieu, was "able to provide for the security of the united body;" as defined by Alexander Hamilton, it was "an assemblage of societies, or an association of two or more states into one state." Perhaps most significantly, following James Madison's definition, it was "a government which derives all its powers directly or

---

[47] *JCC, 1774-1789*, June 29, 1775

indirectly from the great body of the people, and is administered by persons holding their offices during pleasure, for a limited period, or during good behavior..."[48]

THE FIRST UNITED AMERICAN REPUBLIC

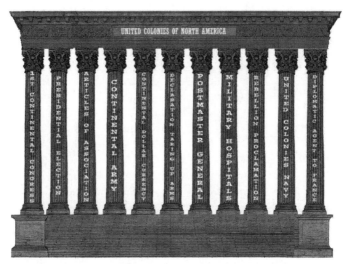

United Colonies Continental Congress Republic Presidents
September 5, 1774, to July 1, 1776

Peyton Randolph	September 5, 1774	October 22, 1774
Henry Middleton	October 22, 1774	October 26, 1774
Peyton Randolph	May 20, 1775	May 24, 1775
John Hancock	May 25, 1775	July 1, 1776

Seats of Government: September 5, 1774, to July 1, 1776

Philadelphia	Sept. 1, 1774 - Caucus Only	City Tavern
Philadelphia	Sept. 5, 1774 to Oct. 24, 1774	Carpenters' Hall
Philadelphia	May 10, 1775 to July 1, 1776	Pennsylvania State House

---

[48] James Madison, "Federalist XXXIX: Conformity of the Plan to Republican Principles." *Independent Journal*, New York: January 16, 1788.

CHAPTER III
THE SECOND UNITED AMERICAN REPUBLIC

Richard Henry Lee's July 2, 1776, Resolution for Independence
Image Courtesy of the Klos Yavneh Collection

THE UNITED STATES OF AMERICA:
THIRTEEN INDEPENDENT STATES UNITED IN CONGRESS
JULY 2, 1776 TO FEBRUARY 28, 1781

The start of the Second American Republic, "Independence Day," has been a matter of debate since the U.S. Continental Congress declared July 4th -- and not July 2nd -- as the "birthday" of the United States of America. Since then, historians have written volumes designating July 4th as U.S. Independence Day – even though independence had, in fact, been declared two days earlier, with the enactment of Richard Henry Lee's *Resolution for Independency:* [49]

> Resolved, that these United Colonies are, and of right ought to be, free and independent states, that they are absolved from all allegiance to the British Crown, and that all political connection between them and the state of Great Britain is, and ought to be, totally dissolved. [50]

Moreover, New York had abstained from both the July 2nd and July 4th declarations, not approving independence of the "more or less" United States until July 9, 1776. [51]

---

[49] Hereinafter referred to as the *Lee's Resolution*.
[50] Op Cit, June 7, 1776
[51] On July 9th, 1776 the New York Provincial Congress assembled in the White Plains Court House and adopted the July 4, 1776 resolution heartedly supported by John Jay who had rushed from New York City to address that body: "That reasons assigned by the Continental Congress for declaring The United Colonies Free and Independent States are cogent and conclusive, and that now we

Notwithstanding New York's July 9th approval, the passage of Lee's *Resolution* on the 2nd, and even John Adams' letter to Abigail declaring that "The Second Day of July 1776, will be the most memorable Epocha, in the History of America," [52] July 4th has been heralded as the birthdate of the United States of America since 1777. Indeed, July 4th has remained sacrosanct despite the enactment of two distinctly different U.S. Constitutions, first in 1781 and again in 1789, that reformulated the United States' federal government.

Since July 1776, all major U.S. legislation signed into law ends with words detailing the country's longevity as an independent nation. For example, the United States in Congress Assembled's *Thanksgiving Day Proclamation of 1782* concludes: "Done in Congress, at Philadelphia. The eleventh day of October, in the Year of Our Lord One thousand seven hundred and eighty two, and of our Sovereignty and Independence the seventh. John Hanson President."[53] This practice continued through the 19th century[54] and the *Emancipation Proclamation*, for example, concludes "and of the Independence of the United States of America the eighty-seventh." [55]

---

approve the same, and will at the risque of our lives and fortunes, join with the other colonies in supporting it." - New York Provincial Congress, *Resolution supporting the Declaration of Independence*, July 9, 1776.

[52] Letter from John Adams to Abigail Adams, 3 July 1776. Original manuscript from the Adams Family Papers, Massachusetts Historical Society. "But the Day is past. The Second Day of July 1776 will be the most memorable Epocha, in the History of America. I am apt to believe that it will be celebrated, by succeeding Generations, as the great anniversary Festival. It ought to be commemorated, as the Day of Deliverance by solemn Acts of Devotion to God Almighty. It ought to be solemnized with Pomp and Parade, with Shews, Games, Sports, Guns, Bells, Bonfires and Illuminations from one End of this Continent to the other from this Time forward forever more".

[53] John Hanson, "United States in Congress Assembled Proclamation. *"The Freeman's Journal*, October 16, 1782, Number LXXVII, p. 3.

[54] In the first three United American Republics, the signature of U.C. and U.S. Presidents are not required to enact any Congressional legislation. These founding presidents, unlike the current U.S. Presidents, had one vote in their respective state delegations in the *"one state one vote"* unicameral congressional system. In the Fourth American Republic, Article I of the Current U.S. Constitution requires every bill, order, resolution or other act of legislation by the Congress of the United States to be presented to the U.S. President for his approval. The President can either sign it into law, return the bill to the originating house of Congress with his objections to the bill (a veto), or neither sign nor return it to Congress. If he does the latter and Congress remains in session for ten days exempting Sundays, the bill becomes law. If during those ten days Congress adjourns than the bill does not become a law.

[55] *Emancipation Proclamation*, January 1, 1863, Original Manuscript, *The Charters of Freedom*, US National Archives and Records Administration.

Emancipation Proclamation Image Courtesy of the U. S. National Archives [56]

Similarly, the 20th-Century *Nuclear Test Ban Treaty* was signed by John F. Kennedy "… in the year of our Lord one thousand nine hundred and sixty-three and of the Independence of the United States of America the one hundred and eighty-eighth."

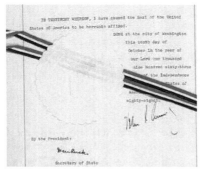

Nuclear Test Ban Treaty Image Courtesy of the Library of Congress

U.S. governmental authorities universally agree that the birth year of the current U.S. Republic is 1776 and not 1781 (when the Articles of Confederation was ratified), nor 1784 (when the Treaty of Paris was ratified ending the war with Great Britain), nor September 17, 1787 (when the Philadelphia Convention produced the current U.S. Constitution), or March 4, 1789, when the current tripartite political system began to govern the United States of America under the *Constitution of 1787*. It is remarkable, however, that, while July 4th, 1776, stands as the nation's birthdate John Hancock, the DOI's presidential signer, is passed over by the same

---

[56] *Ibid.*

governmental authorities as the first U.S. Head of State. Similarly, Samuel Huntington, the first President under the Articles of Confederation, is also passed over as President of the United States in America in Congress Assembled (the title given by the Articles of Confederation to the President of unicameral First Federal Congress). In contrast, these same officials recognize Benjamin Franklin as the first Postmaster General, even though he served not under the current U.S. Constitution but under the Articles of Association since his position was created by a United Colonies' resolution dated July 26th, 1775. (Postmaster General Franklin served in this capacity until November 10th, 1776.).

Setting these inconsistencies aside, the foremost U.S. Founding question pertinent to this chapter remains: *Why does the U.S. Government, since 1777, celebrate the 4th of July as Independence Day and not the 2nd of July?*

When the twelve United Colonies of America declared their independence on July 2nd, the Declaration of Independence (DOI) was already before the Colonial Continental Congress for its consideration. The first draft was read before the delegates on Friday June 28th, 1776, and then laid the Declaration of Independence on the table over the weekend for the Delegates to review. Congress was called to order on July 1st at 9 am and the Delegates were made aware of a large British Fleet's presence just of Sandy Hook from a June 29th George Washington letter to Congress that was read on the floor.

The Accounts communicated yesterday thro' Lieut.Davis0n's Letter are partly confirmed, and I dare say will turn out to be true in the whole. For two or three days past three or four Ships have been droping in and I just now received an Express from an Officer appointed to keep a look out on Staten Island, that forty five arrived at the Hook today, some say more, and I suppose the whole fleet will be in within a day or two. I am hopeful before they are prepared to attack, that I shall get some reinforcements but be that as it may, I shall attempt to make the best disposition I can for our Troops, in order to give them a proper reception, and to prevent the ruin and destruction they are meditating against us.[57]

Serious debate on independence, in the wake of the pending British invasion of New York, consumed most of that hot and humid Monday as evidenced by the following account:

---

[57] George Washington, *The Writings of George Washington from the Original Manuscript Sources, 1745-1799, Volume 5,* By George Washington, John Clement Fitzpatrick, David Maydole Matteson, Government Printing Office:1976, page 200.

On Monday the 1st of July the house resolved itself into a committee of the whole and resumed the consideration of the original motion made by the delegates of Virginia, which being again debated through the day, was carried in the affirmative by the votes of N. Hampshire, Connecticut, Massachusetts, Rhode island, N. Jersey, Maryland, Virginia, N. Carolina, and Georgia.

South Carolina and Pennsylvania voted against it. Delaware having but two members present they were divided: the delegates for New York declared they were for it themselves, and were assured their constituents were for it, but that their instructions, having been drawn near a twelvemonth before, when reconciliation was still the general object, they were enjoined by them to do nothing which should impede that object, they therefore thought themselves not justifiable in voting on either side, and asked leave to withdraw from the question, which was given them, the committee rose and reported their resolution to the house.

Mr Rutlege of South Carolina then requested the determination might be put off to the next day, as he believed his colleagues, though they disapproved of the resolution, would then join in it for the sake of unanimity, the ultimate question whether the house would agree to the resolution of the committee, was accordingly postponed to the next day. [58]

The Continental Congress opened again on July 2nd as planned, but, with the British Fleet anchored in their harbor, the New York delegation felt it imprudent to vote without authorization from its Provincial Congress. The Pennsylvania Delegation, consisting of only three delegates, voted 2 to 1 for independence because neither Robert Morris nor John Dickinson, each of whom had voted "no" on July 1st, attended the July 2nd session.

Although a British fleet had arrived in South Carolina's harbor on June 1st, Edward Rutledge urged his fellow delegates to vote for the resolution. Arthur Middleton, son of First Continental Congress President Henry Middleton, shucked his father's loyalist wishes and joined his fellow Delegates in changing the colony's position from a July 1st "no" to a unanimous "aye" for independence. Finally Caesar Rodney of Delaware, who had been summoned by fellow delegate Thomas McKean, arrived, suffering from a serious facial cancer and afflicted by asthma after riding 80 miles through the rain and a lightning storm. He broke Delaware's 1 to 1 deadlock by casting the third vote for independence. The *Resolution for Independency* was thus

---

[58] Journals of the Continental Congress, 1774-1789, Volume 6, by United States Continental Congress, Worthington Chauncey Ford, Gaillard Hunt, John Clement Fitzpatrick, Roscoe R. Hill, Kenneth E. Harris, and Steven D. Tilley, U.S. Government Printing Office, 1906 page 1092

passed by the 12 colonies empowered to vote; independence from Great Britain was declared as follows:

Resolved, That these United Colonies are, and of right ought to be, free and independent states, that they are absolved from all allegiance to the British Crown, and that all political connection between them and the State of Great Britain is, and ought to be, totally dissolved. [59]

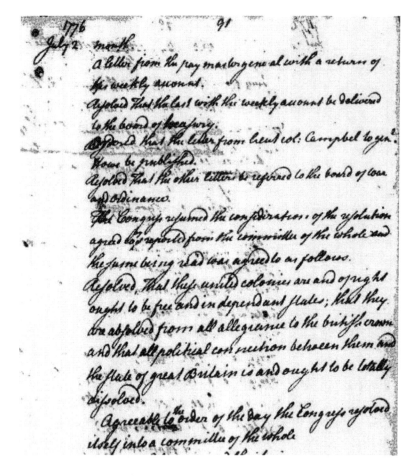

Journal of Congress manuscript open to July 2, 1776, recording the Resolution for Independency's passage. -- *Image courtesy of the U.S. National Archives*

---

[59] *Resolution for Independency* Manuscript, dated July 2, 1776, from the US National Archives.

Voting on the actual Declaration of Independence, however, was still another matter; at the request of Committee of the Whole Chairman Benjamin Harrison, the members agreed to continue deliberations the following day.

On July 3rd, the Continental Congress considered, debated and passed several pressing war resolutions before taking up the Declaration of Independence resolution. Once again, not having sufficient time to finalize the proclamation, Chairman Benjamin Harrison requested more time and the U.S. Continental Congress tabled deliberation until the following day. On the morning of July 4th, 1776 the delegates debated and passed the following war resolution: [60]

> ... that an application be made to the committee of safety of Pennsylvania for a supply of flints for the troops at New York: and that the colony of Maryland and Delaware be requested to embody their militia for the flying camp, with all expedition, and to march them, without delay, to the city of Philadelphia.[61]

The Continental Congress then took up, finalized, and passed the Declaration of Independence: "Mr. Benjamin Harrison reported, that the committee of the whole Congress have agreed to a Declaration, which he delivered in. The Declaration being read again was agreed to ..."[62]

The Declaration's detailed explication of why "... these United Colonies are, and, of right, ought to be, Free and Independent States ..."[63] served to justify the Colonial Continental Congress vote of July 2nd. Indeed, although the Declaration itself was not passed until the 4th, the eloquent and convincingly-argued rhetoric of this document -- whose first draft had been read on June 29th -- rather than the simple language of *Lee's Resolution,* exacted the vote for independence on July 2nd, 1776, from the 12 state delegations. One might argue that the "decent respect to the opinions of mankind" evoked in the opening paragraph required not just the vote but an explanation thereof, before independence could truly occur. Moreover, there is a second reason for the July 4th birthdate: the Declaration proclaimed the nomenclature of this second United American Republic, something *Lee's Resolution* failed to do, for the new name, the United States of America, was not utilized on any of the

---

[60] A Committee of the Whole is a device in which a legislative body or other deliberative assembly is considered one large committee.
[61] *JCC, 1774-1789,* July 4, 1776
[62] *Ibid.*
[63] *JCC, 1774-1789,* July 2, 1776

Continental Congress resolutions or bills passed after *Lee's Resolution* was enacted on July 2nd up until the passage of the Declaration of Independence on July 4th, 1776.

It is true that in Thomas Jefferson's drafts, the word "States" was simply substituted for *"Colonies"* in the stile, or name, "United Colonies of America." In fact, Jefferson's substitution was in accordance with *Lee's Resolution,* which asserted the *"*United Colonies*"* were to be *"free and independent States."* The new republic, however, was not named the "United States" until the adoption of the Declaration of Independence.

The naming of this new republic was no small matter, and the topic would be addressed again in later deliberations on both the Articles of Confederation and the current U.S. Constitution, respectively. [64] As noted earlier, the 1775 *Articles of Confederation* and *Declaration for Taking up Arms* initially named the First United American Republic the *United Colonies of North America.* The name was informally shortened by the Continental Congress to the *United Colonies of America* in 1776 but the name *United Colonies of North America* was still utilized in 1776. We must, therefore, pay heed to the fact that the new nation's name was adopted on July 4th, 1776, with the passage of the Declaration of Independence and not on July 2nd with the enactment of *Lee's Resolution.* This circumstance, coupled with the nearly completed Declaration of Independence being laid before the members on June 28th and present during the July 2nd vote, explicates why the 4th and not the 2nd was ultimately designated *Independence Day* by the Continental Congress.

Nevertheless, we must be precise in determining the start of the *Second United American Republic.* The United Colonies of America severed their allegiance to Great Britain on July 2nd, 1776. The new independent republic of free and independent states enacted resolutions on the 2nd, 3rd, and 4th of July before passing the Declaration of Independence.[65] This Assembly (just like the unnamed Congress

---

[64] At the Philadelphia Convention on May 30, 1787, Virginia Governor and member Edmund Randolph moved to rename the United States, the *"National Government of America."* This name would remain as part of the current U.S. Constitution draft until June 20th, 1787, when it was moved by Mr. Oliver Ellsworth, seconded by Mr. Nathaniel Gorham *"... to amend the first resolution reported from the Committee of the whole House so as to read as follows -- namely, Resolved that the government of the United States ought to consist of a Supreme Legislative, Judiciary, and Executive. On the question to agree to the amendment it passed unanimously in the affirmative."* Max Farrand, *The Records of the Federal Convention of 1787.* New Haven: Yale University Press, 1911.
[65] After the passage of *Lee's resolution* the Continental Congress enacted that *"In obedience to their order, Captain Whipple and Captain Saltonstal were come to Philadelphia; Whereupon, Resolved,*

that had met at Carpenters' Hall from September 5th to October 20th, 1774)[66] formed a new *United American Republic* when it enacted bills, resolutions and other legislation on behalf of the nation consisting of 12 States. July 2nd, 1776, therefore, marks the end of the United Colonies of North America and the beginning of the *Second United American Republic:* The United States of America. It is, however, appropriate that the birth of the United States of America be celebrated on July 4th because on that date, the new nation was formally named with the passage of the *"Declaration By the Representatives of the United States of America in General Congress Assembled."* [67]

Having established the starting point for the *Second United American Republic*, we – like the Continental Congress – now turn to a consideration of that Republic's governance. As we shall see, the process of articulating the document that became the "Articles of Confederation" was not simple. Moreover, although this first constitution of the United States of America was passed by the U.S. Continental Congress on November 15th, 1777, the Articles required unanimous ratification – something that did not occur until March 1st, 1781. For three years the U.S. Continental Congress would govern under a hodge-podge of laws drawn from previous congressional resolutions along with regulations proposed in the Articles of Confederation.

With the passage of *Lee's Resolution* and the Declaration of Independence, the U.S. Continental Congress was now faced with the challenge of transforming the voluminous United Colonies' legislation into a constitution capable of uniting and governing the 13 independent states. Even before the acceptance of those two momentous documents, the matter of drafting a constitution had gained the serious attention of Congress on June 12th, 1776, when it resolved to appoint a committee of thirteen to propose a governing document for the new republic:

That the Marine Committee be directed to enquire into the complaints exhibited against them, and report to Congress." On the third of July seven different resolutions were passed, and finally on the Fourth of July they *"Resolved, That an application be made to the committee of safety of Pennsylvania for a supply of flints for the troops at New York: and that the colony of Maryland and Delaware be requested to embody their militia for the flying camp, with all expedition, and to march them, without delay, to the city of Philadelphia."* All were enacted before the Declaration of Independence was adopted. *Journals of the Continental Congress*, July 2-4, 1776.
[66] On September 5, 1774 the delegates first assembled at Carpenters Hall but did not formalize the name of that body as a "Continental Congress," until October 20, 1784.
[67] *Declaration By the Representatives of the United States of America in General Congress Assembled, JCC, 1774-1789*, July 4, 1776.

Resolved, that the committee to prepare and digest the form of a confederation to be entered into between these colonies, consist of a member from each colony:

- for New Hampshire ... Mr. [Josiah] Bartlett
- Massachusetts ... Mr. S[amuel] Adams
- Rhode Island ... Mr. [Stephen] Hopkins
- Connecticut ... Mr. [Roger] Sherman
- New York ... Mr. R[obert R.] Livingston
- New Jersey ...
- Pennsylvania ... Mr. [John] Dickinson
- Delaware ... Mr. [Thomas] McKean
- Maryland ... Mr. [Thomas] Stone
- Virginia ... Mr. [Thomas] Nelson
- North Carolina ... Mr. [Joseph] Hewes
- S. Carolina ... Mr. [Edward] Rutledge
- Georgia ... Mr. [Button] Gwinnett[68]

One month later, on July 12th, 1776, the committee presented the first draft Articles of Confederation of the United States of America. The Continental Congress resolved:

That eighty copies, and no more, of the confederation, as brought in by the committee, be immediately printed, and deposited with the secretary, who shall deliver one copy to each member: That a committee be appointed to superintend the press, who shall take care that the foregoing resolution [Articles of Confederation].

That the printer be under oath to deliver all the copies, which he shall print, together with the copy sheet, to the secretary, and not to disclose either directly or indirectly, the contents of the said confederation: That no member furnish any person with his copy, or take any steps by which the said confederation may be re-printed, and that the secretary be under the like injunction.[69]

As in the Congress' earlier deliberations, secrecy was of the essence. But the greatest challenge faced by the delegates during their constitutional negotiations was that the British were on the march to conquer Philadelphia, forcing the Continental Congress to flee the city and reconvene in the Henry Fite House on Market Street in Baltimore. As we shall see, Congress would move an additional three times before passing the Articles of Confederation in November, 1777.

---

[68] *JCC, 1774-1789,* Wednesday June 12, 1776.
[69] *JCC,* July 12, 1776

First, George Washington, with a surprise Christmas Eve attack on Trenton, defeated the garrison and stopped the British advance on Philadelphia. Accordingly, the U.S. Continental Congress returned to the Philadelphia State House on March 4th, 1777, but their residency and deliberations on the Articles of Confederation there lasted only six months. In August, a re-organized British army began its advance on Philadelphia and on September 14th, Congress resolved that if it should be necessary to remove from Philadelphia, "Lancaster shall be the place which they shall meet."[70] This resolution was passed none too soon, as President John Hancock and the Continental Congress were forced to abandon the city on September 18th, 1777. Robert Morton, a Philadelphia Tory, wrote,

> Sept. 19, 1777. This morning about 1 o'clock an express arrived to Congress giving an account of the British Army having got to the Swedes Ford on the other side of Schuylkill, which so much alarmed the gentlemen of the Congress, the military officers, and other friends to the general cause of American Freedom, that they decamped with the utmost precipitation and in the greatest confusion; insomuch that one of the delegates, by name of Fulsom, was obliged in a very Fulsome manner to ride off without a saddle. Thus we have seen the men, from whom we have received, and from whom we still expect protection, leave us to fall into the hands of (by their accounts) a barbarous, cruel and unrelenting enemy.[71]

The members rode off separately to Lancaster, a small river town in central Pennsylvania. Their routes were often circuitous, like that of the new South Carolina delegate, Henry Laurens, who first traveled to Bristol to collect the recuperating French Marquis de Lafayette, wounded in the Battle of Brandywine. Laurens was then forced by British patrols to travel north, rather than west, to Bethlehem. His carriage moved southwest through the Lehigh Valley into Reading and finally headed south to Lancaster. Here, Henry Laurens discovered that the Lancaster Inns were already overcrowded because the displaced citizens of Philadelphia had flooded into the small community along with the State government of Pennsylvania. Laurens wrote:

> Here [Lancaster] Congress were soon convened but hearts were still fluttering in some bosoms & a motion made for adjourning to this Town [York-Town], [72]

---

[70] *Ibid.*
[71] Winthrop Sargent, *The Life and Career of Major John Andre, Adjutant-general of the British.* New York: William Ahbatt, 1902.
[72] James McClure, *Nine Months in York Town.* York, PA: York Daily Record, 2001.

On the other side of the Susquehanna, a river offering a protective natural barrier to British invasion, sat the small hamlet of York-Town (now known as York, Pennsylvania). York had an underutilized courthouse readily available to reconvene Congress in safety. The 35-year-old town of about 300 dwellings and 2,000 residents also offered numerous accommodations to house the delegates comfortably and onn September 30th, the Continental Congress moved in. John Adams, once settled, wrote Abigail:

It is now a long Time, since I had an Opportunity of writing to you, and I fear you have suffered unnecessary Anxiety on my Account. -- In the Morning of the 19th. Inst., the Congress were alarmed, in their Beds, by a Letter from Mr. Hamilton one of General Washington's Family, that the Enemy were in Possession of the Ford over the Schuylkill, and the Boats, so that they had it in their Power to be in Philadelphia, before Morning. The Papers of Congress, belonging to the Secretary's Office, the War Office, the Treasury Office, &c. were before sent to Bristol. The President, and all the other Gentlemen were gone that Road, so I followed, with my Friend Mr. Merchant [Marchant] of Rhode Island, to Trenton in the jersies. We stayed at Trenton, until the 21st when we set off, to Easton upon the Forks of Delaware. From Easton We went to Bethlehem, from thence to Reading, from thence to Lancaster, and from thence to this Town, which is about a dozen Miles over the Susquehanna River. -- Here Congress is to sit.

In order to convey the Papers, with safeties, which are of more Importance than all the Members, We were induced to take this Circuit, which is near 180 Miles, whereas this Town by the directest Road is not more than 88 miles from Philadelphia. This Tour has given me an Opportunity of seeing many Parts of this Country, which I never saw before.[73]

Philadelphia was lost, Fort Ticonderoga also captured, and now the British, under the command of General John Burgoyne, were marching down the Hudson Valley to cut off New England from the Middle Atlantic States.[74] These were perilous days but the Continental Congress pressed on with what increasingly appeared to be a failing war effort. Nevertheless, the delegates were prodigious in their efforts to formulate the first U.S. Constitution, the Articles of Confederation. Their letters report that Congress typically met from 10 am to 1 pm and recessed until 4 pm, with

---

[73] Letter from John Adams to Abigail Adams, 30 September 1777. Original manuscript from the Adams Family Papers, Massachusetts Historical Society.
[74] General John Burgoyne (24 February 1722 – 4 August 1792) was a British army officer charged with gaining control of Lake Champlain and the Hudson River valley. This would divide New England from the southern colonies ending the rebellion. On 17 October, 1777, during the Saratoga campaign he surrendered his army of 6,000 men to General Horatio Gates and the northern Continental Army.

"after recess sessions" often lasting well into the evening. Numerous additional committee duties filled any remaining free time. John Hancock wrote to his wife Dorothy during this period:

> I sat in the Chair yesterday & Conducted the Business Eight hours, which is too much, and after that had the Business of my office to attend to as usual ... I cannot Stand it much longer in this way" [75]

John Adams wrote to Abigail Adams of his tenure in York that "War has no Charms for me ... If I live much longer in Banishment, I shall scarcely know my own Children. Tell my little ones, that if they will be very good, Papa will come home." [76] Charles Carroll of Carrollton, a Maryland Delegate, complained of his own York experience that

> The Congress still continues the same noisy, empty & talkative assembly it always was since I have known it. No progress has been made in the Confederation tho' all seem desirous of forming one. A good confederation I am convinced would give us great strength & new vigor. This State is in a great degree disaffected, & the well affected are inactive & supine. This supiness & inactivity I attribute to the government & to the men who govern; they want wisdom, influence, & the confidence of a very great portion of the People, particularly of those whose abilities & activity might in short time set things to rights. [77]

An atmosphere of dread enveloped the convention, as the Delegates grew painfully aware that French monetary aid would not be forthcoming without a constitution forming 13 independent states into one nation. Delegate James Lovell informed General Horatio Gates in Saratoga on October 5th, 1777,

> I believe we shall be able to get speedily thro' the Articles of Confederation, and shall sit faithfully about the Means of keeping our Currency in some sort of Credit. [78]

But there were details still to be resolved as the first constitutional convention dragged on into a crisp and cool central Pennsylvania fall. Freshman delegate Henry Laurens impressed the members of Congress with his "nonpartisan" deliberations,

---

[75] John Adams, 30 September, 1777, *op. cit.*
[76] *Ibid.*
[77] Letter from Charles Carroll of Carrollton, October 5, 1777. In Paul H. Smith, et al., eds, *Letters of Delegates to Congress, 1774-1789*. 25 volumes, Washington, D.C.: Library of Congress, 1976-2000). Cited hereafter as *LDC, 1774-1789.*
[78] Letter from James Lovell to General Horatio Gates, October 5, 1777. In as *LDC, 1774-1789.*

remaining steadfast against the nationalists' proposal to allow control of the proposed new federal government by the wealthy. He was also against Virginia's proposal to have one delegate in Congress for every 30,000 inhabitants, permitting each representative one vote and thereby allowing the largest states to control the new federal government.

In an unusual position, Laurens voted for the new governing body (to be called United States, in Congress Assembled - USCA) to have the authority to decide disputes between the States. Perplexingly, however, Laurens would later vote no on the establishment of an autonomous and separate governmental branch necessary for such judicial matters to be employed. This failure to separate the judicial duties of government from the legislative federal body plagued the United States until the adoption of the current U.S. Constitution in 1789.

Significantly, Laurens voted against Virginia's last attempt to gain more power in the federal government based on population. Under the new constitution, nine votes (2/3 of the 13 states) would be necessary to confirm matters of importance to the new "Perpetual Union"; Virginia's amendment proposed that the nine votes must be from the states containing a majority of the white population. The measure failed largely because of Laurens' efforts, as well as the objections of the other smaller states. That the South Carolinian's vote did not follow the "southern block" clearly indicates Laurens was free from sectional bias. Again and again, he put forth and supported articles and concepts that would work to forge 13 individual States into one unified nation, striving to form a constitution that would empower a central government to act for the benefit of all states equally. This philosophy, along with his wealth, made him a leading candidate for the Presidency to replace the ailing John Hancock in October of 1777.

Meanwhile, on October 20th, 1777, the Continental Congress learned of General Burgoyne's defeat at Saratoga;[79] the British plan to sever the States by controlling the Hudson River Valley had resulted in the capture of the British General and his 6,000 troops. This was the news Congress and their Foreign French Commissioner, Benjamin Franklin, desperately needed to convince France to form an alliance with the United States. The Franco-American Alliance, however, would require a constitutionally formed United States of America to enact such a treaty. Work on the Articles of Confederation, therefore, accelerated, progressing steadily under what

---

[79] *JCC, 1774-1789*, October 20, 1777.

would be the last few days of John Hancock's Presidency. Key amendments and changes to the Articles were agreed on in the sessions of October 27th, 28th, and even the 29th, when Hancock tendered his official resignation as President. So intent was Congress on completing the Constitution that they re-convened immediately after Hancock's departure under the temporary presidency of Secretary Charles Thomson. The Journals report:

Congress resumed the consideration of the 14 article of confederation, whereon it was moved to strike out the words "general officers" in the 24 line, and insert "all officers:" and to add after "United States," "excepting regimental officers." And on the question put, the same was agreed to. It was then moved to strike out the next paragraph, and in the following paragraph, after the word "forces" to insert these words, "and commissioning all officers whatever." And on the question put, the same was agreed to.

The president having taken leave of Congress. Four o'Clock, pm. Met at 4' O'clock, Resolved, That the secretary officiate as president until a new choice is made. On motion, Ordered, That the secretary wait upon the president and request him to furnish the house with a copy of the speech with which he took leave of Congress. [80]

Congress would meet only once more, on October 30th, 1777, to debate and revise the Articles of Confederation with acting President Charles Thomson presiding. The Articles, however, could not be finalized until a new President of the U.S. Continental Congress was elected.. On October 31st, 1777, acting President Thomson turned to other business and presented congress with General Horatio Gates' official notification of the Saratoga Convention. The Continental Congress Journals report:

A letter, of the 18 October, from General Gates, with the copy of the convention at Saratoga, whereby General Burgoyne surrenders himself and his whole army; and another, of the 20th, enclosing the copy of a letter from him to Major General John Vaughan, were read.[81]

The spirit of the delegates soared as the thorough defeat of General Burgoyne was far more than anyone had anticipated. The following day, to Henry Laurens' astonishment, the Chair nominated him to be the President. The vote was taken and, with unanimous approval, Laurens was elected the fourth President of a very festive United States Continental Congress.

---

[80]*Debates on the Articles of Confederation and Hancock request for two months leave*, October 29, 1777. *JCC, 1774-1789.*
[81] *Ibid*, October 31, 1777

Henry Laurens' first official act as the President was to vote for a Day of Thanksgiving and *"to adore the superintending providence of Almighty God"*. In his first letter to the 13 States, President Laurens declared:

Dear Sir, The Arms of the United States of America having been blessed in the present Campaign with remarkable Success, Congress have Resolved to recommend that one day, Thursday the 18th December next be Set apart to be observed by all Inhabitants throughout these States for a General thanksgiving to Almighty God. And I have it in command to transmit to you the enclosed extract from the minutes of Congress for that purpose. [82]

Laurens did not reconvene the Congress until November 4th, when they officially thanked General Horatio Gates[83] and his army for their defense against Burgoyne's invasion as well as various other officers and units for their defense of the Delaware. After another recess, Congress reconvened on November 7th to reorganize the Board of War and agreed to resume debate to finalize the Articles of Confederation. The constitutional deliberations resumed on the 10th, with the Delegates working until the morning of November 15th, 1777, concluding the session with the passage of the Articles of Confederation.

Under this new constitution, the Continental Congress would cease to exist and a new body, "the United States, in Congress Assembled" (USCA), would become the federal government of a "Perpetual Union between the states of New Hampshire, Massachusetts-bay, Rhode Island and Providence Plantations, Connecticut, New York, New Jersey, Pennsylvania, Delaware, Maryland, Virginia, North Carolina, South Carolina and Georgia." [84]

The *Articles* constituted a feeble constitution, a confederation of sovereign states that formed a Not Quite Perpetual Union based on mutual respect and a central government with no taxing power. The federal government also had no power to regulate trade between the States. The national government would have to ask the States for money to wage war, establish federal departments, hire employees,

---

[82] *Ibid, Thanksgiving Proclamation*, November 1, 1777
[83] Horatio Lloyd Gates (1727–1806) was a British soldier who became an American general during the Revolutionary War. He took credit, over Benedict Arnold who led the attack, for the American victory at the Battle of Saratoga. He was promoted to head the Board of War and from there sought to replace George Washington as commander-in-chief. The Conway Cabal failed and Gates was eventually given the Southern Command where he was thoroughly defeated by General Cornwallis in the Battle of Camden.
[84] *JCC, 1774-1789*, Articles of Confederation, November 15, 1777, first paragraph.

maintain a judicial system and carry out the host of laws Congress passed to govern the new United States of America. The States were expected, in a most gentlemanly fashion, to comply with all constitutional requests, bequeathing the federal government with money and land to fund its national endeavors.

The legislative, executive and judicial systems were all entrusted to one body: the "United States in Congress Assembled." Each State had only one vote despite its population or its size, *"all equal in the eyes of God."* Presidents served only one year and Congress rotated candidacy between North and South. The Presidents and Commander-in-Chief accepted only expenses for their services. It was a furtive commune where all members pledged secrecy and service to the people of their respective States that were freely united and desperately seeking peace.

In summary, the first constitution's Articles:

I.   Establish the name of the nation as "The United States of America;"
II.   State that "Each state retains its sovereignty, freedom, and independence, and every power, jurisdiction, and right, which is not by this Confederation expressly delegated" to the new federal government called the "United States, in Congress Assembled" (USCA);[85]
III.   Establish the Sovereign States as one Sovereign nation *". . . for their common defense, the security of their liberties, and their mutual and general welfare, binding themselves to assist each other, against all force offered to, or attacks made upon them . . . ;"*
IV.   Establish the freedom of citizens to pass freely between states, excluding *"paupers, vagabonds, and fugitives from justice."* All the people were also entitled to the rights established by the State into which they traveled. If a crime were committed in one state and the perpetrator to flee to another state, the citizen would be extradited to and tried in the State in which the crime had been committed;
V.   Equality was established in the United States in Congress Assembled with only one vote to each State, regardless of size, but delegations might have from two to seven members. Members of the USCA were elected or appointed by state legislatures and could serve no more than three out of any six years;[86]

---

[85] This language would later be reformulated and added as the 10th Amendment to the current U.S. Constitution that states: *"The powers not delegated to the United States by the Constitution, nor prohibited by it to the States, are reserved to the States respectively, or to the people."*

[86] The concept of one vote to each State would be adopted under the current U.S. Constitution in the formation of any future constitutional conventions and the passage of all amendments. The representation would also be incorporated in the U.S. Senate with each State, regardless of size, having two votes.

VI.	Only the USCA was permitted to conduct foreign relations and to declare war. No states were permitted to have navies or standing armies, or engage in war, without permission of USCA. State militias were encouraged;
VII.	When an Army was raised for common defense, colonels and military ranks below colonel were to be named by the state legislatures;
VIII.	Expenditures by the USCA were paid by funds raised by State legislatures and apportioned based on the real property values of each;
IX.	The ninth- article defined the powers of the central government:

    a. USCA sends and receives ambassadors

    b. USCA enters into treaties and alliances, provided that no treaty of commerce shall be made whereby the legislative power of the respective States shall be restrained from imposing such imposts and duties on foreigners, as their own people are subjected to, or from prohibiting the exportation or importation of any species of goods or commodities whatsoever;

    c. USCA establishes the rules for deciding, in all cases, what captures on land or water shall be legal, and in what manner prizes taken by land or naval forces in the service of the United States shall be divided or appropriated;

    d. USCA grants letters of marque (diplomacy) and reprisal in times of peace;

    e. USCA appoints courts for the trial of piracies and felonies committed on the high seas and establishes courts for receiving and determining finally appeals in all cases of captures, provided that no member of Congress shall be appointed a judge of any of the said courts;

    f. USCA fixes the standards of weights and measures throughout the United States;

    g. USCA regulates the trade and management of all affairs with Indians, not members of any of the States, provided that the legislative right of any State within its own limits be not infringed or violated;

    h. USCA establishes or regulates post offices from one State to another, throughout all the United States. They also exact postage on the papers passing through the post office to defray the expenses of the bureau;

    i. USCA appoints all officers of the land forces, in the service of the United States, excepting regimental officers;

    j. USCA appoints all the officers of the naval forces, and commissions all officers whatever in the service of the United States;

    k. USCA makes rules for the government and regulation of the said land and naval forces, and direction of their operations;

    l. USCA serves as a final court for disputes between states;

    m. USCA defines a Committee of the States to be a government when Congress is not in session;

    n. USCA elects one of their members to preside, provided that no person be allowed to serve in the office of president more than one year in any term of three years;

| X. | The Committee of the States, or any nine of them, shall be authorized to execute, in the recess of USCA, such of the powers of the USCA. The President of the USCA is to chair the Committee of the States; |

XI.	Nine states required to approve the admission of a new state into the confederacy; pre-approves Canada, should it apply for membership;
XII.	Reaffirms that the Confederation accepts war debt incurred by the Continental Congress before the Articles;
XIII.	Declares that the Articles of Confederation are perpetual, and can only be altered by approval of Congress with ratification by all the state legislatures.[87]

The Continental Congress, after 16 months of debate and deliberations, had forged this *Constitution of 1777*, creating one nation empowered to govern. There was, however, one caveat: All 13 States were required to ratify the Articles of Confederation before it would officially take effect. [88]

Most delegates believed that the ratification of this constitution would take less than nine months, but by autumn of 1780, two President terms and three years had elapsed since the passage of the still-unratified Articles of Confederation. The 1778 treaties with France after Burgoyne's surrender at Saratoga were now in jeopardy because the constitutional formation of the United States of America was still in doubt. Many States had called on the U.S. Continental Congress to dissolve itself and set up the new government of the United States in Congress Assembled (USCA) without Maryland, the lone holdout on ratification, as part of the Perpetual Union. The 1778-1780 Presidents John Jay and Samuel Huntington, along with other conservative leaders in the Congress, refused to adopt any such measure. Instead, they continued to broker a resolution to settle the western land disputes between Maryland, New York and Virginia that were holding-up the *"Old Line State's"* ratification.

Meanwhile, the fortunes of the Americans in 1780, instead of improving, had grown worse to the point of desperation. France's aid was waning due to the States' failure to act under one constitution, the southern Continental Army had been defeated, and the American dollar, as discussed below, wasn't worth a *"Continental."*

Early in 1776, one paper continental dollar was worth a Spanish milled dollar -- about 92% fine silver and weighing .89 troy ounces. By the end of 1776, the need to

---

[87] Format and some information gathered from Wikipedia's Articles of Confederation http://en.wikipedia.org/wiki/Articles_of_Confederation. Fact checked against author's research and *JCC, 1774-1789*, ed. Worthington C. Ford et al.

[88] *"City of York - The First Capital of the United States,"* http://yorkcity.org/history, Copyright 2014 City of York, Pennsylvania - 101 South George Street, York, PA 17401.

issue more war dollars forced the new States to remove the redeemable clause for Spanish milled dollars on the currency. The States then refused to tax their citizens to support the new fiat dollar currency.[89] Loans and subsidies furnished by France from the Franco-American Alliance in 1778 brought considerable sums into the federal treasury but not nearly enough to fund the war effort. Meanwhile, the U.S. Continental Congress continued to issue excessive amounts of fiat currency tied to neither gold nor silver. By April of 1779, 20 U.S. dollars were equal to one Spanish Milled Dollar. Continental Congress President John Jay wrote George Washington that "... the state of our currency is really serious. Where or by what means the progress of the depreciation will be prevented is uncertain." [90]

Congress, in an effort to pay for the war and prop up the economy, had issued over $241,500,000 of continental bills of credit by 1780. The States increased their own currency emissions to more than $200,000,000,[91] heavily overburdening their citizens with taxes to meet the demands on the notes. Congress recalled the dollar on March 18, 1780, adopting measures for redeeming bills in circulation at the ratio of 40 to 1.[92] With the swoop of the pen the national debt was effectively reduced from $200 million to $5 million. The fiat dollar would collapse by the end of 1780.

Mr. Pelatiah Webster, a merchant of Philadelphia wrote that "we have suffered more from this than from every other cause of calamity; it has killed more men, pervaded and corrupted the choicest interests of our country more, and done more injustice than even the arms and artifices of our enemies. [93] John Witherspoon, the New Jersey signer of the Declaration of Independence and President of what is now Princeton University said, "For two or three years we constantly saw and were informed of creditors running away from their debtors, and the debtors pursuing

---

[89] Fiat currency is paper declared by a government to be legal tender. The term derives from the Latin *fiat*, meaning, "let it be done". Fiat money achieves value because a government requires it in payment of taxes and deems it as "tender" to pay all debts. It is not tied to a commodity such as gold or silver.

[90] John Jay to George Washington April 1779. John Jay Papers, Columbia University.

[91] Charles Jesse Bullock, *Essays on the monetary history of the United States*, Macmillan and Company, 1900, pp. 63-64.

[92] *JCC, 1774-1789*, March 18, 1780

[93] Cited in Charles Gide and Charles William August Veditz, *Principles of Political Economy*, D.C. Heath & Co., 1903, p. 270. Mr. Webster would go on to write *Political Essays on the Nature and Operation of Money, Public Finances, and other Subjects, published during the American War* (1791), which is required reading for anyone interested in the history of U.S. currency.

them in triumph, and paying them without mercy.[94] Thomas Jefferson remarked that:

> It continued to circulate and to depreciate till the end of 1780, when it had fallen to 75 for 1, and the money circulated from the French army ... being by that time sensible in all the States north of the Potomac, the paper ceased its circulation altogether in those States. In Virginia and North Carolina it continued a year longer, within which time it fell to 1,000 for 1 and then expired, as it had done in the other States ...[95]

Consequently, on the front lines the Continental Army was clothed in rags, half-starved and not paid. The desertions to the British lines averaged more than 100 soldiers a month. The British had changed their strategy and launched a southern spring campaign. The English successfully captured key southern ports in the Carolinas and Georgia. Former Colonial Continental Congress President Henry Middleton surrendered with the fall of Charleston, taking an oath of allegiance to King George III. Even Commander-in-Chief George Washington wrote during this period that he "had almost ceased to hope."[96]

It was on March 31, 1780 that Samuel Huntington presided over another challenge to the war effort, the court-marshal of General Benedict Arnold. In what became known as the "Charming Nancy Affair," Arnold, with some Philadelphia businessmen, invested in a schooner called the *Nancy* which, laden with supplies, was captured by NJ privateers and forced to dock in Egg Harbor, New Jersey. The military commander, fearful of losing the supplies, sent twelve wagons belonging to the people of Pennsylvania on an eight day trip to get a cargo of goods from the schooner.

At this time, the Executive Council of Pennsylvania was headed by Joseph Reed, a former aide who had conspired to remove Washington as Commander-in-Chief in 1778. Reed had been keeping meticulous records of any complaints lodged on Arnold since the latter's appointment as Philadelphia's Military Commander and, upon learning of Arnold's "war profiteering," the Executive Council brought formal charges before Congress against him. President Samuel Huntington was forced to

---

[94] Harold Glenn Moulton, Principles *of Money and Banking: A Series of Selected Materials, with Explanatory Introduction*s, University of Chicago Press, 1916.

[95] Thomas Jefferson, *The Works of Thomas Jefferson.* Ed. Paul Leicester Ford, 12 vols., 1904-1908, vol. IX, p. 248.

[96] William George Smith, William Gifford, *et. al.,* "The Rise and Progress of Popular Disaffection", , *The Quarterly Review*, John Murray, 1817, p. 553.

take off his legislative hat and act as "Chief Justice," presiding over a hearing that took almost the entire day. Arnold was acquitted on six charges but found guilty of illegally permitting ships to dock in Philadelphia and using public wagons to transport his partnership's cargo from Egg Harbor to Philadelphia. George Washington, who had great respect for Arnold's military field accomplishments, issued only a gentle reprimand.

It was shortly after these events that the very disgruntled Benedict Arnold sought the command of West Point through his friend General Philip John Schuyler, who believed the patriot deserved an important military post outside of Philadelphia. Both Schuyler and NY Delegate Livingston lobbied Huntington as well as the Commander-in-Chief, and, in August, Washington approved the command with the backing of Congress. The stage was now set for a betrayal that is now legendary in American History. Benedict Arnold would use this post, granted to him by his most influential political and military benefactors (including President Samuel Huntington and George Washington), as the means to betray the States and, potentially, to end the war in Great Britain's favor.

Benedict Arnold showed no shame in his defection and wielded propaganda by posting statements in newspapers to justify his betrayal. Congress was enraged over Arnold's letter and ordered a thorough investigation into his service as a Continental General. In mid-October, President Huntington wrote Governor Jonathan Trumbull of Connecticut of the initial findings: "The treason of Benedict Arnold hath been a topic of much conversation, and many of his scandalous transactions are brought to light that were before concealed."[97]

President Huntington condemned Arnold's betrayal, making a public spectacle of signing the Presidential Order to erase the traitor's name from the register of Continental Army officers.

Resolved, that the Board of War be and hereby are directed to erase from the register of the names of the officers of the army of the United States, the name of Benedict Arnold.[98]

This public denunciation did not faze Arnold one bit as the British, fresh from victories on all land fronts, were now making trade impossible for the States on the

---

[97] *LDC, 1774-1789,*Letter from Samuel Huntington to Jonathan Trumbull, Sr. October 17, 1780.
[98] *JCC, 1774-1789*, Wednesday, October 4, 1780

high seas and intrastate waterways. The British Admiralty launched a river-plundering 27-ship naval expedition, commanded by Arnold, landing in Virginia on January 14, 1781. General Arnold showed no leniency in the captured territories. He burned Richmond as they searched for Virginia's leadership. Governor Thomas Jefferson narrowly escaped Arnold, learning of the impending invasion just in time to vacate the city. James Madison, in his letter to Jefferson, warned of Arnold's departure and blamed the failure to ratify the Articles of Confederation as the major reason behind France's unwillingness to check British naval power. The States were not united:

Another embarkation has taken place at New York supposed to consist of two thousand five Hundred land forces, whose destination is not yet know. The fleet fell down to the Hook on Wednesday last. Our Conjecture is that they are destined to the Southward, and indeed all the Enemy's political & military maneuvers seem to indicate their Intention of making a Vigorous effort against the Southern States, this Winter. We are Sorry to inform yr. Excellency that we receive very little Authentic Intelligence of the Steps which are taking to counteract those vigorous operations, that we are in a great measure uninformed of the progress that has been made in raising the new army, and on what terms, of what has been, and will be, done in establishing Magazines for its Support, and above all, of the measures perusing to cancel the old money and give an effectual Support to the new, by providing for its punctual and final redemption with Specie. This is a crisis at which we conceive a most assiduous application to these great objects to be necessary, and (next to the completion of the Confederacy which is perhaps the Basis of the whole) of the first importance to America therefore highly importing us to know, as the measures of so large a state as ours cannot but have considerable effects on the other states in the Union.[99]

Adding to the ills of Arnold's Virginia campaign, Congress was unable redress the Continental Army's grievances of no pay and scarce supplies. The New Jersey militia mutinied on January 20th and, fearing the total dissolution of the army, George Washington was forced to deal with the new crisis in a most severe fashion. The Commander-in-Chief ordered General Robert Howe from West Point to suppress the mutiny and immediately execute the most extreme ringleaders, thus stopping the rebellion.

Inexplicably, during this period Congress began to make headway on reorganizing itself in anticipation of Maryland's ratification of the Articles of Confederation. A debate on a resolution establishing a department of foreign affairs headed by a secretary charged with managing all diplomatic activities was about to be passed. In

---

[99] *LDC, 1774-1789.* Virginia Delegates to Thomas Jefferson, January 1st. 1781

early February, Congress resolved to appoint executive officers to direct the war, navy, and treasury departments. On February 19th, Robert Morris, a private citizen, was appointed Superintendent of Finance to oversee the treasury. Morris' powers were analogous to that of Secretary of the Treasury. His appointment was a boost of confidence for the states and the national government. Under Morris, treasury resources were stabilized and began to cash flow enough to enable Washington and his Generals to continue waging what many Americans had believed only six months earlier to be a lost war for freedom.

For two years the U.S. Continental Congress had been the stage for incessant wrangling over the Maryland Plan, which sought that Northwest Territorial state land claims be ceded to the federal government. On September 6th, 1780, Congress passed a resolution urging the states to release their land claims to the USCA. President Huntington sent this circular letter to each of the states:

> I am directed to transmit Copies of this report and the several Papers there in mentioned to the Legislatures of the several States, that they may all be informed of the Desires & Endeavors of Congress on so important a Subject, and those particular States which have Claims to the Western Territory, & the State of Maryland may adopt the Measures recommended by Congress in Order to obtain a final ratification of the Articles of Confederation. Congress, impressed with a Sense of the vast Importance of the Subject, have maturely considered the same, and the result of their Deliberation is contained in the enclosed report, which being full & expressive of their Sentiments upon the Subject; without any additional Observations: it is to be hoped, and most earnestly desired, that the Wisdom, Generosity & Candor of the Legislatures of the several States, which have it in their Power on the one Hand to remove the Obstacles, and on the other to complete the Confederation, may direct them to such Measures, in Compliance ...[100]

Maryland, happy that Hanson, Huntington and others were brokering Northwest Territorial land concessions from numerous states, finally passed an act to empower their delegates to subscribe and ratify the Articles of Confederation on January 30th, 1781. On February 2nd, Governor Thomas Sim Lee signed the empowerment into law. The last State, after 39 long months, had finally agreed to ratify the Articles of Confederation, thus ending the *Second American Republic: United States of America: Thirteen Independent States United in Congress*. This ratification empowered Congress to set a date to enact the new Articles of Confederation, dissolve the old U.S. Continental Congress and convened the new United States in Congress Assembled Constitutional government.

---

[100]*LDC, 1774-1789*, Samuel Huntington to the States, September 10. 1780.

1. The *United States of America: Thirteen Independent States United in Congress'* day of origin is July 2nd, 1776 when 12 Colonies declared their Independence from Great Britain;
2. John Hancock, by virtue of the resolution for Independency, became the first President of the Continental Congress of the United States of America on July 2nd, 1776;
3. Charles Thomson continued as Secretary of the Continental Congress of the United States of America on July 2nd, 1776;
4. George Washington continued to serve as Commander-in-Chief of the Continental Army;
5. Although the first constitution of the United States of America was passed by the U.S. Continental Congress on November 15th, 1777, the Articles of Confederation required unanimous ratification, which did not occur until February 2nd, 1781.
6. Burgoyne's defeat at Saratoga emboldened France to sign the *Franco-American Treaty of Amity and Commerce*, a military pact in which the French provided military supplies, troops, and loans to support the U.S. War for Independence. The treaty was negotiated by Benjamin Franklin, Arthur Lee and Silas Deane for the U.S. and Conrad Alexandre Gérard for France. The treaty was signed on February 6th, 1778.
7. For three years, the Continental Congress would govern under a body of laws that were co-mingled with the proposed Articles of Confederation constitution.
8. The States, during this period, were required to have only one delegate present to cast a vote in Congress.
9. Congress required only a quorum of seven States to enact crucial wartime legislation.
10. The president, who at times cast the only vote for his state in quorums as small as seven States, also retained the authority to receive all official mail directed to the United States of America, to set the agenda on what legislative, executive, and judicial matters came before Congress, and in what order those matters would be addressed.

THE SECOND UNITED AMERICAN REPUBLIC
Continental Congress of the United States Presidents
July 2, 1776 to February 28, 1781

John Hancock	July 2, 1776	October 29, 1777
Henry Laurens	November 1, 1777	December 9, 1778
John Jay	December 10, 1778	September 28, 1779
Samuel Huntington	September 29, 1779	February 28, 1781

THE SECOND UNITED AMERICAN REPUBLIC'S
Seats of Government
July 2, 1776 to February 28, 1781

Philadelphia	July 2, 1776 to Dec. 12, 1776	Pennsylvania State House
Philadelphia	May 10, 1775 to Dec. 12, 1776	Pennsylvania State House
Baltimore	Dec. 20, 1776 to Feb. 27, 1777	Henry Fite House
Philadelphia	March 4, 1777 to Sep. 18, 1777	Pennsylvania State House
Lancaster	September 27, 1777	Lancaster Court House
York	Sept. 30, 1777 to June 27, 1778	York-town Court House
Philadelphia	July 2, 1778 to July 19, 1778*	College Hall - PA State House
Philadelphia	July 19, 1778 to February 28, 1781	PA State House
	* True Dates Unknown	

50

CHAPTER IV
THE THIRD UNITED AMERICAN REPUBLIC

THE UNITED STATES OF AMERICA
A NOT QUITE PERPETUAL UNION
March 1, 1781 to March 3, 1789

All eyes in the Union were on the State of Maryland when the New Year commenced in 1781. On January 30th, 1781, after delegates such as John Hanson, Daniel Carroll, James Madison, Samuel Huntington had brokered land cessions from other states, the Maryland legislature, was finally persuaded to pass an act to empower their delegates to subscribe to and ratify the Articles of Confederation. On February 2nd, 1781, Governor Thomas Sim Lee signed the Maryland Delegate empowerment into law. The following day, the legislature passed legislation "certifying that John Hanson, Daniel of St. Thomas Jenifer, Daniel Carroll and Richard Potts Esquires are elected Delegates to represent this State in Congress for the Year One thousand seven hundred and Eighty one."

Delegate Daniel Carroll arrived in Philadelphia on February 20th and presented Maryland's ratification resolution and his delegate credentials to the US Continental Congress. On that day he wrote Charles Carroll of Carrollton:

On the first day of my appearing in Congress, I delivered the Act empowering the Delegates of Maryland to Subscribe the Articles of Confederation &c. It was read, & entered on the Journals. [101]

---

[101]JCC, 1774-1789, February 20th, 1781.

With John Hanson's arrival in Philadelphia two days later, all the delegates sitting in Congress had now been duly appointed **after their respective states had ratified the Articles of Confederation**. Congress, which had been waiting for the final state's approval since February 1779, decided to enact the new constitution and unanimously resolved that:

The delegates of Maryland having taken their seats in Congress with powers to sign the Articles of Confederation: Ordered, That Thursday next [March 1, 1781] be assigned for compleating the Confederation; and that a committee of three be appointed, to consider and report a mode for announcing the same to the public: the members, [Mr. George] Walton, Mr. [James] Madison, Mr. [John] Mathews. [102]

After 39 months of ratification consideration, the *Third United America Republic* – a self-designated *"Perpetual Union"* -- was finally to become a constitutional reality.

Although the entry was not included in the official printing of *the Journals of Congress, and of the United States in Congress Assembled, for the year 1781* , (David C. Claypoole: Philadelphia), the manuscript Journals of Congress for February 28th, 1781, clearly concludes the business of the Continental Congress:

Resolved That several matters now before Congress be referred over & recommended to the attention of the United States in Congress Assembled, & that the committees who have not yet reported, make report to them.

Adjourned to 10 o' clock tomorrow. [103]

This manuscript entry in the original Journals of Congress clearly signals the conclusion of the U.S. Continental Congress and the start of the Articles of Confederation government that the Journal of Congress properly titles: *The United States in Congress Assembled.*

---

[102]LDC, *1774-1789*, Samuel Huntington to the States, September 10. 1780.
[103]Journals of Congress, Manuscript, National Archives of the United States, February 28th, 1781.

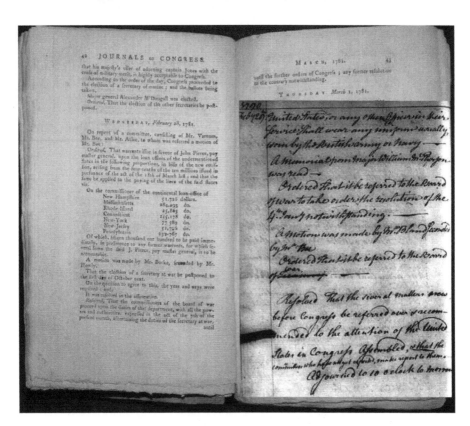

U.S. Continental Congress text comparison between the original Journals of Congress Manuscript (courtesy of the National Archives of the United States) and *the Journals of Congress, and of the United States in Congress Assembled, for the year 1781, Vol. VII" By Order of Congress. David C. Claypoole: Philadelphia, 1781.* The 1781 printing omits the concluding entry: "Resolved that several matters now before Congress be referred over & recommended to the attention of the United States in Congress Assembled, & that the committees who have not yet reported, make report to them. Adjourned to 10 o clock tomorrow."

The following day, March 1st, 1781, the original manuscript of the Journals of Congress reports the credentials of each of the state's delegates, concluding with those from Maryland:

According to the order of the day the Hon John Hanson and Daniel Carrol two of the Delegates for the State of Maryland in pursuance of the act of the legislature of that State entitled "An Act to Empower the Delegates of their State in Congress ti subscribe and ratify the Articles of Confederation which was received in Congress the 18th of February last and a copy thereof entered on the minutes in behalf of the said State of Maryland sign and ratify the said articles, by which act the Confederation of the United States of America was completed, each and every of the thirteen United States from

New Hampshire to Georgia both included having adopted and confirmed and by their Delegates in Congress ratified the same. [104]

The manuscript journals end here on March 1st, 1781, but the Claypool printing includes the complete text of the Articles of Confederation that begins (bold for emphasis):

Articles of Confederation and perpetual Union between the states of New Hampshire, Massachusetts-bay, Rhode Island and Providence Plantations, Connecticut, New York, New Jersey, Pennsylvania, Delaware, Maryland, Virginia, North Carolina, South Carolina and Georgia.

I. **The Stile** of this Confederacy shall be **The United States of America.**

II. Each state retains its sovereignty, freedom, and independence, and every power, jurisdiction, and right, which is not by this Confederation expressly delegated to the **United States, in Congress assembled.**

III. The said States hereby severally enter into a firm league of friendship with each other, for their common defense, the security of their liberties, and their mutual and general welfare, binding themselves to assist each other, against all force offered to, or attacks made upon them, or any of them, on account of religion, sovereignty, trade, or any other pretense whatever ...

XIII. **Every State shall abide by the determination of the United States in Congress assembled,** on all questions which by this confederation are submitted to them. And the Articles of this Confederation shall be inviolably observed by every State**, and the Union shall be perpetual;** nor shall any alteration at any time hereafter be made in any of them; unless such alteration be agreed to in a Congress of the United States, and be afterwards confirmed by the legislatures of every State. [105]

---

[104]Journals of Congress, Manuscript, National Archives of the United States, March 1, 1781.
[105] *Journals of Congress, and of the United States in Congress Assembled, for the year 1781, Vol. VII" By Order of Congress. David C. Claypoole: Philadelphia,*, March 1, 1781

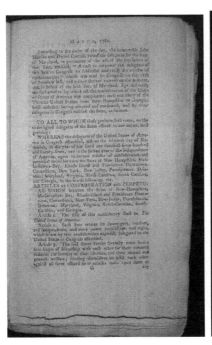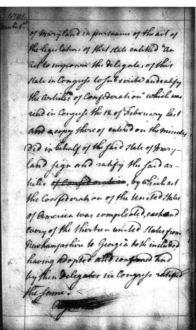

Above is the Claypool Journal printing of the March 1, 1781, ratification entry, which adds the Articles of Confederation text alongside the original manuscript Journal March 1st entry, which omits either a written or printed insertion of the Articles of Confederation.

By virtue of this ratification, the ever-fluid Continental Congress ceased to exist, replaced by a new governing body designated by the Articles as "the United States in Congress Assembled." As reported in the Pennsylvania Gazette's summary of the March 1st ratification festivities, the elated Minister of France was the first diplomat to address Samuel Huntington as *"His Excellency the President of the United States in Congress Assembled"*:

In pursuance of an Act of the Legislature of Maryland, entitled, 'An Act to empower the Delegates of the State in Congress to subscribe and ratify the Articles of Confederation,' the Delegates of the said State, on Thursday last, at twelve o, signed and ratified the Articles of Confederation; by which act the Confederation of The United States Of America was completed, each and every of the Thirteen States, from New Hampshire to George, both included, having adopted and confirmed, and by their Delegates in Congress ratified the same.

This happy event was immediately announced to the public by the discharge of the artillery on land, and the cannon of the shipping in the river Delaware. At two o'clock his Excellency the President of Congress received on this occasion the congratulations of the Hon. Minister Plenipotentiary of France, and of the Legislative and Executive Bodies of this State, of the Civil and Military Officers, sundry strangers of distinction in town, and of many of the principal inhabitants.

The evening was closed by an elegant exhibition of fireworks. The Ariel frigate, commanded by the gallant John Paul Jones, fired a feu de joye, and was beautifully decorated with a variety of streamers in the day, and ornamented with a brilliant appearance of lights in the night.

Thus will the first of March, 1781, be a day memorable in the annals of America, for the final ratification of the Confederation and perpetual Union of the Thirteen States of America --- A Union, begun by necessity, cemented by oppression and common danger, and now finally consolidated into a perpetual confederacy of these new and rising States: And thus the United States of America, having, amidst the calamities of a destructive war, established a solid foundation of greatness, are growing up into consequence among the nations, while their haughty enemy, Britain, with all her boasted wealth and grandeur, instead of bringing them to her feet and reducing them to unconditional submission, finds her hopes blasted, her power crumbling to pieces, and the empire which, with overbearing insolence and brutality she exercised on the ocean, divided among her insulted neighbors.[106]

On March 2nd, the title, *"The United States, in Congress Assembled,"* was placed at the head of the first page of the new official Journal of Congress, which reported:

The ratification of the Articles of Confederation being yesterday completed by the accession of the State of Maryland: The United States met in Congress, when the following members appeared: His Excellency President Samuel Huntington for Connecticut ...[107]

---

[106] Pennsylvania Gazette 1728-1800 on-line publication by Accessible Archives Malvern, PA, John Nagy, Editor - http:www.accessible.com
[107] *JCC, 1774-1789*, March 2, 1781

Image comparison of the manuscript copy and official Claypool printing of the USCA Journals for Tuesday, March 2nd, 1781.

Note that the primary source manuscript differs slightly from the official Journals of the United States in Congress Assembled printed by order of Congress, which states: "His Excellency Samuel Huntington Delegate for Connecticut, President" [108]. The placement of President is a nuance, nevertheless it demonstrates yet another variance between the print and written versions of the USCA Journals.

That same day, the USCA voted to send out the first USCA Presidential circular letter to each of the States:

> By the Act of Congress herewith enclosed your Excellency will be informed that the Articles of Confederation & perpetual Union between the thirteen United States are formally & finally ratified by all the States. We are happy to congratulate our Constituents on this important Event, desired by our Friends but dreaded by our Enemies. Your Excellency's most obedient humble Servant, Samuel Huntington, President.[109]

March 12th, 1781, marks the first recorded foreign diplomat's use of the new Articles of Confederation Presidential title for Samuel Huntington, when the U.S. Treasury office took up the matter of a letter "from the Honorable Minister of France to His Excellency the President of the United States in Congress Assembled.".

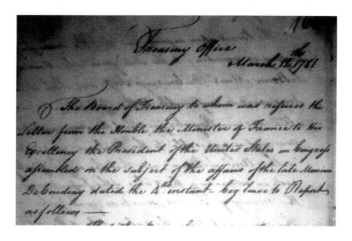

Treasury letter, Samuel Huntington, President of the United States in Congress Assembled [110]

---

[108] *JCC, 1774-1789*, March 2, 1781
[109] Samuel Huntington to the States, March 2, 1781. *LDC, 1774-1789*.
[110] *Ibid.*

The Articles of Confederation not only retitled the President and his Congress; the new constitution also created the *First Federal Congress* of the United States of America. The Articles of Confederation was recognized as a federal constitution by the states, including, for example, Maryland, the last state to ratify, when, in an "Act of Appointment of, And Conferring Powers in, Deputies from this State to the Federal Convention" it affirmed that it would join with other states "… in considering such alterations, and further provisions, as may be necessary to render the federal constitution adequate to the exigencies of the union."

Maryland Act of 1787 – Image Courtesy of Historic.us

The term "federal constitution" was also utilized repeatedly by the US government, in **resolutions** ("and further provisions as to render the federal Constitution adequate to the Exigencies of the Union"),[111] **treaties** ("That these United States be considered in all such treaties, and in every case arising under them, as one nation, upon the principles of the federal constitution"),[112] in reference to **finances** ("The federal constitution authorizes the United States to obtain money by three means; 1st. by requisition; 2d., by loan; and 3d., by emitting bills of credit")[113] and in the **debates of the congressional delegates**:

A requisition of Congress on the States for money is as much a law to them as their revenue Acts when passed are laws to their respective Citizens. If, for want of the faculty or means of enforcing a requisition, the law of Congress proves inefficient, does

---

[111] *JCC, 1774-1789,* , March15, 1787
[112] *JCC, 1774-1789,* March 26, 1784
[113] *Ibid,* February 3, 1786

it not follow that in order to fulfill the views of the federal constitution, such a change sd. Be made as will render it efficient? Without such efficiency the end of this Constitution, which is to preserve order and justice among the members of the Union, must fail; as without a like efficiency would the end of State Constitutions, which is to preserve like order & justice among its members. [114]

Indeed, the U.S. founding acts and laws include a resolution empowering the USCA President to reconvene the *"federal government"* in New Jersey after he and the Congress fled Independence Hall from mutinous United States soldiers:

There is not a satisfactory ground for expecting adequate and prompt exertions of this State for supporting the dignity of the federal government, the President ... be authorized and directed to summon the members of Congress to meet on Thursday next at Trenton or Princeton, in New Jersey. [115]

These recurrent references clearly indicate that the congress operating under the Articles of Confederation considered itself a federal congress. Unfortunately, this evidence is not recognized by the current U.S. Congress, the Supreme Court, or even the Executive offices of the U.S. government, which continually refer to the congress of this Third United American Republic as the "Continental Congress." Even the Library of Congress, the steward of the many primary sources cited above, refers to the Presidents of the "United States in Congress Assembled" as "Continental Congress Presidents" in their important *Biographical Directory of the United States Congress* (2005).[116] The same error is made by the scholars at George Washington University, in their otherwise excellent *Documentary History of the First Federal Congress, 1789-1791.* Yet, as we have seen, the Congress of 1789-1791 was by no means the "First Federal Congress." It was the "First Federal Bicameral Congress." Moreover, the USCA was not the "Continental Congress." The *Articles of Association* in 1774 named its assembly a Continental Congress, which reconvened in 1775 and eventually enacted the *Resolution for Independency*, thus creating the Second United American Republic. That Continental Congress was dissolved with the enactment of the Articles of Confederation in 1781, which, as clarified above, named its new congress the "United States in Congress Assembled." It is also important to note that after March 1, 1781, there are no recording in the Journals or other official records, letters, resolutions, treaties, or commissions of the USCA referring to Congress as the "Continental Congress." Because these primary

---

[114] *Ibid*, January 28, 1783
[115] *Ibid*, June 21, 1783
[116] http://www.gpo.gov/fdsys/pkg/GPO-CDOC-108hdoc222/pdf/GPO-CDOC-108hdoc222.pdf

source-based facts have been convoluted by every branch of the federal department and its corresponding federal departments, libraries, museums, and even the Archives of the United States, it is crucial that we explore this question of nomenclature.

NAMING THE U.S. CONGRESSES

In developing their "Articles of Confederation," the U.S. Continental Congress considered numerous names for the proposed new governing body. For example, the original title of "General Congress," which was to manage the new union's "General Continental Business," was rejected by Congress in 1775. The name United States Assembled, which was proposed in the draft of July 12th, 1776, along with the earlier Continental Congress versions, was also ultimately rejected by Congress.

The federal government's official name, the "United States in Congress Assembled," first appears in late 1776 in various drafts of the Articles of Confederation. The Articles' drafts of 1777 also record the term "United States in Congress Assembled." Finally, "United States in Congress Assembled" appears in the Journals of Congress on November 15th, 1777, when the Continental Congress passes the Articles of Confederation and sends it to the 13 States for ratification .

Looking at the document itself, Article 2 of the proposed constitution names the governing body the "United States in Congress Assembled":

Each State retains its sovereignty, freedom and independence, and every power, jurisdiction, and right, which is not by this confederation expressly delegated to the United States, in Congress assembled.[117]

The designation "United States in Congress Assembled" appears another 25 times in the *Articles of Confederation*. Nowhere, however, is Congress referred to as the "Congress of the Confederation," the "Confederation Congress" or the "Continental Congress." The term "United States in Congress Assembled" does not recur in the Journals until February 28th, 1781, except on October 19th, 1778, where it is referred to only in the context of the 8th Article of the *Articles of Confederation*:

A letter, of 17, from Major General Lord Stirling, was read: Whereas, by the 8th article of the articles of confederation and perpetual union, agreed upon for the United States of North America, it is provided, that all expenses for the common defense or general welfare, and allowed by the United States in Congress assembled, shall be defrayed out of a common treasury to be supplied by the several states, in proportion to the value of all lands within each State, granted to, or surveyed for any person, as such land, and the buildings and improvements thereon, shall be estimated, according to such mode as the United States in Congress assembled shall, from time to time, direct and appoint:

And, whereas, the value aforesaid must, from the nature of things, frequently change, and frequent valuations thereby become necessary: therefore, Resolved, That it be recommended to the several states to instruct their delegates to fix the period of such valuation. Resolved, That in the opinion of Congress five years will be a proper term for that purpose.[118]

In fact, the next use of the title by the U.S. Continental Congress on February 28th, 1781, in that congress' last resolution, clearly indicates that the "United States in Congress Assembled" is recognized as a different legal entity from the "U.S. Continental Congress":

Resolved That several matters now before Congress be referred over & recommended to the attention of the United States in Congress Assembled, & that the committees who have not yet reported, make report to them.[119]

Several colleagues have suggested that the name "United States in Congress Assembled" (USCA) was used by the U.S. Continental Congress on commissions before the March 1st, 1781, ratification of the Articles of Confederation. Such

---

[117] *JCC, 1774-1789*, October 19, 1778
[118] *JCC, 1774-1789*, November 15, 1777
[119] *JCC, 1774-1789*, February 28, 1781

assertions, however, are inaccurate. While the term "United States of America in Congress Assembled" (USACA) was used on commissions, [120] federal forms,[121] Court of Appeals Appointments[122] and commissioner appointments[123] that were standardized by the U.S. Continental Congress in anticipation of the Articles of Confederation, the name "United States in Congress Assembled" was not used. That designation was reserved only for its constitutional use by the Congress established *after* the ratification of the Articles of Confederation.

And from the ratification of the Articles of Confederation on March 1st, 1781, until March 3rd, 1789, the Journals record no use of the "United States of America in Congress Assembled" or USACA for the USCA.

During its entire 1774-1781 tenure, the U.S. Continental Congress governing body never used, was known by, or referred to as the "United States in Congress Assembled.". Although numerous Continental Congress resolutions, commissions, and letters utilize other conflicting names such as "Congress of the United States of America," "Congress of the United States of North America," and "General Continental Congress" for the governing body, the constitutional term "United States in Congress Assembled" was unequivocally set aside for the Congress that would form under the ratified Articles of Confederation.

Accordingly, the proper to use of Congressional terms is as follows:
1. September, 1774-February 28th, 1781: "Continental Congress"
2. March 1st, 1781, to March 3rd, 1789: "United States in Congress Assembled"

---

[120] *JCC, 1774-1789*, December 11th, 1778, Adoption of the Board of War's recommendation to print up military commission documents with the heading "United States of America in Congress Assembled;" April 20, 1780 - United States of America in Congress Assembled name in the form of a commission for the naval officers; September 26, 1780 - United States of America in Congress Assembled name in the form when it addresses the language for privateers.
[121] *JCC, 1774-1789*, June 26, 1778, Resolution adopting the proper language, "United States of America in Congress Assembled," for the States to use in Articles of Confederation ratification conventions.
[122] *JCC, 1774-1789*, February 2, 1780 - Congress approved the use of the United States of America in Congress Assembled name in Court of Appeals Appointments.
[123] *JCC, 1774-1789*, October 15, 1779 - Commission for John Jay, Minister Plenipotentiary at the Court of Madrid; October 30, 1779 - "Standardize a commission for the person appointed to negotiate a loan;" November 1, 1779 - "committee appointed to prepare a commission for the commissioner appointed to negotiate a treaty of amity and commerce:" June 20, 1780, "United States of America in Congress Assembled," for the Commissions to John Adams and Henry Laurens.

3. March 4th, 1789 to the present: "House of Representatives and Senate in the United States in Congress Assembled."

SESSIONS OF UNITED STATES IN CONGRESS ASSEMBLED

This First Federal Congress, constituted under the Articles of Confederation, would convene in eight different "United States in Congress Assembled" sessions. The first session, as noted, commenced on March 1st, 1781, with the adoption of the Articles of Confederation and Samuel Huntington presiding as President. The eighth and last USCA session commenced under President Cyrus Griffin and ended on October 10th, 1788, because the Delegates failed to achieve any further quorums. The ninth USCA, which was supposed to assemble on November 3rd, 1788, failed to achieve a quorum, nor were subsequent attempts (in November, December and January) successful in garnering the required representation of at least seven states by at least two delegates each. Cyrus Griffin's term as President expired on January 21st, 1789, and, on January 27th, 1789, USCA Delegate Tench Coxe wrote James Madison:

I have been here about a Fortnight during which time we have not made a Congress. South Carolina, Virginia, Pennsylvania, New Jersey, & Massachusetts are represented. There is one Member from each of the States of Rhode Island, N. Carolina & Georgia, but none from New Hampshire, Connecticut, New York, Delaware or Maryland. I very much wish we may make a house in a week or ten days, as I think the Appearance in Europe, & perhaps even here, of the old Congress being in full operation and tranquilly yielding the seats to the new would have a good effect. The misrepresentations in Europe have been extremely gross, and must have an unfavorable effect upon Emigration in the poorer ranks of life. Col. Wadsworth has been mentioned as President. I respect him much, but I wish to give appearance to the old System by a Character of rather more celebrity. Mr. Adams would meet my Judgment better than any member of the present house. The principal Objection is his Absence, which I fear will deprive him of his chance. [124]

---

[124] *LDC, 1774-1789,* Tench Coxe letter to James Madison, January 27th, 1789.

Articles of Confederation Congress
United States in Congress Assembled (USCA) Sessions

USCA	Session Dates	USCA Convene Date	President(s)
First	11-05-1780 to 11-04-1781*	03-02-1781	Samuel Huntington & Thomas McKean
Second	11-05-1781 to 11-03-1782	11-05-1781	John Hanson
Third	11-04-1782 to 11-02-1783	11-04-1782	Elias Boudinot
Fourth	11-03-1783 to 10-31-1784	11-03-1783	Thomas Mifflin
Fifth	11-01-1784 to 11-06-1785	11-29-1784	Richard Henry Lee
Sixth	11-07-1785 to 11-05-1786	11-23-1785	John Hancock & Nathaniel Gorham
Seventh	11-06-1786 to 11-04-1787	02-02-1787	Arthur St. Clair
Eighth	11-05-1787 to 11-02-1788	01-21-1788	Cyrus Griffin
Ninth	11-03-1788 to 03-03-1789**	None	None

* The Articles of Confederation was ratified by the mandated 13th State on February 2, 1781, and the dated adopted by the Continental Congress to commence the new United States in Congress Assembled government was March 1, 1781. The USCA convened under the Articles of Confederation Constitution on March 2, 1781.

** On September 14, 1788, the Eighth United States in Congress Assembled resolved that March 4th, 1789, would be commencement date of the *Constitution of 1787's* federal government thus dissolving the USCA on March 3rd, 1789.

THE HANSONITE CHALLENGE

A review of the above-referenced primary sources appears, irrefutably, to establish the starting point of Third United American Republic as March 1st, 1781. Unfortunately, both the federal and state governments have spent millions of taxpayers' dollars purporting that the United States in Congress Assembled government commenced on November 5th, 1781, rather than on March 1st, and that, therefore, John Hanson, not Samuel Huntington, was the first USCA President to serve under the ratified Articles of Confederation.

The challenge to the March 1st, 1781, start date was birthed on a national platform by the ancestors of John Hanson, who sought to have the President's statue included in U.S. Capitol's National Statuary Hall as one of the two allotted to the State of Maryland in 1903**. The "Hansonites" were well-funded, politically connected, and managed – correctly -- to convince the Maryland State Assembly that the *Articles of Confederation* had been the first true United States Constitution. Unfortunately, they also convinced the Maryland Governor and the State Assembly that John Hanson was the first to serve as President of the United States under the *Articles of Confederation* and therefore was the first President of the United States. The Hansonites assertion can be summarized as follows:

The United States in Congress Assembled government was not formed until no less than two delegates from each state, elected or appointed under the ratified Articles of Confederation, formed a quorum of at least seven states. Delegates, duly elected and/or appointed by the states under the fully ratified Articles of Confederation, did not form a Congress until November 5th, 1781. On that date, the Delegates elected John Hanson as the first President of the United States in Congress Assembled. Samuel Huntington's March 1st, 1781, Presidency (according to this argument) was merely a carryover from the chair of the old Continental Congress and therefore not a legitimate presidency under the Articles of Confederation. Furthermore, John Hanson was the first President elected and also the first to serve the prescribed full one-year term (1781-82) under the Articles of Confederation. Accordingly, John Hanson, under the Articles of Confederation constitution, is the first President of the United States.

The Maryland State Assembly agreed with the above argument, and enacted the necessary legislation to include a statue of John Hanson, along with one of Charles Carroll of Carrollton, in the National Statuary Hall Collection at the United States Capitol. This decision resulted in the U.S. Federal government's acknowledgment of John Hanson as the first President of the "United States in Congress Assembled" during the January 31, 1903, national acceptance ceremony at the U.S. Capitol. The official acceptance of Hanson's statue, along with the speeches of U.S. Senators and other dignitaries maintaining that John Hanson was the first President to serve under the Articles of Confederation, were officially recognized by Congress in the 111-page *Proceedings in the Senate and House of Representatives Upon the Reception and Acceptance from the State of Maryland of the Statues of Charles Carroll of Carrollton and of John Hanson, Erected in Statuary Hall of the Capitol: January 31, 1903*, which Congress ordered be printed and distributed by the U.S. Government Printing Office. It is from this U.S. Congressional printing that the "John Hanson First Presidential Myth" alleged by Hansonites, gained its dreadful foothold in the annals of Congressional blunders. The book explicitly records numerous distinguished politicians, including prominent U.S. Senators, wrongfully claiming that John Hanson was the first President to serve under the *Articles of Confederation*. For example, the speech of Louis Emory McComas (1846 - 1907), U.S. Senator of Maryland, outright maintains:

The confederation of the States was now complete, and on November 5, 1781, John Hanson was elected the first president of the Congress of the Confederation. This elevation to the Presidency was a signal compliment and a great honor to Maryland. It has a much larger meaning as we look back now over the stately procession of the great Commonwealths successively entering the Union. [125]

Similarly, the address of Senator Augustus Octavius Bacon of Georgia (1839 - 1914) contributes to the confusion by asserting:

John Hanson was the first President of the United States in Congress Assembled, and a Virginian was the first President of the United States under the Constitution. [126]

Even more astoundingly, the speech of George Louis Wellington (1852 - 1927), U.S. Senator of Maryland, also published in the book, is often quoted by numerous Hansonites as evidence that the surrender of Cornwallis occurred not under the USCA Presidency of Thomas McKean, but during the term of President John Hanson:

John Hanson, of Maryland, was chosen as President, and thus became President of the United States in Congress Assembled, occupying that exalted position until 1782, during the eventful period when American armies, in conjunction with their French allies, finally triumphed, when beneath the rays of an October sun George Washington received the sword of his captive, Cornwallis... He was the first President of the United States in Congress Assembled. [127]

Despite the numerous primary sources recording that Thomas McKean, not John Hanson, was the President of the United States in Congress Assembled when Cornwallis surrendered on October 19th, 1781 (a date clearly prior to the Hansonites' asserted November 5th start date of the *Articles of Confederation* presidency). Claims such as Wellington's are prevalent in post-1903 accounts of the war's conclusion.

Thirty years later, the 1903 volume inspired journalist Seymour Wemyss Smith to expand its specious rhetoric and write his own biography, *John Hanson: Our First President* (New York, 1932). This book, filled with an enormous amount of misinformation, asserts:

---

[125] *Proceedings in the Senate and House of Representatives Upon the Reception and Acceptance from the State of Maryland of the Statues of Charles Carroll of Carrollton and of John Hanson, Erected in Statuary Hall of the Capitol: January 31, 1903*, Washington: Government Printing Office, 1903. Page 14.
[126] *Ibid. page 55.*
[127] *Ibid.* pps 58-70.

The Revolution had two distinct and separate phases. One was the military outcome of the war, under the leadership of George Washington. The other was purely political under the leadership of John Hanson.[128]

Since then, the assertion that John Hanson was the first President under the *Articles of Confederation* has been perpetuated by books,[129] articles,[130] the State of Maryland, the Library of Congress,[131] the Smithsonian Institute [132] and even the U.S. Post Office. [133] Maryland's claim carries special weight with the Federal Government because the home of the major repository for the National Archives and Records Administration for United States documents and the Library of Congress official records is located in Rockville, MD.

In the 21st Century, the Hanson First U.S. President craze is currently led by Peter H. Michael, the President of the *John Hanson Memorial Association*. His book, *Remembering John Hanson, The First Lincoln: A biography of the first president of the original United States government* (Adamstown, Maryland, 2011), has become a media darling; even NPR and the Military History Channel embrace its specious claims that go far beyond the First President John Hanson Myth. Even after the public information giant Wikipedia finally reversed its support of John Hanson as the nation's first President, Mr. Michaels still managed to get an entire paragraph added to the John Hanson Wiki page that states:

_____

[128] Seymour Wemyss Smith, *John Hanson: Our First President*, New York: Brewer, Warren & Putnam, 1932, *page 39*
[129] See for example, Herbert J. Stoeckel, "The Strange Story of John Hanson, First President of the United States." *A Guide to Oxon Hill Manor and Mulberry Grove in Maryland*. Hartford, Conn.: Hanson House, 1932. Reprint 1956.
[130] See, for example, John W. Cavanaugh, "Our Two First Presidents, John Hanson and George Washington." *The Gold Book of United States History, Full of Gold Nuggets*. New York: N.p., and Amandus Johnson, , *John Hanson: First President of the United States Under the Articles of Confederation*. Philadelphia: Swedish Colonial Society, 1966.
[131] "John Hanson 1715-1783." Bibliography Directory of the United States Congress, , Extended Bibliography, bioguide.congress.gov/scripts/bibdisplay.pl?index=H000177
[132] Smithsonian Institute, The American Presidency – *"John Hanson mug - John Hanson served as the first president of the Continental Congress under the Articles of Confederation from 1781 to 1782. The Congress elected a president annually from among its members, but the position bore no relationship to the presidency established under the Constitution. When Hanson became the first president of the new independent nation, it was more an honorary position than a powerful office"* http://americanhistory.si.edu/presidency/2a1a.html 2008.
[133] *John Hanson President of the Continental Congress*. The National Postal Museum, United States Post Office, 2008. - http://arago.si.edu/index.asp?con=1&cmd=1 &mode=2&tid=2039383

In 2009 the *John Hanson Memorial Association* was incorporated in Frederick, Maryland to create the John Hanson National Memorial and to both educate Americans about Hanson as well as counter the many myths written about him. The Memorial includes a statue of President John Hanson and an interpretive setting in Frederick, Maryland, where Hanson lived between 1769 and his death in 1783. The Memorial is in the Frederick County Courthouse's courtyard at the corner of Court and West Patrick Streets. Leaders of the Memorial include President Peter Hanson Michael, Vice President Robert Hanson and Directors John Hanson Briscoe and John C. Hanson.

The Wikipedia site then directs the public to the *John Hanson Memorial Association's* website touting his book and Hanson as the United States' first President.

Most disturbing, in 2012, the *John Hanson Memorial Association* successfully unveiled a Maryland State Assembly-funded seven-foot tall statue of John Hanson in his hometown, maintaining the "First President of the United States" myth. Additional taxpayer dollars from the Maryland State coffers will also erect a monument to Jane Hanson as *"the nation's first, First Lady."* On an even more poignant historical, note the local Frederick, Maryland history bee was won by a student responding that *"John Hanson was the first President of the United States."*

Maryland and the *John Hanson Memorial Association* are not alone in claiming that the *Third United American Republic* began on November 5th, 1781, and not on March 1st, 1781. For example, in February, 2004, I had the privilege and honor to contribute founding presidential documents from 1774-1789 to the Smithsonian traveling exhibit, *"A Glorious Burden: The American Presidency."* The exhibit began with a photo of President John Hanson, with a caption declaring him "the first President of the Continental Congress."[134]

Smithsonian Exhibit that incorrectly starts the U.S. Presidency lineage with John Hanson as the First President of the Continental Congress. In the background is the author's exhibit including an 18th-Century printing of the USCA Journals recording John Hanson as the 3rd President of the United States under the Articles of Confederation. Photo Courtesy of Author[135]

The John Hanson myth actively promoted by Hansonites, the State of Maryland, and the United States federal government is a serious matter that wastes taxpayer dollars in an unfortunate attempt to re-write U.S. History at its most fundamental founding level. As we shall see, however, primary source evidence clearly indicates that the United States Articles Confederation Republic commenced on March 1st, 1781, and, therefore, that Samuel Huntington was the first President of the United States in Congress Assembled.

---

[134] This claim put forth by the Smithsonian was challenged but the Smithsonian never responded or changed the exhibit.
[135] Photograph of the Smithsonian's traveling exhibit *"A Glorious Burden, The American Presidency,"* at the Heinz History Center in Pittsburgh. Stanley L. Klos, February 2004.

As stated above, the claim that John Hanson was the first president under the *Articles of Confederation* is based in the assertion that the new constitutional government did not officially commence until November 5th, 1781. A review of the historical evidence, however, clearly demonstrates that the *Articles of Confederation* were considered to be fully in force on March 2nd, 1781, and that Samuel Huntington was officially recognized as the president of the newly-constituted United States in Congress Assembled.

The new republic commenced on March 1st, and the United States in Congress Assembled faced its first constitutional challenge on March 2nd. According to the newly ratified *Articles of Confederation*, each state was required to be represented by two delegates in order to vote; by this rule, both New Hampshire and Rhode Island, states with only one delegate physically present in the USCA, were to be excluded from voting. The situation was particularly prickly because, the day before, the two delegates had each voted as quorum members of the Continental Congress on numerous Treasury and Board of War resolutions required to conduct the war against Great Britain. The March 2nd diary entry of Delaware Delegate Thomas Rodney explains the conundrum faced by the USCA:

> The States of New Hampshire and Rhode Island having each but one Member in Congress, they became unrepresented by the Confirmation of the Confederation-By which not more than Seven nor less than two Members is allowed to represent any State -Whereupon General Sullivan, Delegate from New Hampshire moved - That Congress would appoint a Committee of the States, and Adjourn till those States Could Send forward a Sufficient number of Delegates to represent them-Or that they would allow their Delegates now in Congress To give the Vote of the States until one More from each of those States was Sent to Congress to Make their representation Complete.

> He alleged that it was but just for Congress to do one or the other of them-for that the act of Congress by completing the Confederation ought not to deprive those States of their representation without giving them due Notice, as their representation was complete before, & that they did not know When the Confederation Would be Completed. Therefore if the Confederation put it out of the power of Congress to Allow the States vote in Congress because there was but one member from each them, they ought in justice to those States to appoint a Committee of the States, in which they would have an Equal Voice. This Motion was Seconded by Genl. Vernon from Rhode Island and enforced by Arguments to the same purpose.

> But all their Arguments were ably confuted by Mr. Burke of N.C. and others, and the absurdity of the motion fully pointed out, So that the question passed off without a Division -But it was the general Opinion of Congress that those members might

Continue to Sit in Congress, and Debate & Serve on Committees though they could not give the vote of their States. [136]

Despite the New Hampshire delegates argument that his state was being deprived of representation without due notice, the USCA unanimously agreed on March 2nd, 1781, that the *Articles of Confederation* was in full force and that, unlike the requirements for the U.S. Continental Congress, for a state to have a vote in the new Congress,, two or more delegates were required, in accordance with Article V: "No State shall be represented in Congress by less than two, nor more than seven members."

A comparison of two different entries from the Journals of Congress serves as further evidence that President Samuel Huntington's USCA was obliged to comply with the Articles of Confederation. The first entry, reproduced below, is the December 24th 1778, vote tally taken while U.S. Continental Congress President Henry Laurens was presiding. Although the states of New Hampshire, Delaware, Rhode Island, and Georgia each had only one delegate present, their votes were registered as "ay" and counted in the tally:

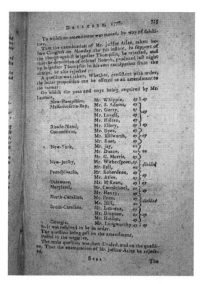

Thursday, December 24, 1778 Journals of Congress entry of the US Continental Congress vote on " *the support of the charge against Brigadier Thompson, be*

---

[136] *LDC, 1774-1789*, Delegate Thomas Rodney Diary entry March 2nd, 1781

rejected, and that the deposition of Colonel Noarth, produced last night by Brigadier Thompson in his own exculpation from the charge, be also rejected ... passed in the negative" Journals of Congress Containing the proceedings from January 1st, 1779 to Jan. 1st, 1780 PUBLISHED BY ORDER OF Congress, Philadelphia, by David Claypoole, VOLUME V. -- Image courtesy of the Historic.us Collection.

In contrast, the March 22nd 1781, United States in Congress Assembled vote tally taken with President Samuel Huntington presiding, shows that the states of New Hampshire, Maryland, Rhode Island, and Georgia each had only one delegate present, and that therefore their state votes of "no" were registered as " * " and not tallied.

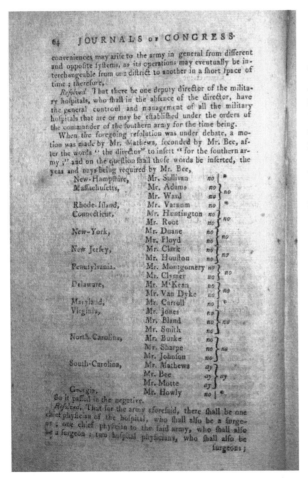

Thursday, March 22nd, 1781 Journals of Congress entry of the USCA vote "Resolved, That there be one deputy director of the military hospitals, in the Southern district subject to the general control of the director... So it passed in the negative." The Journals of Congress and the United States in Congress Assembled, For the Year 1781, Published By Order of Congress, Volume VII New York: Printed by John Patterson. -- *Image courtesy of the Historic.us Collection*

A similar entry from the USCA Journal record from Hanson's presidency demonstrates that the same voting rules were in effect as during Huntington's service earlier that year: On November 14th, 1781, the states of Connecticut and North Carolina each had only one delegate present, and the States' votes of "ay" were recorded as " * ", again with no effect on the tally.

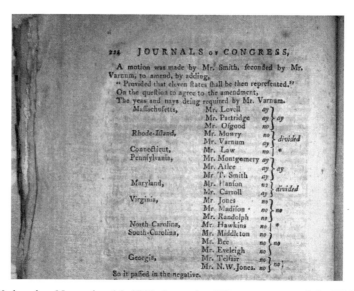

Wednesday, November 14, 1781, Journals of Congress entry of the USCA vote "That the first Tuesday of December next, be assigned for the consideration of the report of the committee, to whom were referred the cessions of New York, Virginia, Connecticut, and the petitions of the Indiana, Vandalia, Illinois, and Wabash companies. A motion was made by Mr. Smith, seconded by Mr. Varnum, to amend, by adding, "provided that eleven states shall be then represented." On the question to agree to the amendment, the yeas and nays being required by Mr. Varnum, ... So it passed in the negative." The Journals of Congress and the United States in Congress Assembled, For the Year 1781, Published By Order of Congress, Volume VII New York: Printed by John Patterson. -- Image courtesy of the Historic.us Collection.

It is true that, unlike John Hanson, Samuel Huntington did not complete a full year as USCA President, the maximum term permitted under the Articles of Confederation. Huntington had assumed the USCA's presidency already exhausted from his long service as a U.S. Continental Congress President, which had begun on September 29th, 1779 and ended with the expiration of the old Congress on February 28th, 1781. Yet despite serving as the USCA's first President for only four months, the record reflects that he issued copious letters, resolutions, military commissions and proclamations under that title, including one calling for the first national "Day of Humiliation, Fasting, and Prayer" under the new constitution:

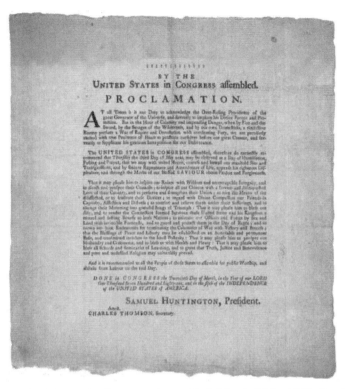

The United States in Congress Assembled, March 20th, 1781, Proclamation signed by Samuel Huntington as President, calling for the first National "Day of Humiliation, Fasting, and Prayer" under the Articles of Confederation - in part: "The United States in Congress assembled, therefore do earnestly recommend, that Thursday the third day of May next, may be observed as a day of humiliation, fasting and prayer, that we may, with united hearts, confess and bewail our manifold sins and transgressions, and by sincere repentance and amendment of life, appease his righteous displeasure, and through the merits of our blessed Saviour, obtain pardon and forgiveness …"

Not only was Huntington exhausted; during his short term, the USCA voted to reduce the already limited powers of the presidency. Now that the Articles of Confederation had raised the USCA quorum level to two delegates per state with at least nine (as opposed to the Continental Congress' seven) states required to assent to crucial legislation, presidential authority in the new central government would be extremely limited. No longer would a president be able to cast his vote as the sole delegate present for his home State in a quorum of Seven States on crucial national legislation, judicial findings, or executive orders. Moreover, on May 4th, 1781, after three months of committee work and a final debate, Huntington's USCA adopted thirty-five *"Rules for conducting the Business in the United States Congress Assembled"* under the Articles of Confederation (with Delegate John Hanson absent from the congress). The new rules stripped the USCA Presidential office of its important political power to formulate the agenda of Congress, and prod Delegates to move in directions he considered proper.

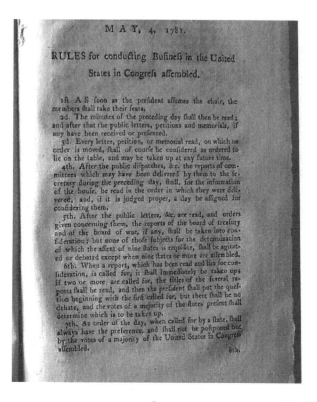

Rules for Conduction Business, in the United States in Congress Assembled dated May 4th, 1781, in this entry of The Journals of Congress and the United States in Congress Assembled, For the Year 1781, Published By Order of Congress, Volume VII New York: Printed by John Patterson. -- *Image courtesy of the Historic.us Collection*

It is no wonder that President Samuel Huntington resigned and on July 8th, 1781. Delegate Thomas McKean would write to Samuel Adams, about the upcoming presidential election:

A new President of Congress is to be chosen tomorrow, as Mr. Huntington will not continue any longer; this honor is going a begging; there is only one Gentleman, and he from the Southward, who seems willing to accept, but I question whether he will be elected. There are some amongst us, who are so fond of having a great and powerful man to look up to, that, tho' they may not like the name of King, seem anxious to confer kingly powers, under the titles of Dictator, Superintendent of Finance, or some such, but the majorities do not yet appear to be so disposed. [137]

To add to the mountains of primary sources recording Samuel Huntington's service as the first President under the *Articles of Confederation* , the USCA Journals report that two presidential elections occurring after Huntington's resignation and before John Hanson's Presidency,. The first presidential election under the ratified *Articles of Confederation* occurred on July 9th, 1781, when North Carolina Delegate Samuel Johnston was chosen as Huntington's successor.

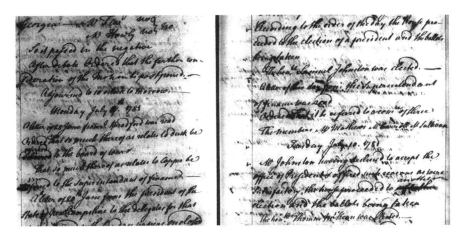

Journal of the United States in Congress Assembled manuscript open to July 9-10th, 1781, recording the elections of Samuel Johnston and Thomas McKean as USAC Presidents. The handwritten July 9th, 1781, Journal of the USCA does record Johnston as the new President and an order that was passed after Johnston's election. Consequently, if Johnston took the chair then he was the USCA President for a day because no oath of office was required by the Articles of Confederation. The USCA Journals, however, are unclear on who chaired the USCA after Johnston's election: "The honble. Samuel Johnston was elected. A letter of this day, from the superintendent of finance [Robert Morris] was read: Ordered, That it be referred to a committee of three: The members, Mr. [John] Mathews, Mr. [Daniel] Carroll, Mr. [John] Sullivan. -- *Image courtesy of the National Archives of the United States.*"

---

[137] LDC, 1774-1789, July 8, 1781, USCA Delegate Thomas McKean to Samuel Adams

Although it is unclear from the record whether or not Johnston may have actually served as president on July 9th during a brief decision referring a letter from the superintendent of finance to committee discussion, on the following day the USCA Journals report that Samuel Johnston "declined" rather than "resigned" the office of President and that Thomas McKean was elected President.

Mr. [Samuel] Johnston having declined to accept the office of President, and offered such reasons as were satisfactory, the House proceeded to another election; and, the ballots being taken, the Hon. Thomas McKean was elected. [138]

Thomas Rodney's July 10th letter to Caesar Rodney also indicates that Samuel Johnston, although elected, never accepted or served as the second USCA President.

Congress has been endeavoring some time past to elect a new President Mr. Huntington having often applied for leave to go home on account of his health and private affairs, and yesterday Mr. Johnson of N. Carolina was appointed but he declined it on account of his bad state of health, and today Mr. McKean was appointed and prevailed on to serve till October next at which time he says he is determined to decline serving in Congress any longer. [139]

Delegate Thomas McKean accepted the USCA Presidential office and began to preside over Congress on July 10th, 1781, four months before John Hanson was elected to the USCA Presidency. President Thomas McKean, like Samuel

Huntington, executed numerous resolutions, proclamations, and letters as the second USCA President to serve under the Articles of Confederation. The following September 7th, 1781, USCA Journal entry is one example of numerous documents officially recording Thomas McKean as a President of the United States in Congress Assembled.

---

[138] JCC, 1774-1789, July 10th, 1781
[139] LDC, 1774-1789, Thomas Rodney letter to Caesar Rodney July 10th, 1781

F R I D A Y, *September* 7, 1781.

A memorial from the honorable the minister plenipotentiary of France was read, enclosing a commission of the sieur Philip Joseph de l'Etombe, consul general of France in the states of New-Hampshire, Massachusetts, Rhode-Island and Providence plantations, and Connecticut; whereupon,

Ordered, That the said commission be registered; and that the act of recognition be in the following words:

By the United States in Congress assembled.

It is hereby made known to all whom it may concern, that full credence and respect are to be paid to Philip Joseph de l'Etombe, as consul general of France for the states of New-Hampshire, Massachusetts, Rhode Island and Providence Plantations, and Connecticut, which states are called upon respectively, by virtue of the powers delegated by the confederation to the United States in Congress assembled, to furnish the said Mr. de l'Etombe with their exequatur or notification of his quality, delivering one copy thereof to the said Mr. de l'Etombe, and causing another to be published in one or more gazettes. Done at Philadelphia, this seventh day of September, in the year of our Lord one thousand seven hundred and eighty-one, and in the sixth year of our independence:

By the United States in Congress assembled.
THOMAS McKEAN, President.

Attest. CHARLES THOMSON, *Secretary.*

Resolved, That the president inform the supreme executive power of the states aforesaid, that Congress recommend the following form of the exequatur, to wit.

Above is the September 7th, 1781 Journal of the USCA Claypoole printing, which is taken from the Manuscript September 7th, 1781 Journal of the USCA entry pictured below. Both entries record Thomas McKean as President of the United States in Congress Assembled duly elected under the Articles of Confederation. – *Images courtesy of the Historic.us Collection and the National Archived of the United States.*

On October 23, 1781, however, President Thomas McKean submitted his letter of resignation to USCA Secretary Charles Thomson:

Sir: I must beg you to remind Congress, that when they did me the honor of electing me President, and before I assumed the Chair, I informed them, that as Chief Justice of Pennsylvania, I should be under the necessity of attending the Supreme Court of that State, the latter end of September, or at farthest in October. That court will be held today; I must therefore request, that they will be pleased to proceed to the choice of another President. [140]

The United States in Congress Assembled resolved: *"That the resignation of Mr. [Thomas] McKean is accepted. Ordered, That the election of a President be postponed until to-morrow."* [141] But the USCA was not yet aware that Cornwallis had surrendered. The following day, Secretary Charles Thomson presented Commander-in-Chief George Washington's letter to Congress, "giving information of the reduction of the British army under the command of the Earl of Cornwallis, on the 19th instant with a copy of the articles of capitulation." An elated USCA resolved, among other resolutions, that:

Unanimously, That Mr. [Thomas] McKean be requested to resume the chair, and act as President till the first Monday in November next; the resolution of yesterday notwithstanding.

That it be an instruction to the said committee, to report what in their opinion, will be the most proper mode of communicating the thanks of the United States in Congress Assembled, to General Washington, Count de Rochambeau and Count de Grasse, for their effectual exertions in accomplishing this illustrious work; and of paying respect to the merit of Lieutenant Colonel Tilghman, aid-de-camp of General Washington, and the bearer of his despatches announcing this happy event" [142]

---

[140] JCC, 1774-1789, October 23rd, 1781
[141] Ibid
[142] Ibid, October 24th, 1781

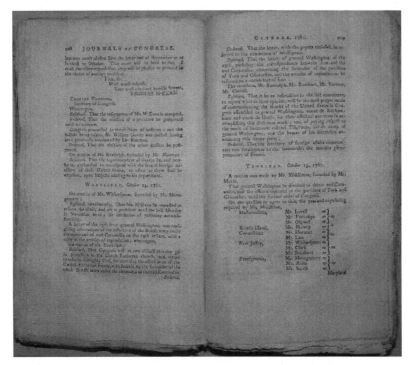

October 24th, 1781 Journals of the United States in Congress Assembled concerning. President Thomas McKean's letter of resignation, News of Yorktown, and United States in Congress Assembled resolutions of thanks -*The Journals of Congress and the United States in Congress Assembled, For the Year 1781, Published By Order of Congress, Volume VII New York: Printed by John Patterson - Image Courtesy of Historic.us*

Delegate Thomas McKean agreed to remain President, while serving as Pennsylvania's Chief Justice, until the second United States in Congress Assembled convened on the "first Monday of November" as prescribed in the Articles of Confederation. On October 26th, 1781, the USCA passed a Thanksgiving Proclamation signed by Thomas McKean as president:

By The United States in Congress Assembled - Whereas, it hath pleased Almighty God, the supreme Disposer of all Events father of mercies, remarkably to assist and support the United States of America in their important struggle for liberty, against the long continued efforts of a powerful nation: it is the duty of all ranks to observe and thankfully acknowledge the interpositions of his Providence in their behalf. Through the whole of the contest, from its first rise to this time, the influence of divine

Providence may be clearly perceived in many signal instances, of which we mention but a few .... Thomas McKean, President[143]

Indeed, McKean spent his remaining term presiding over a jubilant Congress and sending out official letters of thanks, with the proclamation enclosed, to various military officers, including an October 31st, 1781, letter to French Admiral Comte de Grasse:

Sir, Philada October 31, 1781. The Thanks of the United States in Congress assembled is the highest honor that any of their citizens can receive for the most distinguished services. I feel myself peculiarly happy in being the instrument of conveying these Thanks to your Excellency in Obedience to their Act of the 29th instant, a copy of which I have the honor to enclose herewith.(1) Be pleased therefore to accept, what in the name of the United States of America in Congress assembled I most cheerfully give you, Their Thanks for the display of your skill and bravery in attacking and defeating the British Fleet off the Bay of Chesapeake, and for your zeal and alacrity in rendering with the Fleet under your command the most effectual and distinguished aid & support to the operations of the allied Army in Virginia.

I will only add, Sir, that your name will be ever dear to the good people of these States as long as gratitude is a virtue. Your wisdom, your attachment to the essential interests of this country, your effectual completion of the wishes of your Sovereign, and your whole conduct justly endear you to us, and entitle you to every mark of honor that we can possibly confer upon you. May you long retain the smiles and approbation of your Prince, and of all good men, and enjoy all the happiness this world can afford.

I have the honor to be, with every sentiment of gratitude & respect, Sir, Your Excellency's most humble and obedient servant,

Thomas Mc Kean President[144]

This letter, along with the enclosed proclamation leave, no doubt that Thomas McKean was the President of the United States in Congress Assembled during and following the surrender of General Cornwallis at Yorktown, just as Samuel Huntington had been president when the new government had started under the Articles of Confederation. On what basis, then, do the Hansonites claim John Hanson to have been first president?

---

[143] JCC, 1774-1789, October 26, 1781
[144] LDC, 1774-1789, October 31, 1781

On the first Monday of November at the convening of the second USCA, the credentials of the Delegates were entered into the record, just as they had been entered on March 1st, at the start of the previous session. The USCA Journals of Congress then report the election of President Hanson:

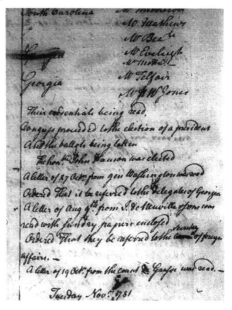

> Their credentials being read, Congress proceeded to the election of a President; and the ballots being taken, the honorable John Hanson was elected. [145]

How did this election differ from the previous elections discussed in this chapter? According to the John Hanson Memorial Association (JHMA), unlike Hanson, Presidents Samuel Huntington and Thomas McKean presided over an "interim Congress of the Confederation":

> On March 2, 1781, the Second Continental Congress is succeeded by the interim Congress of the Confederation with scant powers with the same delegates and officers as from the Second Continental Congress. On November 4th the Confederation goes out of existence to be replaced by the United States in Congress Assembled ... November 5, 1781, the United States in Congress Assembled, the nation's first government, springs into being ... as its first act, the new United States in Congress Assembled unanimously elects John Hanson of Frederick, Maryland, to a one year term as the nation's first president. Hanson becomes first president under any form of the United States government elected to a stated fixed term. President Hanson becomes first in the nation's history to be recognized at home or abroad as head of state. [146]

---

[145] JCC, 1774-1789, November 5, 1781
[146] John Hanson Memorial Association, *Timeline of John Hanson's Life, Roles In the Birth of the United States, Presidency and Remembrances Since His Death* accessed March 1, 2014 http://johnhansonmemorial.org/The_John_Hanson_National_Memorial/Timeline_files/John_Hanson_Timeline.pdf - hereafter referred to as JHMA Timeline

March 1, 1781	Second Continental Congress passes into history.
March 2, 1781-November 4, 1781	On March 2, the Second Continental Congress is succeeded by the interim Congress of Confederation with scant powers and with same delegates and officers as from the Second Continental Congress
March 2-July 9, 1781	Samuel Huntington continues as president of the new body, serves 130 days. Congress of the Confederation meets once during this time on July 9 to elect a new president on Huntington's request.
June 29, 1781	John and Jane Hanson's son Dr. Samuel Harrison Hanson, is killed in the Revolutionary War less than four months before its end
July 9-10, 1781	Samuel Johnston elected President of the Congress of Confederation on July 9. Refuses to serve when learning of election on July 10 saying he does not want to preside over a temporary government which was not meeting often and only waiting for the United States in Congress Assembled to commence in 120 days.
July 10, 1781	Thomas McKean of Delaware elected "Provisional President" understanding that he would retire from the position upon the presidential election on the first Monday of November that year as provided for in the Articles of Confederation.
July 10-November 4, 1781	Thomas McKean of Delaware serves 118 days as President of Congress of the Confederation. Before November, had to be persuaded not to resign for the same reason which Johnston cited.
September 20, 1781	John Hanson's will filed in Frederick County
October 12 , 1781	Cornwallis surrenders at Yorktown. Colonies win independence.
November 4, 1781	Congress of the Confederation goes out of existence to be replaced by the United States in Congress Assembled largely with the same delegates
The Hanson Administration	
November 5, 1781	United States in Congress Assembled, the nation's first government, springs into being
November 5, 1781	As its first act, the new United States in Congress Assembled unanimously elects John Hanson of Frederick, Maryland, to a one-year term as the nation's first president. Hanson becomes first president under any form of United States government elected to a stated fixed term. President Hanson becomes first in the nation's history to be recognized at home or abroad as head of state.

The primary sources we have reviewed above contradict many of these assertions; we need only recall, for example, the congratulations received by Huntington from the French Minister Plenipotentiary, and the many documents signed by him as "president." The Hansonite argument thus would require us to accept that what this book recognizes as the first USCA was in fact an "interim congress" – a contention based on two claims:

1) That the Articles of Confederation required that the new USCA could only be formed on the first Monday of each November.

2) That the Delegates be duly elected by the States after the Articles of Confederation's enactment.

According to these contentions, since the Delegates that formed the March 1st, 1781 congress were not duly elected by their respective States after the enactment of the Articles of Confederation and since they were not convened on the first Monday in November, the actual first USCA was the one formed on November 5th, and Hanson the first true president

The *Articles of Confederation*, however, say nothing about when the first USCA must form. Article IX does state, in clause V, that:

For the most convenient management of the general interests of the United States, delegates shall be annually appointed in such manner as the legislatures of each State shall direct, to meet in Congress on the first Monday in November, in every year, with a power reserved to each State to recall its delegates, or any of them, at any time within the year, and to send others in their stead for the remainder of the year. [147]

Although the *Articles* direct the states to appoint delegates to meet in Congress on the first Monday in November, the text does not state that the only time the first or, indeed, any new United States in Congress Assembled could convene would be at that time. And certainly such was not the consistent practice of the USCA. Of the nine USCA sessions, the Journals of Congress record only three sessions actually convening on the "First Monday in November." As we have seen, the first USCA convened in March because the Articles of Confederation had not been ratified in time to begin the 1780-1781 session on the "First Monday in November"; three additional sessions – the fifth, sixth, seventh, and eighth -- also failed to convene for the first time on the "First Monday," and the ninth, despite several attempts, failed to convene at all.

Why, then, should the 1780-1781 USCA convened for the first time on March 2nd, 1781 be any less of an official USCA Congress than the Seventh 1786-1787 USCA, which convened for the first time on February 2, 1787.

Just as it was the duty of the 1787-1788 USCA, after the required ninth state's ratification of the *Constitution of 1787*, to enact legislation setting a start date for the new government (March 4th, 1789), it was similarly the responsibility of the U.S. Continental Congress, after the ratification of the *Articles* on February 2, 1781, to enact legislation to begin government under that document (March 1st, 1781). It is, therefore, nonsensical for the Library of Congress, State of Maryland, and JHMA to maintain that all the laws enacted, officials appointed, rules adopted and Presidents elected under the ratified Articles of Confederation by the United States in Congress Assembled from March 1st, 1781 until November 4th, 1781, were done under some other form of quasi-government simply because the first USCA session commenced on March 1st, 1781.

The second argument, that the USCA could only legitimately be formed by Delegates elected or appointed by their respective States after the Articles of Confederation's enactment on March 1st, 1781, is also a condition found nowhere in

---

[147] JCC, 1774-1789, November 5, 1781

the document itself. But if we accept this assertion as true, then the USCA 1781-1782 Congress of John Hanson similarly fails to meet this constitutional provision:

The Journals of Congress record that the credentials presented on November 5th, 1781 to the USCA by the delegates from the state of Delaware were "outdated" because the delegates had been appointed on February 10th, 1781 -- 18 days before the March 1st enactment of the Articles of Confederation.

> In the general assembly of the Delaware State, at New Castle, Saturday, A.M. February 10, 1781. The Council and House of Assembly, having met in the State-House, agreeable to the Order of the Day, proceeded, by joint Ballot, to the Election of Delegates to represent this State in the Congress of the United States of America, for the ensuing year, and the Box containing the Ballots being examined, The Honorable Thomas Rodney, Thomas McKean and Nicholas Vandyke, Esquires, are declared duly elected. Extract from the Minutes, James Booth Clerk of Assembly. [148]

Ironically, even the Maryland Delegation fails this Hansonite test because, as the November 5th Journals of Congress make clear, Maryland's delegate appointments for both the March 1st, 1781, and November 5th, 1781, sessions occurred on February 3rd -- 25 days before the enactment of the *Articles*.. By this measure, then, John Hanson himself was not appointed as a duly "enacted" Articles of Confederation Delegate:

> Maryland, Annapolis 3 Feb. 1781. We hereby certify that John Hanson, Daniel of St. Thomas Jenifer, Daniel Carroll and Richard Potts Esquires are elected Delegates to represent this State in Congress for the Year One thousand seven hundred and Eighty one. - James Maccubbin, Clerk. [149]

Even if we were to maintain that the new constitution required an Articles of Confederation Congress to be formed by Delegates duly elected or appointed by their respective States **after** February 2nd, 1781 (i.e., the date upon which Maryland's action completed the *Articles'* required unanimous ratification, rather than the date the *Articles* took effect), several of the states' credentials would still have been out of compliance on November 5th, when the Journals of the USCA record that:

---

[148] JCC, 1774-1789, November 5, 1781
[149] Ibid

1. The State of Pennsylvania's Delegate credentials were issued "In the General Assembly, Thursday 23rd. November 1780.," and that
2. The State of New Hampshire's credentials were issued "In Council January 18th, 1781." [150]

If we accept the arguments put forth by the Library of Congress, Maryland, and other Hansonite supporters, because these New Hampshire and Pennsylvania delegations had been appointed before Maryland ratified the *Articles of Confederation* on February 2nd, 1781, these States were not qualified to participate in the USCA 1781-1782 session nor to elect John Hanson, President. By this Hansonite logic, then, John Hanson himself must also have been an interim "Congress of the Confederation" President. Why? Without including the New Hampshire and Pennsylvania Delegations in Congress, only six States formed the 1781-1782 USCA on November 5th, 1781—one fewer than the seven states (with two or more delegates to be in attendance) required by the *Articles* to elect a President. Therefore, one must conclude that the election of John Hanson, like Samuel Huntington and Thomas McKean, was a JHMA-proclaimed "Congress of the Confederation" Presidency.

Despite the enthusiasm (and sloppy scholarship) that have allowed the continuation, and, indeed, propagation of the Hanson myth by the Maryland State Legislature, the Library of Congress, the Smithsonian and various departments of the federal government for over 110 years, the evidence indicates that the USCA delegates of both the March 1st and November 5th sessions, were credentialed by their respective states after each of those states had ratified the Articles of Confederation. Accordingly, Samuel Huntington, Thomas McKean, and John Hanson each served as President presiding over the United States in Congress Assembled.

---

[150] JCC, Ibid

Smithsonian

The National Museum of
AMERICAN HISTORY

The Foundations

Defining the Presidency | The President's Job | Limits of Power
The New Republic | George Washington
Continental Congress | Constitutional Convention

J, Hanson
md Trade for
— ever —

John Hanson mug
John Hanson served as the first president of the Continental Congress under the Articles of Confederation from 1781 to 1782. The Congress elected a president annually from among its members, but the position bore no relationship to the presidency established under the Constitution. When Hanson became the first president of the new independent nation, it was more an honorary position than a powerful office.

Smithsonain Institue online exhibit *The Foundations: Defining the Presidency* heralding John Hanson as the "first president of the Contiental Congress under the Articles if Confederation."

The fact remains that all the USCA delegates of the March 1st and November 5th, 1781 sessions, were credentialed by their respective states after each one had ratified the Articles of Confederation. Therefore, Presidents Samuel Huntington, Thomas McKean, and John Hanson were all Presidents presiding over the United States in Congress Assembled.

Although there are numerous other claims on the JHMA's *Articles of Confederation* timeline to refute, I will only address one more: that is, that John

Hanson was the first president under any form of the United States government elected to a stated fixed term. [151]

This assertion is based on a misunderstanding of the president's term of office under the *Articles of Confederation*. Although presidents were limited to one year of service in the USCA, such service could span across two different sessions, as long as the President's term did not exceed 365 days. Specifically, Article IX states of the presidency that the USCA has the power:

> ... to appoint one of their members to preside, provided that no person be allowed to serve in the office of president more than one year in any term of three years. [152]

As opposed to the current U.S. Presidency as prescribed in the *Constitution of 1787*, there was no stated "fixed term" for USCA President A prime example of this flexibility was the presidency of Cyrus Griffin, elected by the 8th USCA Congress on January 21st, 1788. When the 9th USCA Congress failed to form on the "First Monday in November" in 1788, since he had not served 365 days, Griffin continued in the office as President. In fact, the 9th USCA Congress never mustered enough delegates even after Griffin's constitutional office expired on the 366th day, January 21st, 1789. Despite the end of his term, Congress recognized Griffin as the last President under the Articles of Confederation, at George Washington's inauguration:

> That seats be provided in the Senate-Chamber sufficient to accommodate the late President of the United States in Congress Assembled [Cyrus Griffin], the Governor of the Western territory [Arthur St Clair], the five persons being the heads of the three great departments [Secretary of Foreign Affairs John Jay, Secretary of War Henry Knox, Commissioners of the Treasury Arthur Lee, Walter Livingston, and Samuel Osgood].... [153]

Finally, there is one additional piece of evidence that Hanson was not the first president under the *Articles of Confederation*. Putting aside the complexities of the delegates' credentials, the start date of USCA sessions, and the length of a presidential term, we have Hanson's presidential letter, dated November 10th, 1781, issuing the "official thanks" of the USCA to President Thomas McKean and affirming to him that President Hanson "has the honor of being your Successor":

---

[151] JHMA Timeline
[152] JCC, 1774-1789, March 1, 1781 – Articles of Confederation
[153] Broadside Announcing Ceremonial for Washington's Inauguration, 29 April 1789 - Library of Congress Collection

It is always a pleasing task to pay a just tribute to distinguished Merit. Under this impression give me leave to assure you, that it is with inexpressible satisfaction that I present you the thanks of the United States in Congress assembled, in testimony of their approbation of your conduct in the Chair and in the execution of public business; a duty I am directed to perform by their Act of the 7th instant, a copy of which I have the honor of enclosing.

When I reflect upon the great abilities, the exemplary patience and unequalled skill and punctuality, which you so eminently displayed in executing the important duties of a President, it must unavoidably be productive of great apprehensions in the one who has the honor of being your Successor. But the Choice of Congress obliges me for a moment to be silent on the subject of my own inability: And altho' I cannot equal the bright example that is recently set me, yet it shall be my unremitting study to imitate it as far as possible; and in doing this the reflection is pleasing that I shall invariably pursue the sacred path of Virtue, which alone ought to preserve me free from censure.[154]

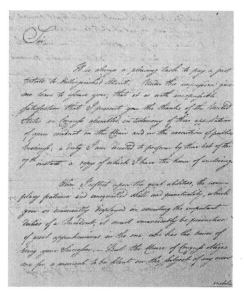

John Hanson autographed letter signed as President, dated November 10th, 1781, issuing the *"official thanks"* of the USCA to Thomas McKean for his service as President of the United States in Congress Assembled, page 2. - Image taken by Stan Klos at Library of Congress, 2001

---

[154] LDC, 1774-1789, John Hanson letter to Thomas McKean, November 10th, 1781.

John Hanson, the self-proclaimed *"successor"* to USCA President Thomas McKean, understood that he himself was not the first President of the United States in Assembled. The historical evidence adduced clearly corroborates that The *Third American Founding Republic* was birthed on March 1st, 1781, and not November 5th, 1781. Samuel Huntington, not John Hanson, was the first President of the United States under the Articles of Confederation. Thomas McKean, duly elected on July 10th, 1781, served as the second President under the Articles of Confederation. John Hanson, duly elected on November 5th, 1781, as the third President under the Articles of Confederation was the first to fully serve the prescribed one year term.

TREATY OF PARIS CHALLENGE:

Another challenge to the March 1st, 1781, start date for the *Third United American Republic* comes from various historians who maintain the United States did not achieve its sovereignty until September 3rd, 1783, when Great Britain and United States Commissioners executed the *Definitive Treaty of Peace in Paris,* thus ending the Revolutionary War. In this Treaty, Great Britain specifically agreed that

His Britannic Majesty acknowledges the said United States, viz., New Hampshire, Massachusetts Bay, Rhode Island ..., Connecticut, New York, New Jersey, Pennsylvania, Maryland, Virginia, North Carolina, South Carolina and Georgia, to be free sovereign and independent states, that he treats with them as such, and for himself, his heirs, and successors, relinquishes all claims to the government, propriety, and territorial rights of the same and every part thereof.

According to the Treaty of Paris proponents, the United States of America did not exist as a sovereign nation on July 4th, 1776, nor throughout the Revolutionary War. New Hampshire, Massachusetts Bay, Rhode Island, Connecticut, New York, New Jersey, Pennsylvania, Maryland, Virginia, North Carolina, South Carolina and Georgia, they argue, remained colonies of Great Britain until this *Definitive Treaty of Peace in Paris* in 1783.

Although at first glance this argument appears unsupported by the historical record, the execution and subsequent ratification of the Treaty of Paris did end the Revolutionary War and achieve international recognition of the United States of America as a sovereign nation. It is, therefore, prudent to examine this historic achievement as one of the possible start dates of *America's Four Republics*.

First, in considering September 3rd, 1783 as the inception date for the United States of America, it is important to note that U.S. Peace Commissioner John Jay, one year earlier, had refused to continue treaty negotiations with Great Britain in Paris unless the United States was recognized as a foreign nation. Additionally Jay, against the direct orders of the United States in Congress Assembled, persuaded fellow Commissioners John Adams and Benjamin Franklin to exclude France from the treaty negotiations. The three Commissioners in 1782, therefore, unanimously required the British Ministry to formulate a new commission authorizing Peace Commissioner Richard Oswald to negotiate a treaty without France or Spain and with the United States of America as a sovereign nation. The absence of France and Spain in the negotiations came as a great relief to Great Britain because it took off the negotiation table their claims to North American territory in the area being claimed by the United States. On September 21st, 1782, Parliament passed an act empowering Commissioner Oswald to enact a treaty with United States of America as a sovereign nation:

An act to enable his Majesty to conclude a peace or truce with certain colonies in North America therein mentioned, it is recited ... And it is our royal will and pleasure, and we do hereby authorize, empower and require you, the said Richard Oswald, to treat, consult of, and conclude with any commissioners or persons veiled with equal powers, by, and on the part of the Thirteen United States of America, viz. New Hampshire,

Massachusetts Bay, Rhode Island, Connecticut, New York, New Jersey, Pennsylvania, the three Lower Counties on Delaware, Maryland, Virginia, North Carolina, South Carolina, and Georgia, in North America, a peace or a truce with the said Thirteen United States, any law, act or acts of parliament, matter or thing, to the contrary in any wise notwithstanding.[155]

This date of September 21st, 1782, therefore, rather than September 3rd, 1783, marks Great Britain's recognition of United States' sovereignty. Commissioner John Jay wrote to Foreign Secretary Robert R. Livingston:

Dear Sir, I have only time to inform you that our objections to Mr. Oswald's first commission have produced a second, which arrived yesterday. It empowers him to treat with the Commissioners of the Thirteen United States of America. I am preparing a longer letter on this subject, but as this intelligence is interesting, I take the earliest opportunity of communicating it.[156]

On October 5th, 1782, with the "colonies" now recognized by Great Britain as the United States of America, John Jay turned over their treaty plan to Oswald. The plan included the new clauses relating to independence, the territorial boundaries and the articles on the fisheries. Oswald, in enclosing the plan to his government, wrote: *"I look upon the treaty as now closed."*

One only has to glimpse a 1780's map of North America (such as the one included in the *Life of Shelburne*, showing *"the boundaries of the United States, Canada, and the Spanish possessions, according to the proposals of the court of France"*) to understand what Commissioners John Jay, John Adams, Benjamin Franklin and Henry Laurens[157] accomplished with the 1783 *Definitive Treaty of Peace in Paris.*

---

[155] King George III, *An act to enable His Majesty to conclude a peace or truce with certain Colonies in North America Colonies in North America therein Mentioned.* Printed Charles Eyre and William Strahan, London, September 21, 1782.

[156] *The Diplomatic Correspondence of the American Revolution*, Published By. John C. Rives, Washington, DC: 1857, page 462. (hereinafter *DCAR, 1857*)

[157] A fourth U.S. Peace Commissioner, former President Henry Laurens, arrived in Paris in late November 1782. John Adams wrote ... *that Congress had, three or four years ago, when they did me the honor to give me a commission to make a treaty of commerce with Great Britain, given me a positive instruction not to make any such treaty without an article in the treaty of peace acknowledging our right to the fishery; that I was happy Mr. Laurens was now present, who, I believed, was in Congress at the time and must remember it. Mr. Laurens upon this said, with great firmness, that he was in the same case and could never give his voice for any articles without this. Mr. Jay spoke up, and said it could not be a peace; it would only be an insidious truce without it.* -- John Adams diary 37, 22 - 30 November 1782. Original manuscript from the Adams Family Papers, Massachusetts Historical Society, page three.

If the American commissioners had followed the USCA's instructions to govern themselves by the opinion of French Minister Vergennes,[158] the treaty would have deprived the United States of Alabama and Mississippi, the greater part of Kentucky and Tennessee. The lands consisting of Ohio, Michigan, Indiana, Illinois, Wisconsin, parts of Minnesota and the navigation of the Mississippi River would also been excluded in the treaty proposed by France.

John Jay, who insisted that France and Spain be removed from the negotiations, was the territorial sage who produced the land-rich Treaty that would end the war with Great Britain. So complete were the negotiations that nothing was lost after France and Spain learned that a *Preliminary Definitive Treaty of Peace in Paris* had been executed by the United States and Great Britain on November 30th, 1782. The final treaty, which was signed by U.S. Commissioners John Jay, John Adams and Benjamin Franklin, along with His Britannic Majesty's Minister Plenipotentiary David Hartley on the 3rd day of September, 1783, withstood France's and Spain's challenges to the 1782 preliminary agreement. It began:

> **In the name of the most holy and undivided Trinity.** It having pleased the Divine Providence to dispose the hearts of the most serene and most potent Prince George the Third, by the grace of God, king of Great Britain, France, and Ireland, defender of the faith, duke of Brunswick and Lunebourg, arch- treasurer and prince elector of the Holy Roman Empire etc., and of the United States of America, to forget all past misunderstandings and differences that have unhappily interrupted the good correspondence and friendship which they mutually wish to restore, and to establish such a beneficial and satisfactory intercourse , between the two countries upon the ground of reciprocal advantages and mutual convenience as may promote and secure to both perpetual peace and harmony...[159]

Like the Articles of Confederation, the treaty had a provision for ratification. Unlike the Articles, however, the ratification required approval only by nine of the 13 United States and Great Britain to become law.

---

[158] comte de Vergennes Charles Gravier (1717—1787) was a French Foreign Minister serving during the reign of Louis XVI during the American War of Independence. In 1777, he informed the United Colonies commissioners that France recognized the United States and together they formed the Franco-American Alliance. Vergennes was circumvented by the commissioners in 1782-83 when they negotiated an end to the Revolutionary War with Great Britain without France's participation.
[159] *JCC, 1774-1789*, Treaty of Paris, Proclamation by the USCA, January 14, 1784

The solemn ratifications of the present treaty expedited in good and due form shall be exchanged between the contracting parties in the space of six months or sooner, if possible, to be computed from the day of the signatures of the present treaty... [160]

The first order of business for newly-elected USCA President, Thomas Mifflin was to ensure the treaty was ratified within the time constraint set forth in the agreement. The fourth USCA reconvened in Annapolis, and Mifflin scheduled a ratifying session on December 15th, 1783. The delegates, however, failed to achieve a quorum and the proposed vote was then rescheduled to coincide with the last great act of the Revolutionary War, George Washington's resignation as Commander-in-Chief.

On December 17th, 1783, Congress convened with seven states. The treaty, however, required a nine-state quorum to issue a formal ratification resolution and proclamation. George Washington's impending audience to resign as Commander-in-Chief was the next major order of business and the delegates were certain that at least two of the missing five states' representatives would attend that most momentous event. The Commander-in-Chief was scheduled to arrive on December 22nd and, according to nineteenth-century historian David Ramsay, the citizens of the United States were well aware of Washington's intentions:

In every town and village, through which the General passed, he was met by public and private demonstrations of gratitude and joy. When he arrived at Annapolis, he informed Congress of his intention to ask leave to resign the commission he had the honor to hold in their service, and desired to know their pleasure in what manner it would be most proper to be done. They resolved that it should be in a public audience. [161]

Congress arranged for a dinner in Washington's honor on Monday, the twenty-second. On December 23rd, the USCA gave the Commander-in-Chief a public audience in their legislative chamber. The stage was set for one of the most remarkable events of United States' history, witnessed by citizens all throughout the neighboring States:

In one of the galleries, which was "bright with a beautiful group of elegant ladies," sat Mrs. Martha Washington and her two grandchildren, Nelly and Parke Custis. Staff officers accompanied Washington as he entered the hall. In his right hand he held his commission and a copy of his address; and in his left hand his sheathed sword. Charles Thomson, the faithful secretary, met and led him to his seat by the President's chair. All

---

[160] The Definitive Treaty of Peace 1783, Article 10, September 3, 1783.
[161] David Ramsay, *The History of the American Revolution Published*. Trenton: James J. Wilson, 1811

delegates stood uncovered — an unusual honor. When President Mifflin signified the readiness of Congress to receive the commission, Washington, in a short farewell, gave up his command. Having handed over the commission and a copy of his address, he resumed his seat; but, when Mifflin replied, he arose and stood until the President had ceased to speak. Great the solemnity; deep the feeling; indeed, it is doubtful whether Monroe, or any other patriotic witness of the ceremony, ever allowed the scene to fade out of his recollection.[162]

What made this action especially remarkable was that George Washington surrendered his commission to a President who had previously conspired in the *Conway Cabal* to replace Washington as Commander-in-Chief with Horatio Gates.[163] Washington, upon surrendering his commission to President Mifflin, stated:

Mr. President -- The great events on which my resignation depended having at length taken place; I have now the honor of offering my sincere Congratulations to Congress & of presenting myself before them to surrender into their hands the trust committed to me, and to claim the indulgence of retiring from the Service of my Country.

Happy in the confirmation of our Independence and Sovereignty, and pleased with the opportunity afforded the United States of becoming a respectable Nation, I resign with satisfaction the Appointment I accepted with diffidence—A diffidence in my abilities to accomplish so arduous a task, which however was superseded by a confidence in the rectitude of our Cause, the support of the Supreme Power of the Union, and the patronage of Heaven.

The Successful termination of the War has verified the more sanguine expectations— and my gratitude for the interposition of Providence, and the assistance I have received from my Countrymen increases with every review of the momentous Contest.

---

[162] George Morgan, *The life of James Monroe*. Small, Maynard and Company, 1921, p. 100.

[163] The Conway Cabal refers to a series of 1777-1778 events that sought George Washington be replaced as Commander-in-Chief. Opposing Washington's command in Pennsylvania was former quartermaster, General Thomas Mifflin. He viewed Washington as a rank amateur and was supported by U.S. Continental Congress delegates Richard Henry Lee, Benjamin Rush as well as Continental Army French officers Johann de Kalb, Louis Lebègue Duportail, and Thomas Conway whose private letters criticizing Washington were forwarded to the U.S. Continental Congress. Conway's letters were made public and supporters of Washington mobilized to assist him politically. General Horatio Gates, the leading candidate to replace Washington, apologized for his role in the cabal and General Conway ended up resigning from the army. Gates, the "Hero of Saratoga," was eventually reassigned as the Commander of the Southern Army. On August 16, 1780, Gates was routed by General Charles Cornwallis at the Battle of Camden, ending his military career. George Washington would effectively end the War for Independence with Cornwallis' Virginia defeat at Yorktown on October 19, 1781.

While I repeat my obligations to the Army in general, I should do injustice to my own feelings not to acknowledge in this place the peculiar Services and distinguished merits of the Gentlemen who have been attached to my person during the War. It was impossible the choice of confidential Officers to compose my family should have been more fortunate. Permit me Sir, to recommend in particular those, who have continued in Service to the present moment, as worthy of the favorable notice & patronage of Congress.

I consider it an indispensable duty to close this last solemn act of my Official life, by commanding the Interests of our dearest Country to the protection of Almighty God, and those who have the superintendence of them, to his holy keeping.

Having now finished the work assigned me, I retire from the great theatre of Action— and bidding an Affectionate farewell to this August body under whose orders I have so long acted, I here offer my Commission, and take my leave of all the employments of public life.[164]

President Thomas Mifflin replied with the following answer:

Sir, -- The United States, in Congress Assembled receive with emotions, too affecting for utterance, the solemn deposit resignation of the authorities under which you have led their troops with safety and triumph success through a long, a perilous and a doubtful war. When called upon by your country to defend its invaded rights, you accepted the sacred charge, before they it had formed alliances, and whilst they were without funds or a government to support you. You have conducted the great military contest with wisdom and fortitude, through invariably regarding the fights of the civil government power through all disasters and changes. You have, by the love and confidence of your fellow-citizens, enabled them to display their martial genius, and transmit their fame to posterity. You have persevered, till these United States, aided by a magnanimous king and nation, have been enabled, under a just Providence, to close the war in freedom, safety and independence; on which happy event we sincerely join you in congratulations.

Having planted and defended the standard of liberty in this new world: having taught a lesson useful to those who inflict and to those who feel oppression, you retire from the great theatre of action, loaded with the blessings of your fellow-citizens, but your fame and the glory of your virtues will not terminate with your official life the glory of your many virtues will military command, it will continue to animate remotest posterity ages and this last act will not be among the least conspicuous .

---

[164] *JCC, 1774-1789,* December 23, 1783.

We feel with you our obligations to the army in general; and will particularly charge ourselves with the interests of those confidential officers, who have attended your person to this interesting affecting moment.

We join you in commending the interests of our dearest country to the protection of Almighty God, beseeching him to dispose the hearts and minds of its citizens, to improve the opportunity afforded them, of becoming a happy and respectable nation. And for you we address to him our earnest prayers that a life so beloved may be fostered with all his care; that your days may be happy, as they have been illustrious; and that he will finally give you that reward which this world cannot give. [165]

Despite the historic magnitude of this event, the fourth USCA was unable to ratify the *Definitive Treaty of Peace* because the necessary nine-state quorum failed to materialize.

Quorum challenges at Annapolis became more complex after Washington's resignation. The severe winter of 1783–1784 due to the volcanic eruption of Laki in Iceland prevented delegates from five of the thirteen States from attending the USCA. The Treaty stipulated that the USCA was required to approve and return the document to England within six months of September 3rd, 1783. It was now January 3rd, 1784, four months into the timeframe and a ratified treaty would take 45 days to cross the Atlantic. The deadline for the treaty ratification was at hand yet only delegates from seven states had remained assembled in Annapolis in an attempt to achieve a quorum.

One faction of the USCA maintained that the accord could be ratified because they were merely approving and not entering into a treaty. Furthermore, it was unlikely that the required two additional state delegations would reach Annapolis before the ratification deadline of March 2nd, 1784. Thomas Jefferson, however, led the delegate faction that insisted a full nine state USCA quorum was required to ratify the treaty. Any less, Jefferson argued, would be chicanery and a "dishonorable prostitution" of the Great Seal of the United States. Additionally, a seven state ratified treaty would open the door to Great Britain declaring it null and void at a later date when the King learned the United States did not meet its constitutional nine state requirements.

---

[165] *JCC, 1774-1789,* December 23, 1783.

With time running out, Jefferson agreed to head a committee of both factions and they arrived at a compromise. The USCA would ratify the treaty with only seven states present if the vote was unanimous and if it were universally agreed that such action would not set a precedent for future decisions. The treaty would be forwarded to the U.S. Commissioners in Europe who would be instructed to request a delay of three months. If Great Britain should insist on meeting the deadline, then the Commissioners would present the seven-state treaty ratification. Shortly after the committee submitted the recommendation to Congress an eighth state, arrived and was in favor of the treaty's ratification. On January 13th, the convention needed only one more delegate to gain the nine states necessary to ratify the treaty under the Articles of Confederation. The following day, South Carolina Representative Richard Beresford, who was ill, arrived in Maryland, thus achieving a USCA nine-state quorum. The vote was immediately taken and on January 14th, 1784, the treaty passed unanimously.

The USCA resolved: Unanimously, nine states being present, that the said definitive treaty be, and the same is hereby ratified by the United States in Congress assembled, in the form following A Proclamation To all persons to whom these presents shall come greeting: Whereas definitive articles of peace and friendship between the United States of America and his Britannic majesty, were concluded and signed at Paris on the 3d day of September, 1783, by the plenipotentiaries of the said United States, and of his said Britannic Majesty, duly and respectively authorized for that purpose; which definitive articles are in the words following:

'The Most Holy and Undivided Trinity ... Done at Paris, this third day of September, in the year of our Lord, one thousand seven hundred and eighty-three. (L. S.) D. Hartley, (L. S.) John Adams, (L. S.) B. Franklin, (L. S.) John Jay.' In testimony whereof, we have caused the seal of the United States to be hereunto affixed. Witness his Excellency Thomas Mifflin, our President, this fourteenth day of January in the year of our Lord one thousand seven hundred and eighty four and in the eighth year of the sovereignty and independence of the United States of America.

Resolved, that the said ratification be transmitted with all possible despatch, under the care of a faithful person, to our ministers in France, who have negotiated the treaty, to be exchanged. Resolved, that Colonel Josiah Harmar be appointed to carry the said ratification. [166]

---

[166] JCC, 1774-1789, Proclamation by USCA, January 14, 1784

Three copies were sent by separate couriers to ensure delivery. King George III did not ratify the treaty for Great Britain until April 9th, 1784, when his signature officially ended the American War for Independence.

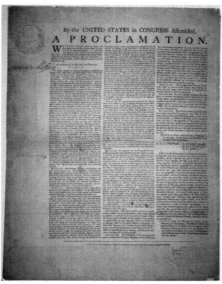

United States, in Congress Assembled Treaty of Paris Proclamation[167]

Although September 3rd, 1783, January 14th, 1784 and April 9th, 1784, were momentous dates in ending the war with Great Britain, the third United American Republic that approved the *Definitive Treaty of Peace* was formulated under the ratified Articles of Confederation on March 1st, 1781. September 3rd, 1783, January 14th, 1784, and April 9th, 1784, are not dates establishing the United States of America as a sovereign nation. They are, however, three important dates that together enacted the *Definitive Treaty of Peace in Paris,* ending the war between the United States and Great Britain.

Having considered the historical role of the *Treaty of Paris* and what was accomplished on particular dates in its negotiation, signing and ratification, the earlier conclusion remains sound: The implementation date of March 1st, 1781, for

---

[167] Treaty of Paris Proclamation Broadside, Original Manuscript, the United States National Archives Administration

the Articles of Confederation marks the birth of the *Third United American Republic: The United States of America: A Not Quite Perpetual Union.*

The Post War United States in Congress Assembled

After the *Treaty of Paris* was ratified and the remaining British troops exited New York and South Carolina, the United States was faced with a war-torn economy and a weak federal government. By the summer of 1786, former veterans, merchants and money lenders deluged Congress daily, in person and with letters, to be remunerated their back pay, money and goods "loaned" to the United States. Even former Presidents took to the cause of patriots burdened with federal receivables, but the federal treasury was empty.

Inflation was rampant due to war reparations owed to Great Britain under the *Definitive Treaty of Peace* and there was no U.S. currency, because the dollar had been recalled five years earlier. The States were also heavily in debt, embroiled in border and trade disputes. It was evident that the *Third American United Republic* adopted under the Articles of Confederation was collapsing.

On January 21st, 1786, Virginia invited all the states to attend a conference to discuss ways to facilitate commerce by establishing intrastate rules and regulations under the Articles of Confederation. The meeting was held in Annapolis but only five of the 13 States sent delegations. The host state of Maryland, wary of expanding the federal powers, sent no delegates. The group of five state delegations, led by nationalists John Dickinson (Chairman-DE), James Madison (Virginia) and Alexander Hamilton (New York), resolved on September 14th, 1786:

Your Commissioners, with the most respectful deference, beg leave to suggest their unanimous conviction, that it may essentially tend to advance the interests of the union, if the States, by whom they have been respectively delegated, would themselves concur, and use their endeavors to procure the concurrence of the other States, in the appointment of Commissioners, to meet at Philadelphia on the second Monday in May next, to take into consideration the situation of the United States, to devise such further provisions as shall appear to them necessary to render the constitution of the Federal Government adequate to the exigencies of the Union; and to report such an Act for that purpose to the United States in Congress assembled, as when agreed to, by them, and afterwards confirmed by the Legislatures of every State, will effectually provide for the same.[168]

U.S. Foreign Secretary John Jay, then the most influential official in the federal government, agreed with the commission, writing:

... to vest legislative, judicial, and executive powers in one and the same body of men, and that, too, in a body daily changing its members, can never be wise. In my opinion those three great departments of sovereignty should be forever separated, and so distributed as to serve as checks on each other. [169]

Earlier in the summer, rebellious mobs stormed the courthouse in Northampton, Massachusetts to prevent the trial and imprisonment of citizen debtors. This turmoil precipitated outright rebellion and in September 1786, former Revolutionary War Captain Daniel Shays and about 600 armed farmers stormed the courthouse in Springfield, Massachusetts. The Sixth USCA, presided over by Massachusetts Delegate Nathaniel Gorham, was impotent to aid the state militia due to the disbandment of the federal army and a lack of funds to assemble new troops. This USCA had begun with high hopes, electing John Hancock President. Hancock never reported for duty and Gorham, along with South Carolina Delegate David Ramsey, served as USCA Chairman. Hancock finally resigned and on June 6th, 1786, Chairman Gorham was elected President. He served until November 3rd, 1786.   In adjourning, the USCA referred "the several matters now before Congress" to the new Congress scheduled to meet "on Monday next," November 6th.[170]   The Seventh USCA, however, failed to form a quorum of the minimum seven states on that date or on any quorum call in November, December and even into January 1787.   The Annapolis Convention's resolution, a congressional action against Shays Rebellion, as well as all federal matters requiring USCA action remained in quorum limbo for nearly three months.

On January 25th, 1787, Daniel Shays led 2000 rebels to Springfield, Massachusetts to storm the arsenal. The USCA was still not in session and the nation had no

---

[168] Frederick Newton Judson, *The Law of Interstate Commerce and Its Federal Regulation,* *"Proceedings of commissioners to remedy defects of the federal government, Annapolis in the State of Maryland, September 11th 1786.   At a meeting of Commissioners, from the States of New York, New Jersey, Pennsylvania, Delaware and Virginia,* Chicago: the Flood & Co. 1905, p. 4.
[169] George Pellew, *John Jay,* Houghton, Mifflin and Company Boston: 1890, p. 221.
[170] *JCC, 1774-1789,* November 3, 1786.

President or Commander-in Chief to lead a U.S. effort with the newly mustered Massachusetts State Militia to put down the armed rebellion.

...The Rebels formed and fired on our people, killed a Mr. Gleason of Stockbridge, a Mr. Porter of Barrington, and wounded three others. The fire was returned, which killed two and wounded five, among whom was their commander. At this instant, our troops in sleighs came up; but before the men could form, the Rebels broke and took to the woods. We have made prisoners of 25 of them, retook all our friends and their property...We have been very much harassed since out troops left this point. The malice of the Rebels can be equaled only by no order of beings but Devils. - *Connecticut Courant 1787*

The Seventh USCA began with only eight states assembling in New York City on February 2nd, 1787. Despite an ominous beginning that many Americans thought marked the end of the *"Perpetual Union,"* this 1787 USCA would enact the most eventful, enlightened and important legislation in United States history.

Serving among the delegates of the USCA was Major-General Arthur St. Clair. Four years earlier, General St. Clair had been a key figure in averting a national crisis when an uprising of several hundred federal soldiers stationed in Lancaster and Philadelphia marched on the Philadelphia State House. The soldiers surrounded the building where both the Third USCA, headed by President Elias Boudinot, and the Pennsylvania Supreme Executive Council, headed by President John Dickinson were assembled. The march on Independence Hall created a constitutional crisis because it raised the question of which police power under the Articles of Confederation, federal or state, was the ultimate authority in putting down the mutiny of federal troops:

The mutinous soldiers presented themselves, drawn up in the street before the State House, where Congress had assembled. The executive Council of the State sitting under the same roof, was called on for the proper interposition. President Dickinson came in, and explained the difficulty under actual circumstances, of bringing out the militia of the place for the suppression of the mutiny. He thought that without some outrages on persons or property, the temper of the militia could not be relied on. Genl St. Clair then in Philadelphia was sent for, and desired to use his interposition, in order to prevail on the troops to return to the Barracks. His report gave no encouragement.

In this posture of things, it was proposed by Mr. Izard that Congress, should adjourn. It was proposed by Mr. Hamilton, that General St. Clair in concert with the Executive Council of the State should take order for terminating the mutiny. Mr. Reed moved that the General should endeavor to withdraw the troops by assuring them of the disposition of Congress to do them justice. ... In the meantime the Soldiers remained in their position, without offering any violence, individuals only occasionally uttering offensive words and wantonly pointed their Muskets to the Windows of the Hall of Congress. No danger from premeditated violence was apprehended, but it was observed that spirituous drink from the tippling houses adjoining began to be liberally served out to the Soldiers, & might lead to hasty excesses. [171]

Arthur St. Clair, the Major General in charge of all Pennsylvania troops, was called in to work out an agreement with the soldiers to end the demonstration:

… General St. Clair worked out an agreement with the soldiers to end the demonstration. He asked Council if it would attend a conference with a committee of commissioned and decommissioned officers, to be appointed by soldiers? St. Clair believed the soldiers might be prevailed upon to return to the barracks if Council so agreed. Dickinson returned to the congressman and inquired of Boudinot if it was agreeable to them for the Council to hold conference as proposed by St. Clair. The President of congress declared it was. Whereupon the Council consented to receive a state of claims from the soldiers "if decently expressed and constitutionally presented."[172]

Later that afternoon, General St. Clair escorted President Boudinot and members of the USCA through mutinous soldiers to safety. Two days later, President Boudinot wrote his brother recounting the mutiny, the Pennsylvania Supreme Executive Council's refusal to call out the state militia to protect the USCA, and the decision to move the seat of the federal government to Princeton, New Jersey.

I have only a moment to inform you, that there has been a most dangerous insurrection and mutiny among a few Soldiers in the Barracks here. About 3 or 400 surrounded Congress and the Supreme Executive Council, and kept us Prisoners in a manner near three hours, tho' they offered no insult personally. To my great mortification, not a Citizen came to our assistance. The President and Council have not firmness enough to call out the Militia, and allege as the reason that they would not obey them. In short the political Maneuvers here, previous to that important election of next October, entirely unhinges Government. This handful of Mutineers continue still with Arms in their hands and are privately supported, and it is well if we are not all Prisoners in a short time. Congress will not meet here, but has authorized me to change their place of residence. I mean to adjourn to Princeton if the Inhabitants of Jersey will protect us. I have wrote to the Governor particularly. I wish you could get your Troop of Horse to

---

[171] *JCC, 1774-1789*, Saturday June 21, 1783

[172] Kenneth R. Bowling, *"*New Light on Philadelphia Mutiny of 1783: Federal-State Confrontation at the Close of the War for Independence.*"* *The Pennsylvania Magazine of History and Biography*, Vol. 101, 1977, p. 433.

offer them aid and be ready, if necessary, to meet us at Princeton on Saturday or Sunday next, if required.[173]

The Seat of the U.S. Government remained in Princeton until fall of 1783, moving then to Annapolis, to Trenton, and finally to New York City where the 1787 USCA was now in session. These delegates who were aware of Shays Rebellion and the Annapolis Convention's call to revise the Articles of Confederation shrewdly elected Arthur St. Clair as the ninth USCA President. The five states that had no representation in Congress -- New Hampshire, Rhode Island, Delaware, Maryland, Virginia, and North Carolina -- were notified of the St. Clair Presidency by Secretary Charles Thomson in the hopes that a former Revolutionary War General might encourage them to send delegates to legislate the nation out of its insolvency and chaos.

It was not until February 14th, 1787, that the USCA formed a nine-state quorum that enabled the federal government to enact major legislation. In January, without the backing of the USCA, General Benjamin Lincoln under a Massachusetts Gubernatorial Commission raised 6000 pounds from private citizens and subsequently fielded 3000 militia to put down Shays' Rebellion. On February 4th, Shays' forces were defeated and scattered after a surprise attack on their camp in Petersham, Massachusetts. The crisis had passed and there was no need for federal government military intervention. On February 21st, 1787 the report of the Annapolis Commissioners was brought before the USCA recommending the Articles of Confederation be revised "... *to render the constitution of the Federal Government adequate to the exigencies of the Union.*" The USCA resolved:

> ... that in the opinion of Congress it is expedient that on the second Monday in May next a Convention of delegates who shall have been appointed by the several States be held at Philadelphia for the sole and express purpose of revising the Articles of Confederation and reporting to Congress and the several legislatures such alterations and provisions therein as shall when agreed to in Congress and confirmed by the States **render the federal Constitution** adequate to the exigencies of Government and the preservation of the Union. [174]

This historic resolution produced what is now known as the 1787 Constitutional Convention.

---

[173] *LDC, 1774-1789.* Elias Boudinot to Elisha Boudinot June 23, 1783.
[174] *JCC, 1774-1789,* USCA Resolution to *"render the federal Constitution adequate to the exigencies of Government and the preservation of the Union",* February 21, 1787.

While the Constitutional Convention was in session in Philadelphia, the USCA meeting in New York turned to the matter of managing and selling 260,000 square miles of real estate conceded to the United States by Great Britain in the *Definitive Treaty of Peace*. After three years of hotly contested debates over the vast territory and passages of both the Ordinance of 1784 and the Land Ordinance of 1785, the time was right to enact a sweeping ordinance designed to govern the *Territory Northwest of the Ohio River.* The Ordinance of 1784, proposed by Thomas Jefferson in the USCA Annapolis Session, prescribed that the new states birthed from the territory were to remain forever a part of the United States of America. The ordinance also mandated that the new states bear the same relation to the USCA as the original states, pay their apportionment of the federal debts, and uphold state republican forms.

The Western Land Ordinance of 1785 put the 1784 Land Ordinance into operation by providing a mechanism for selling and settling the land. The federal surveyors divided the land into carefully planned individual square townships. Each side of the township square was to be six miles in length containing thirty-six square miles of territory. The township was then divided

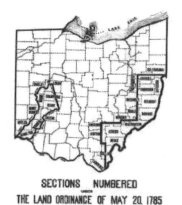

SECTIONS   NUMBERED

THE LAND ORDINANCE OF MAY 20, 1785

into one-square mile sections, with each section receiving its own number and encompassing 640 acres. Section sixteen was to be set aside for a public school and sections eight, eleven, twenty-six, and twenty-nine were to provide veterans of the American Revolution with land as payment for their service during the war, thus greatly reducing the war debt. The government would then sell the remaining sections at public auction at the minimum bid of 640 dollars per section or one dollar for an acre of land in each section. [175]

The Federal Government, however, lacked the resources to manage the newly surveyed lands because Native Americans refused to relinquish a large percentage of the plotted land and most of the territory remained too dangerous for settlement. This situation either required troops to eject the Native Americans or capital to purchase

---

[175] William E. Peters, *Ohio Lands and Their Subdivisions*. W.E. Peters, 1918, p. 308.

their land *"fairly,"* ensuring both peaceful sale and settlement. Additionally the small amount of federal land that was not in dispute by the Native Americans was enthusiastically being occupied by western settlers who had no faith in or respect for the USCA operation as a federal authority. The settlers just claimed the land as squatters and the USCA was unable to muster the capital for magistrates, let alone troops, to enforce the $1.00 per acre fee required for a clear federal land title. With the States no longer in control of the lands and no federal magistrates or troops to enforce the laws, a tide of western squatters flowed into the Northwest Territory with virtually no money flowing into the federal treasury from land sales. The treasury was utterly empty, the United States by 1787 had defaulted on its loan payments to France, opting to pay Holland or risk impressments of its ships. There was an ominous need for the USCA to establish a territorial government to oversee the vast province.

A Committee was formed, chaired by James Monroe, which proposed the replacement of Jefferson's 1784 new states' plan with a colonial system that would result in no less than three or more than five states.[176] Additionally, the Ohio Company of Associates,[177] represented by Manasseh Cutler, made it known that they were willing to purchase 1.5 million acres for private development in what is now southeastern Ohio.

On the morning of July 9th, through the influence of President St. Clair and USCA Treasury Board assistant William Duer, Cutler was permitted to meet with the new committee assigned the task of drafting a new ordinance. Only Edward Carrington and Nathan Dane, two of the five members, were in New York for the meeting because committee members James Madison and Rufus King were in Philadelphia at the Constitutional Convention. In the afternoon, Congress appointed three new members, Richard Henry Lee, John Kean, and Melancton Smith to replace the three absent delegates. Together, they encouraged Cutler's input and together, worked out a plan that would satisfy both Congress and the Ohio Company. The following morning the plan was submitted to Cutler and President St. Clair. Cutler added an educational provision, which was improved by the committee and became part of

---

[176] *JCC, 1774-1789*, March 28, 1787

[177] In 1786, a group of men in Massachusetts, including General Rufus Putnam, Benjamin Tupper, Samuel Holden Parsons and Manasseh Cutler, founded the Ohio Company of Associates, a real estate company. The Ohio Company of Associates agreed to purchase 1,500,000 acres of land, $500,000 immediately and another $500,000 payment once survey the Northwest Ordinance was enacted and surveys completed. The USCA, in the end enacted the Ordinance and also permitted the company to pay for part of the land using military warrants.

Article III. Other revisions were made after input from the President. Cutler, satisfied with the changes, did not remain in New York for the vote in Congress and left for Philadelphia that evening.

The ordinance required seven votes to pass; the States divided four South and five North. The reading by Chairman Nathan Dane on the 11th did not include the provision abolishing slavery. Chairman Dane, the delegate from Massachusetts, who has been credited with drafting the ordinance thought it best to leave the anti-slavery language out so the southern delegations might focus more clearly on the favorable attributes of the ordinance. On July 12th, the ordinance was read again by Dane but this time the anti-slavery provision was added.

In a strange twist of events on July 12th, as the bill was being debated on the floor, President St. Clair decided to take a three-day leave of Congress along with what surely would have been a yes vote from the Commonwealth of Pennsylvania. Eight states remained, evenly divided and neither the President nor the Ohio Company was present to effectuate the required seven state passage of the ordinance. On Friday, July 13th, however, the ordinance passed unanimously.[178] It has been charged that both Arthur St. Clair and Manasseh Cutler left New York to cover up their back room dealings. In rebuttal, President St. Clair's biographer writes:

On the 13th of July he [President Arthur St. Clair] did not preside. He had gone the day before to New Jersey to visit a friend, and he did not return until two days after the passage of the Ordinance. Only eight States out of thirteen voted for that instrument: Pennsylvania was one of the five not represented. When St. Clair returned to New York, he was accompanied by General Irvine, one of his colleagues. In a letter of the latter, written 19th July, and addressed to Colonel Richard Butler, he refers to the Ordinance which had passed two days before his return, and adds: "Who the officers of that government will be I have not heard, nor inquired."

If the name of General St. Clair had been canvassed, or, if he had had any understanding with the New England people, as is alleged, it would have been known to a friend as intimate as General Irvine. But, furthermore, we have his own testimony, which is of the best, to sustain us. In a letter to the Hon. William B. Giles, he says that the office of Governor was, in a great measure, forced upon him by his friends, who thought there would be in it means to compensate for his sacrifices to his country, and provide for his large family. But it proved otherwise. He had " neither the taste nor genius for speculation in land; nor did he consider it consistent with the office." He declared the accepting of the Governorship the most imprudent act of his life, for he

---

[178] *JCC, 1774-1789*, July 13, 1787

was then in possession of a lucrative office, and his influence at home was very considerable. But he had the "laudable ambition of becoming the father of a country, and laying the foundation for the happiness of millions then unborn.[179]

The measure was done and the ordinance's importance is best summed up U.S. Senator Daniel Webster, who remarked:

We are accustomed to praise lawgivers of antiquity ... but I doubt whether one single law of any lawgiver, ancient or modern, has produced the effects of more distinct, marked, and lasting character than the Ordinance of 1787. [180]

In 1787, the world was now put on notice that the land north and west of the Ohio River and east of the Mississippi would be settled and utilized for the creation of *"... not less than three nor more than five territories."* Additionally, this plan for governing the Northwest Territory included freedom of religion, right to trial by jury, the banishment of slavery, and public education as asserted rights granted to the people in the territory. This ordinance was and still remains one of the most important laws ever enacted by the government of the United States and it begins:

An Ordinance for the government of the Territory of the United States northwest of the River Ohio.[181]

Section 1. Be it ordained by the United States in Congress assembled, that the said territory, for the purposes of temporary government, be one district, subject, however, to be divided into two districts, as future circumstances may, in the opinion of Congress, make it expedient. ...[182]

Specifically, this ordinance was an exceptional piece of legislation because Article V permitted the people North and West of the Ohio River to settle their land, form their own territorial government, and take their place as a fully-fledged state, equal to the original 13. The Northwest Ordinance's Article V became the principle that enabled the United States rapid westward expansion, which ended with the inclusion of Alaska and Hawaii as our 49th and 50th states, respectively. This ordinance also

---

[179] Arthur St. Clair and Henry Smith, *The St. Clair Papers: The Life and Public Services of Arthur St. Clair,* Robert Clark and Company 1881, p. 128
[180] Librarian of Congress, The Works of Charles Sumner, Lee and Shepard: 1877 Entered according to Act of Congress, in the year 1877, by Francis V. Balclif, executor, p. 416.
[181] Hereinafter referred to as the Northwest Ordinance or Ordinance of 1787.
[182] *JCC, 1774-1789,* July 13, 1787,*An Ordinance for the government of the Territory of the United States northwest of the River Ohio*

guaranteed that inhabitants of the Territory would have the same rights and privileges that citizens of the original 13 States enjoyed.

Equally important; Article VI provided that slavery and involuntary servitude were outlawed in the Northwest Territory. This was a law that finally gave some merit to the Declaration of Independence's "... *all men are created equal...*" It took three years and a Congress led by Arthur St. Clair to pass this ordinance, making the legislation one of the great documents in American History.

Theism was also openly expressed in the legislation, as Article III stated:

Religion, Morality and knowledge being necessary to good government and the happiness of mankind, Schools and the means of education shall be forever encouraged.[183]

This measure essentially legislated that religion and morality were indispensable to good government but it was not carried out by the federal government because the *Third United American Republic* faded away just after the Northwest Territorial government was barely established. Several state governments, however, adopted similar Article III legislation that provided financial assistance to the Western Christian churches in the 18th and 19th Centuries.

Meanwhile, in 1787 Philadelphia a reasonable quorum of States assembled in convention to "revise" the Articles of Confederation. James Madison reports:

Friday 25 of May ... Mr. Robert Morris informed the members assembled that by the instruction & in behalf, of the deputation of Pennsylvania he proposed George Washington Esqr. late Commander in chief for president of the Convention. Mr. Jno. Rutledge seconded the motion; expressing his confidence that the choice would be unanimous, and observing that the presence of Genl Washington forbade any observations on the occasion which might otherwise be proper.

General (Washington) was accordingly unanimously elected by ballot, and conducted to the chair by Mr. R. Morris and Mr. Rutlidge; from which in a very emphatic manner he thanked the Convention for the honor they had conferred on him, reminded them of the novelty of the scene of business in which he was to act, lamented his want of (better qualifications), and claimed the indulgence of the House towards the involuntary errors which his inexperience might occasion.

---

[183] *JCC, 1774-1789*, July 13, 1787

The "more or less" United States' Assembly was attended by 12 States[184] whose delegates elected George Washington as the Philadelphia Convention's president. Washington began the first session by adopting rules of order which included the provision of secrecy. No paper could be removed from the Convention without the majority leave of the members. The yeas and nays of the members were not recorded and it was the unwritten understanding that no disclosure of the proceedings would be made during the lives of its delegates. At the end of the convention Washington ordered that every record be burned except the Journals which were merely minutes, of which he took personal possession. *"We the People"* of the United States, therefore, knew very little about the Convention until the Journals were finally published in 1819. It was not until the death of President James Madison that his wife, Dolley, revealed she possessed his account of the convention. Dolley Madison sold these journals to the Library of Congress in 1843.

The delegates of the convention were given no authority by the USCA to scrap the Articles of Confederation and construct a new constitution in its place. Throughout the proceedings this fact was addressed in debate and federally-minded delegates led by George Washington, James Madison, Benjamin Franklin, Alexander Hamilton and Charles Pinckney all stood firm on formulating an entirely new constitution. The larger states (by population), especially, were determined to change the one state one vote system adopted under the Articles of Confederation to enact legislation and construct a strong central governmental authority. The smaller states sought to preserve independent state sovereignty and the USCA system of casting votes equally. The two sides, as they did in the York Courthouse[185] formulating the Articles of Confederation in 1777, clashed once again on issue of States rights over federalism.

Edmund Randolph submitted the large states' *"Virginia Plan"* that was primarily drafted by James Madison. There were other plans, most just seeking revisions to the Articles of Confederation. Surprisingly, the 29 year old delegate from South Carolina, Charles Pinckney, provided a plan of a federal structure and powers that was more tangible than any other plan. Pinckney's plan was actually a nascent form

---

[184] Rhode Island sent no delegates.

[185] South Carolina Delegate Henry Laurens, in a final constitutional act, voted against Virginia's attempt to gain more power in the federal government based on population. Specifically, Virginia's amendment to the Articles of Confederation proposed that the nine votes necessary to determine matters of importance in the USCA must come from only the states that contained a majority of the white population.

of the constitution that would be eventually be passed by the Philadelphia convention of States.

The small states formed a sub-committee in an attempt to develop an alternate plan for a newly-proposed bicameral legislature only to emerge still insistent that the one-state one-vote unicameral USCA be retained. The *"New Jersey Plan"*[186] proposed improvements called for a weak federal executive and judiciary branches. The federal government was to remain a confederation with the requirement of at least nine states voting in the positive to enforce their decrees. Although there were many challenges, none was more crucial than the acceptance of a bicameral legislature and how the representatives and senators would be finally numbered in the two newly proposed congressional bodies. The impasse loomed over the proceeding with the large States insisting that all members, in both the House and Senate, be selected based on population. The small States disagreed, but with Rhode Island absent, they lost the convention vote 7-5 on this matter to the large State voting bloc.

State	1776 US Population*	1790 US Census
Virginia	540,000	747,610
Pennsylvania	310,000	434,373
North Carolina	280,000	393,751
Massachusetts	270,000	378,787
New York	240,000	340,120
Maryland	230,000	319,728
South Carolina	180,000	249,073
Connecticut	170,000	237,946
New Jersey	130,000	184,139
New Hampshire	105,000	141,885
Georgia	60,000	82,548
Rhode Island	50,000	68,825
Delaware	45,000	59,096
United States	2,610,000	3,637,881

Author Estimates

---

[186] The New Jersey Plan was the developed by the small States and named after N.J. Delegate William Paterson who presented it on the convention floor.

This embittered many of the small state members. James Madison wrote of one small State delegate:

Mr. L. MARTIN resumed his discourse, contending that the Genl. Govt. ought to be formed for the States, not for individuals: that if the States were to have votes in proportion to their numbers of people, it would be the same thing whether their representatives were chosen by the Legislatures or the people; the smaller States would be equally enslaved; that if the large States have the same interest with the smaller as was urged, there could be no danger in giving them an equal vote; they would not injure themselves, and they could not injure the large ones on that supposition without injuring themselves and if the interests, were not the same, the inequality of suffrage wd. be dangerous to the smaller States: that it will be in vain to propose any plan offensive to the rulers of the States, whose influence over the people will certainly prevent their adopting it: that the large States were weak at present in proportion to their extent: & could only be made formidable to the small ones, by the weight of their votes; that in case a dissolution of the Union should take place, the small States would have nothing to fear from their power; that if in such a case the three great States should league themselves together, the other ten could do so too: & that he had rather see partial confederacies take place, than the plan on the table. This was the substance of the residue of his discourse which was delivered with much diffuseness & considerable vehemence.[187]

On June 28, 1787 the small States gave an ultimatum to the convention that, unless representation in both branches of the proposed legislature was on the basis of equality, one-state one-vote, they would forthwith leave the proceedings. With tempers flaring, Benjamin Franklin rose and called for a recess with the understanding that the delegates should confer with those with whom they disagreed rather than with those with whom they agreed. This recess resulted in a crucial compromise of the convention: The House of Representatives was to be elected by the people based on population, thus providing more representation in the new federal government to the large states. This House, however, was to be checked by the Senate where each state, regardless of size, would have two votes. This resolution to the great Philadelphia Convention crisis enabled the delegates to labor another two months to create one of the most elastic forms of government in human history. And the convention's new plan for the federal government that scrapped the Articles of Confederation consisted of less than four thousand words.

---

[187] Max Farrand, *The records of the Federal convention of 1787*, Volume 1. New Haven: Yale University Press, 1911, p. 444

The innovative *Plan of the New Federal Government* was passed on September 17th, 1787, and rushed to New York by stagecoach. The new constitution was presented to Congress along with a letter from the convention's President, George Washington, to USCA President Arthur St. Clair:

SIR, -- WE have now the honor to submit to the consideration of the **United States in Congress assembled**, that Constitution which has appeared to us the most adviseable. The friends of our country have long seen and desired, that the power of making war, peace and treaties, that of levying money and regulating commerce, and the correspondent executive and judicial authorities should be fully and effectually vested in the general government of the Union: but the impropriety of delegating such extensive trust to one body of men is evident—Hence results the necessity of a different organization. It is obviously impracticable in the federal government of these States, to secure all rights of independent sovereignty to each, and yet provide for the interest and safety of all—Individuals entering into society, must give up a share of liberty to preserve the rest. The magnitude of the sacrifice must depend as well on situation and circumstance, as on the object to be obtained. It is at all times difficult to draw with precision the line between those rights which must be surrendered, and those which may be reserved; and on the present occasion this difficulty was increased by a difference among the several States as to their situation, extent, habits, and particular interests.

In all our deliberations on this subject we kept steadily in our view, that which appears to us the greatest interest of every true American, the consolidation of our Union, in which is involved our prosperity, felicity, safety, perhaps our national existence. This important consideration, seriously and deeply impressed on our minds, led each State in the Convention to be less rigid on points of inferior magnitude, than might have been otherwise expected; and thus the Constitution, which we now present, is the result of a spirit of amity, and of that mutual deference and concession which the peculiarity of our political situation rendered indispensible. That it will meet the full and entire approbation of every State is not perhaps to be expected; but each will doubtless consider, that had her interests been alone consulted, the consequences might have been particularly disagreeable or injurious to others; that it is liable to as few exceptions as could reasonably have been expected, we hope and believe; that it may promote the lasting welfare of that country so dear to us all, and secure her freedom and happiness, is our most ardent wish. With great respect, we have the honor to be, SIR, Your EXCELLENCY'S most obedient and humble Servants,

George Washington, President.
By unanimous Order of the CONVENTION. [188]

---

[188] George Washington, Convention President, *Plan of the New Federal Government*, Printed by Robert Smith, Philadelphia: 1787, Original Document, Stan Klos Collection.

The Convention delegates called for the *Plan of The New Federal Government* to be sent to the states for their consideration with the approval of only 2/3rds of their legislatures being required to discard the Articles of Confederation for the new constitution. The convention overstepped the authority granted by the seventh USCA on February 21st, 1787, first, by discarding the Articles instead of revising that constitution and second, by completely dismissing the modification requirements set forth in Article XIII of the federal constitution, which stated:

Every State shall abide by the determination of the United States in Congress assembled, on all questions which by this confederation are submitted to them. And the Articles of this Confederation shall be inviolably observed by every State, and the Union shall be perpetual; nor shall any alteration at any time hereafter be made in any of them; unless such alteration be agreed to in a Congress of the United States, and be afterwards confirmed by the legislatures of every State.[189]

The proposed obliteration of the Articles of Confederation by convention was to be accomplished without the unanimous approval by the States. It was a constitutional crisis that, to this day, has not been equaled in the United States save by the southern secession of the 1860's which formed the Confederate States of America.[190]

Only sketches of the great debate that ensued in the 1787 USCA exist due to the veil of secrecy that surrounded the sessions. We do know from the notes of New York delegate Melancton Smith, which became available to the public in 1959, that most USCA Delegates believed they had the authority to alter the new proposed Constitution of 1787 before it was sent on to the States. James Madison, Rufus King, and Nathaniel Gorham argued, however, to the contrary.

Since there was no Supreme Court, the USCA was the final authority on the new constitution judicially as well as legislatively. Virginia Delegate Richard Henry Lee would lead the "9-13 opposition" that insisted on unanimous State convention ratification. Lee also sought to amend the new constitution. Melancton Smith writes of Lee:

---

[189] *JCC, 1774-1789*, November 15, 1777, the Articles of Confederation
[190] The Confederate States of America (1861-1865) was a government created by eleven Southern states that had declared their secession from the United States. Secessionists argued that the United States Constitution was a compact among states, an agreement which each state could abandon without consultation. The Union government rejected secession as illegal. A War ensued and the Confederacy was tactically lost with General Robert E. Lee's Army of Northern Virginia surrender at Appomattox Court House, Virginia, on April 9, 1865. President Jefferson Davis was capture the following month and by the end of June 1865 all CSA forces had surrendered.

RH LEE -- The convention had not proceeded as this house were bound; it is to be agreed to by the States & means the 13; but this recommends a new Confederation of nine; the Convention has no more powers than Congress, yet if nine States agree becomes supreme Law. Knows no instance on the Journals as he remembers, opposing the Confederation the impost was to be adopted by 13. This is to be adopted & no other with alteration Why so? good things in it; but many bad; so much so that he says here as he will say everywhere that if adopted civil Liberty will be in eminent danger.[191]

Despite such arguments, Rufus King, James Madison, and Nathaniel Gorham – all delegates to both the Philadelphia Convention and the USCA – maintained that Congress must keep the new constitution intact, sending it on to the States without any changes or amendments despite the unanimous requirement in Article XIII. Smith records Richard Henry Lee's reaction to their position:

Strangest doctrine he ever heard, that referring a matter of report, that no alterations should be made. The Idea the common sense of Man. The States & Congress he thinks had the Idea that congress was to amend if they thought proper. He wishes to give it a candid enquiry, and proposes such alterations as are necessary; if the General wishes it should go forth with the amendment.; let it go with all its imperfections on its head & the amendments by themselves; to insist that it should go as it is without amendments, is like presenting a hungry man 50 dishes and insisting he should eat all or none.[192]

Virginia delegate James Madison's response was:

The proper question is whether any amendments shall be made and that the house should decide; suppose altercations sent to the State, the Acts require the Delegates to the Constitutional Convention to report to them; there will be two plans; some will accept one & some another this will create confusion and proves it was not the intent of the States.[193]

Massachusetts Delegate Nathaniel Gorham, who served as Deputy Chairman of the Philadelphia convention, is reported to have argued against USCA amendments to the new constitution:

Gorham thinks not necessary to take up by paragraphs, every Gentn. may propose amendments; no necessity of a Bill of rights; because a Bill of Rights in state Govts.

---

[191] *LDC, 1774-1789*, Melancton Smith's Notes of Debates
[192] *LDC, 1774-1789*, Melancton Smith's Notes of Debates
[193] *Ibid.*

was intended to retain certain powers, as the [state] legislatures had unlimited powers.[194]

Gorham, although correct in his counsel for the USCA not to amend the constitution, was wrong in his assertion that States' retained enforcement of their *"unlimited powers."* Even the 10th Amendment to the U.S. Constitution enacted passed in the 1790's failed to preserve the "unlimited powers" possessed by state legislatures under the Articles of Confederation.

In addition to the discussions of whether or not the USCA should alter or amend the Constitution, the question: "If not altered how should it be submitted to the States?" was also debated. Smith reports on New Jersey Delegate Abraham Clark:

Clark don't like any proposal yet made; he can't approve it; but thinks it will answer no purpose to alter it; will not oppose it in any place; prefers a resolution to postpone to take up one, barely to forward a copy to the States, to be laid before the Legislatures to be referred to conventions.[195]

It was reported of Virginia Delegate William Grayson:

This is in a curious situation, it is urged all alterations are precluded, has not made up his mind; and thinks it precipitous to urge a decision in two days on a subject that took four Months. If we have no right to amend, then we ought to give a silent passage; for if we cannot alter, why should we deliberate. His opinion they should stand solely upon the opinion of Convention.[196]

Clark argued that *"the motion by Mr. Lee for amendments will do injury by coming on the Journal, and therefore the house upon cool reflection, will think it best to agree to send it out without agreeing."* [197]

The opinions of James Madison and Rufus King won out in the end, earnestly supported by President Arthur St. Clair who, surprisingly, was and remains the only foreign-born President of the United States —a circumstance   outlawed by the new constitution. On September 30th, 1787, James Madison wrote George Washington, summing up the debate that occurred in the United States in Congress Assembled's U.S. Constitution sessions:

---

[194] *Ibid.*
[195] *Ibid.*
[196] *Ibid.*
[197] *Ibid.*

It was first urged that as the new Constitution was more than an alteration of the Articles of Confederation under which Congress acted, and even subverted these articles altogether, there was a Constitutional impropriety in their taking any positive agency in the work.(1) The answer given was that the Resolution of Congress in February had recommended the Convention as the best mean of obtaining a firm national Government; that as the powers of the Convention were defined by their Commissions in nearly the same terms with the powers of Congress given by the Confederation on the subject of alterations, Congress were not more restrained from acceding to the new plan, than the Convention were from proposing it. If the plan was within the powers of the Convention it was within those of Congress; if beyond those powers, the same necessity which justified the Convention would justify Congress; and a failure of Congress to Concur in what was done, would imply either that the Convention had done wrong in exceeding their powers, or that the Government proposed was in itself liable to insuperable objections; that such an inference would be the more natural, as Congress had never scrupled to recommend measures foreign to their Constitutional functions, whenever the Public good seemed to require it; and had in several instances, particularly in the establishment of the new Western Governments, exercised assumed powers of a very high & delicate nature, under motives infinitely less urgent than the present state of our affairs, if any faith were due to the representations made by Congress themselves, echoed by 12 States in the Union, and confirmed by the general voice of the People. An attempt was made in the next place by Richard Henry Lee to amend the Act of the Convention before it should go forth from Congress. He proposed a bill of Rights; provision for juries in civil cases & several other things corresponding with the ideas of Col. M---;---;.(2) He was supported by Mr. Meriwether (3) Smith of this State. It was contended that Congress had an undoubted right to insert amendments, and that it was their duty to make use of it in a case where the essential guards of liberty had been omitted.

On the other side the right of Congress was not denied, but the inexpediency of exerting it was urged on the following grounds. 1. That every circumstance indicated that the introduction of Congress as a party to the reform was intended by the States merely as a matter of form and respect 2. that it was evident from the contradictory objections which had been expressed by the different members who had animadverted on the plan, that a discussion of its merits would consume much time, without producing agreement even among its adversaries. 3. that it was clearly the intention of the States that the plan to be proposed should be the act of the Convention with the assent of Congress, which could not be the case, if alterations were made, the Convention being no longer in existence to adopt them. 4. that as the Act of the Convention, when altered would instantly become the mere act of Congress, and must be proposed by them as such, and of course be addressed to the Legislatures, not conventions of the States, and require the ratification of thirteen instead of nine States, and as the unaltered act would go forth to the States directly from the Convention under the auspices of that Body---;Some States might ratify one & some the other of the plans, and confusion & disappointment be the least evils that could ensue.

These difficulties which at one time threatened a serious division in Congress and popular alterations with the yeas & nays on the journals, were at length fortunately terminated by the following Resolution---;"Congress having recd. the Report of the Convention lately assembled in Philadelphia, Resolved unanimously that the said Report, (4) with the Resolutions & letter accompanying the same, be transmitted to the several Legislatures, in order to be submitted to a Convention of Delegates chosen in each State by the people thereof, in conformity to the Resolves of the Convention made & provided in that case.[198]

This summary, especially in point four, exemplifies James Madison's legal position on why it was constitutional to circumvent Article XIII of the Articles of Confederation. I would argue, however, that George Washington's signature on the new constitution carried more weight with the USCA and fellow Revolutionary War General Arthur St. Clair's Chair than the somewhat specious arguments made by James Madison and his fellow delegates. The September 28th, 1787, resolution passed by President Arthur St. Clair's USCA is recorded as:

Congress having received the report of the Convention lately assembled in Philadelphia: Resolved Unanimously that the said Report with the resolutions and letter accompanying the same be transmitted to the several legislatures in Order to be submitted to a convention of Delegates chosen in each state by the people thereof in conformity to the resolves of the Convention made and provided in that case. [199]

In the final days of the USCA, Arthur St. Clair would be named the first Northwest Territorial Governor under the Ordinance of 1787. Arthur St. Clair's service as Revolutionary War General, USCA President, and now Northwest Territorial Governor, would all but be forgotten, however, by future generations of his fellow Pennsylvanians. Ironically, on February 2nd (the anniversary of St. Clair's Presidency), Western Pennsylvanians expertly market a groundhog burrow emergence, less than 50 miles from the patriot's 18th century home. These citizen efforts have resulted in Punxsutawney Phil's unprecedented international rodent celebrity. It is suggested here, to the mayor of Punxsutawney Pennsylvania, that perhaps a beam of Phil's national February 2nd spotlight might be shined on a forgotten U.S. Presidency that just happened to birth the current Constitution of the United States of America.

The historic 1787 USCA continued to conduct the nation's business into late October, voting to sell 1,000,000 acres of the Northwest Territory to the Ohio Company. In its final November 1-2 session days, the 1787 USCA failed to achieve

---

[198] *LDC, 1774-1789*, James Madison to George Washington, September 30, 1787.
[199] *JCC, 1774-1789*, September 28, 1787

a quorum. On November 5th, 1787 Secretary Charles Thomson called the new USCA to quorum but only five delegates, representing three states, attended. It was not until January 22nd, 1788 that the last USCA would form a quorum, electing Virginia Delegate Cyrus Griffin, President.

At the 1788 USCA session, the delegates were already aware that five states (Delaware, Pennsylvania, New Jersey, Georgia, and Connecticut) had approved the Constitution of 1787. The "Federalist Papers,"[200] authored by James Madison, Alexander Hamilton, and John Jay, made a most persuasive case for ratification. Massachusetts would ratify the constitution on February 6th, 1788, but Rhode Island, a month later, rejected ratification by popular referendum. Maryland and South Carolina stayed the federalist course and voted for ratification. This set the stage for New Hampshire,[201] which became the ninth state to ratify the new constitution on June 21st, 1788, and thus effectively terminated the Articles of Confederation and its government.

Despite that the ratification by New Hampshire met the new constitution's 2/3rds requirement, the USCA was unable to implement the new government the following day, as the Continental Congress had done on March 2nd, 1781, after adopting the *Articles of Confederation.* The unicameral USCA was to be replaced by a complex tripartite government with new officials; the ratifying states, by virtue of the Constitution of 1787's mechanisms, required action by the USCA to establish a plan for the national election of President as well as state elections of U.S Senators and House of Representatives members. Additionally, a start date and location for the new Constitution of 1787 government had to be established by the USCA. The plan to dissolve the confederation and implement the Constitution of 1787 government became the primary objective of the now lame-duck USCA government. Meanwhile three states (Virginia, New York, and North Carolina) had yet to vote on ratification so the USCA bided its time adopting the 9th state's ratification of the new constitution.

---

[200] The Federalist Papers are a series of 85 essays promoting the ratification of the *U.S. Constitution of 1787*. They were written by Alexander Hamilton, John Jay, and James Madison. Seventy-seven of the essays were published serially as articles in the *Independent Journal* and the *New York Packet* between October 1787 and August 1788. A compilation of these and eight others, called The Federalist was published by J. and A. McLean in 1788. The title "Federalist Papers" did not emerge in the U.S. lexicon until the early twentieth century.

[201] Philip Robert Dillon, *American Anniversaries: Every Day in the Year, Presenting Seven Hundred and Fifty Events in United States History*, from the Discovery of America to the Present Day, The Philip R. Dillon: New York 1918

In the Virginia ratification convention, James Madison found himself in direct opposition to Patrick Henry, George Mason, William Grayson, and future President James Monroe. These men and other anti-federalists believed that the new constitution did not protect the individual rights of citizens and created a central government that was too powerful. On June 26th, 1788 Madison and his colleagues were able to secure the necessary votes by including in the ratification resolution "That there be a Declaration or Bill of Rights asserting and securing from encroachment the essential and unalienable Rights of the People in some such manner as the following...".[202] These recommended Virginia amendments to the second U.S. Constitution would eventually become the framework for what we now call the "Bill of Rights," the first ten amendments to the Constitution.

Shortly after receiving the good news of the ratification by Virginia, the largest and 10th state to adopt the new constitution, the USCA acted on New Hampshire's ratification resolution, resolving on July 2nd, 1788:

The State of New Hampshire having ratified the constitution transmitted to them by the Act of the 28 of Sept. last and transmitted to Congress their ratification and the same being read, the president reminded Congress that this was the ninth ratification transmitted and laid before them, whereupon, on Motion of Mr. Clarke seconded by Mr. Edwards - Ordered That the ratifications of the constitution of the United States transmitted to Congress be referred to a committee to examine the same and report an Act to Congress for putting the said constitution into operation in pursuance of the resolutions of the late federal Convention.[203]

The committee consisted of Edward Carrington, Pierpont Edwards, Abraham Baldwin, Samuel Allyne Otis and Thomas Tudor Tucker. They reported and made recommendations to Congress on July 8th, 9th, 14th and 28th but no plan was adopted for the transition. The July USCA deliberations on how to implement the new U.S. Constitution were overshadowed by their host state's ratifying convention being held in Poughkeepsie, New York. If the convention failed to ratify the *Constitution of 1787*, the USCA could not consider convening the new government in their current seat, New York City. Thus a plan could not be debated, let alone adopted, until the ratification votes from the New York Convention were tallied.

---

[202] *Ratification of the Constitution by the State of Virginia; June 26, 1788*, Avalon project, Yale University, http://avalon.law.yale.edu/18th_century/ratva.asp 2011
[203] *JCC, 1774-1789*, July 2, 17888

Federalist leaders, John Jay, Robert R. Livingston, and Alexander Hamilton encountered stiff opposition to the new constitution in Poughkeepsie. Jay advocated ratification, reminding the Convention that:

the direction of general and national affairs is submitted to a single body of men, viz. the congress. They may make war; but are not empowered to raise men or money to carry it on. They may make peace; but without power to see the terms of it observed. They may form alliances, but without ability to comply with the stipulations on their part. They may enter into treaties of commerce; but without power to enforce them at home or abroad. They may borrow money; but without having the means of re-payment. They may partly regulate commerce; but without authority to execute their ordinances. They may appoint ministers and other officers of trust; but without power to try or punish them for misdemeanors. They may resolve; but cannot execute either with dispatch or with secrecy. In short, they may consul & deliberate and recommend and make requisitions; and they who please, may read them. From this new and wonderful system of government, it has come to pass, that almost every national object of every kind is, at this day, unprovided for; & other nations, taking the advantage of its imbecility, are daily multiplying commercial restraints upon us. [204]

Livingston, upon learning of New Hampshire's ratification remarked, "The Confederation was now dissolved. The question before the committee was now a question of policy and expediency."[205] News that Virginia, the home state of George Washington, had also ratified the new constitution all but assured the demise of the Articles of Confederation Republic with or without New York. Jay, Livingston, Hamilton, and their supporters therefore were able to eke out a razor-thin victory with a 30 to 27 ratification vote whose convention also proposed amendments to the new constitution including:

That the People have an equal, natural and unalienable right, freely and peaceably to Exercise their Religion according to the dictates of Conscience, and that no Religious Sect or Society ought to be favored or established by Law in preference of others. That the People have a right to keep and bear Arms; that a well-regulated Militia, including the body of the People capable of bearing Arms, is the proper, natural and safe defense

---

[204] James Hardie, *The Description of the City of New York, A Brief Account and Most Remarkable Events, Which Have Occurred in Its History*, New York: S. Marks Publisher, : 1827, p. 113
[205] Jonathan Elliot and James Madison, *The debates in the several State conventions on the adoption of the federal Constitution, as recommended by the general convention at Philadelphia, in 1787: Together with the Journal of the federal convention, Luther Martin's letter, Yates's minutes, Congressional opinions, Virginia and Kentucky resolutions of '98-'99, and other illustrations of the Constitution*, J. B. Lippincott company, 1891, Volume II, P. 320.

of a free State; ... That the People have a right peaceably to assemble together to consult for their common good, or to instruct their Representatives; and that every person has a right to Petition or apply to the Legislature for redress of Grievances.-That the Freedom of the Press ought not to be violated or restrained.[206]

During the New York Convention, North Carolina delegates had assembled in Hillsborough to consider ratifying the *Constitution of 1787*. Federalists, led by James Iredell, Sr., struggled to mitigate Antifederalists' fears that the *Constitution of 1787* would ultimately concentrate power at the national level permitting the federal government to chip away at states' rights and individual liberties. The abuse of power arising from empowering a central government to levy taxes, appoint government officials, and institute a strong court system was of particular concern to Antifederalists leaders Willie Jones, Samuel Spencer, and Timothy Bloodworth. Antifederalist William Gowdy of Guilford County summed up the majority's opinion in the debates, stating:

Its intent is a concession of power, on the part of the people, to their rulers. We know that private interest governs mankind generally. Power belongs originally to the people; but if rulers be not well guarded, that power may be usurped from them. People ought to be cautious in giving away power.[207]

The North Carolina delegates, who overwhelming distrusted the proposed centralized authority, adjourned on August 4th after they had drafted a *"Declaration of Rights"* and a list of *"Amendments to the Constitution."* Unlike New York and Virginia, these members voted *"neither to ratify nor reject the Constitution proposed for the government of the United States."* James Madison reported to his father:

We just learn the fate of the Constitution in N. Carolina. Rho. Island is however her only associate in the opposition and it will be hard indeed if those two States should endanger a system which has been ratified by the eleven others. Congress has not yet finally settled the arrangements for putting the new Government in operation. The place

---

[206] *Ratification of the Constitution by the State of New York; July 26, 1788*, Avalon project, Yale University, http://avalon.law.yale.edu/18th_century/ratny.asp 2012
[207] Jonathan Elliot and James Madison, *The debates in the several State conventions on the adoption of the federal Constitution, as recommended by the general convention at Philadelphia, in 1787: Together with the Journal of the federal convention, Luther Martin's letter, Yates's minutes, Congressional opinions, Virginia and Kentucky resolutions of '98-'99, and other illustrations of the Constitution*, J. B. Lippincott company, 1891, Volume IV, Page 13.

for its first meeting creates the difficulty. The Eastern States with N. York contend for this City. Most of the other States insist on a more central position.[208]

The dies were now cast. Eleven states, not thirteen, would form a new United American Republic, *We The People* of the United States of America.

Statement of the periods at which the new conftitution has been ratified by the feveral ftates which compofe the new union*.

					Majority.
Delaware,	December	3,	1787,	unanimoufly.	
Pennfylvania,	December	13,		46 to 23,	23
New-Jerfey,	December	19,		unanimoufly.	
Georgia,	January	2,	1788,	unanimoufly.	
Connecticut,	January	9,		128 to 40,	88
Maffachufetts,	February	6,		187 to 168,	19
Maryland,	April	28,		63 to 12,	51
South-Carolina,	May	23,		149 to 73,	76
New Hampfhire,	June	21,		57 to 46,	11
Virginia,	June	25,		89 to 79,	10
New-York,	July	26,		30 to 25,	5

August 1788 Printing of the "More or Less" 11 United States Ratification Statistics

All throughout August and into September, the USCA debated the implementation of the new U.S. Constitution. James Madison wrote Thomas Jefferson, who was serving in France as U.S. Minister:

Congress have not yet decided on the arrangements for inaugurating the new Government. The place of its first meeting continues to divide the Northern & Southern members, though with a few exceptions to this general description of the parties. The departure of Rhode Island, and the refusal of North Carolina in consequence of the late event there to vote in the question, threatens a disagreeable issue to the business, there being now an apparent impossibility of obtaining seven States for any one place. The three Eastern States & New York, reinforced by South Carolina, and as yet by New Jersey, give a plurality of votes in favor of this City [New York]. The advocates for a more central position however though less numerous, seemed very determined not to yield to what they call a shameful partiality to one extremity of the Continent.[209]

---

[208] *LDC, 1774-1789*, James Madison, Jr. to James Madison, August 18, 1788
[209] *LDC, 1774-1789*, James Madison to Thomas Jefferson, August 23, 1788.

The Third United American Republic Summary:

1. *The United States of America: A Not Quite Perpetual Union Republic* day of origin is March 1st, 1781 when the 13 States adopted the first U.S. Constitution, the Articles of Confederation;

2. The Continental Congress of the United States of America was replaced with a new governing body, with the convening of the United States in Congress Assembled on March 1st, 1781;

3. Samuel Huntington, who had served 16 months as President of the Continental Congress, was acknowledged as the First President of the United States in Congress Assembled on March 2nd, 1781, in the USCA Journals;

4. Charles Thomson, who had served six years and six months as Secretary of the Continental Congress was acknowledged as the first Secretary of the United States in Congress Assembled on March 2nd, 1781 in the USCA Journals;

5. Commander-in-Chief George Washington served as Commander-in-Chief under the Articles of Confederation until December 23rd, 1781, when he voluntarily resigned his commission to Thomas Mifflin, President of the United States in Congress Assembled. He had served in this position since June 1775 for eight years and six months serving as Commander-in-Chief in the First, Second, and now the *Third United American Republic*.

6. The United States in Congress Assembled, on January 14th, 1784, and King George III, on April 9th, 1784, ratified the September 3rd, 1783 *Definitive Treaty of Peace* ending the Revolutionary War;

7. The United States in Congress Assembled passed the *Ordinance of 1787* to govern the vast federal lands known as the Northwest Territory;

8. The Philadelphia Convention of 1787, with George Washington as its President, drafted a new plan for the federal government on September 17th, 1787. On September 28th, 1787 the United States in Congress Assembled, without changing a word of it, sent the new U.S. Constitution on to the States for ratification;

9. On October 5th, 1787, the USCA elected Arthur St. Clair Northwest Territorial Governor and on October 21st authorizes the sale of one million acres to the Ohio Company;

10. The last USCA convenes on January 22nd, 1788, electing Virginia Delegate Cyrus Griffin, President;

11. On September 13th, 1788 the USCA adopts a plan for implementing the new 11 state-ratified Constitution on March 4, 1789, over the objections of Articles of Confederation member states North Carolina and Rhode Island;

12. USCA Secretary Charles Thomson makes his last entry in the Journals: *March 2, Mr. Philip Pell from New York is present.*

THE THIRD UNITED AMERICAN REPUBLIC
Presidents of the United States in Congress Assembled
March 1, 1781 to March 3, 1789

Samuel Huntington	March 1, 1781	July 6, 1781
Samuel Johnson	July 9, 1781	Declined Office
Thomas McKean	July 10, 1781	November 4, 1781
John Hanson	November 5, 1781	November 3, 1782
Elias Boudinot	November 4, 1782	November 2, 1783
Thomas Mifflin	November 3, 1783	June 3, 1784
Richard Henry Lee	November 30, 1784	November 22, 1785
John Hancock	November 23, 1785	June 5, 1786
Nathaniel Gorham	June 6, 1786	November 13, 1786*
Arthur St. Clair	February 2, 1787	October 29, 1787*
Cyrus Griffin	January 22, 1788	January 21, 1789

*Last USCA Quorum as President

THE THIRD UNITED AMERICAN REPUBLIC'S SEATS OF GOVERNMENT
March 1, 1781 to March 3, 1789

Philadelphia	July 2, 1776 to Dec. 12, 1776	Pennsylvania State House
Philadelphia	May 10, 1775 to Dec. 12, 1776	Pennsylvania State House
Baltimore	Dec. 20, 1776 to Feb. 27, 1777	Henry Fite House
Philadelphia	March 4, 1777 to Sep. 18, 1777	Pennsylvania State House
Lancaster	September 27, 1777	Lancaster Court House
York	Sept. 30, 1777 to June 27, 1778	York-town Court House
Philadelphia	July 2, 1778 to July 19, 1778*	College Hall - PA State House
Philadelphia	July 19, 1778 to February 28, 1781	PA State House
	* True Dates Unknown	

Articles of Confederation Congress
United States in Congress Assembled (USCA) Sessions

USCA	Session Dates	USCA Convene Date	President(s)
First	11-05-1780 to 11-04-1781*	03-02-1781	Samuel Huntington & Thomas McKean
Second	11-05-1781 to 11-03-1782	11-05-1781	John Hanson
Third	11-04-1782 to 11-02-1783	11-04-1782	Elias Boudinot
Fourth	11-03-1783 to 10-31-1784	11-03-1783	Thomas Mifflin
Fifth	11-01-1784 to 11-06-1785	11-29-1784	Richard Henry Lee
Sixth	11-07-1785 to 11-05-1786	11-23-1785	John Hancock & Nathaniel Gorham
Seventh	11-06-1786 to 11-04-1787	02-02-1787	Arthur St. Clair
Eighth	11-05-1787 to 11-02-1788	01-21-1788	Cyrus Griffin
Ninth	11-03-1788 to 03-03-1789**	None	None

* The Articles of Confederation was ratified by the mandated 13th State on February 2, 1781, and the dated adopted by the Continental Congress to commence the new United States in Congress Assembled government was March 1, 1781. The USCA convened under the Articles of Confederation Constitution on March 2, 1781.

** On September 14, 1788, the Eighth United States in Congress Assembled resolved that March 4th, 1789, would be commencement date of the *Constitution of 1787's* federal government thus dissolving the USCA on March 3rd, 1789.

UNITED STATES STATEHOOD ORDER
Articles of Confederation – 1 to 13 States

	State	State Passes Ratification	Reported to Congress	Delegates Sign
1	Virginia	Dec. 16, 1777	June 25, 1778	July 9, 1778
2	South Carolina	Feb. 5, 1778	June 25, 1778	July 9, 1778
3	New York	Feb. 6, 1778	June 23, 1778	July 9, 1778
4	Rhode Island	Feb. 16, 1778	June 23, 1778	July 9, 1778
5	Georgia	Feb. 26, 1778	June 25, 1778	July 9, 1778
6	Connecticut	Feb. 27, 1778	June 23, 1778	July 9, 1778
7	New Hampshire	March 4, 1778	June 23, 1778	7-9-1778 to 8-8-1778
8	Pennsylvania	March 5, 1778	June 25, 1778	7-9-1778 to 7-9-1778
9	Massachusetts	March 10, 1778	June 23, 1778	July 9, 1778
10	North Carolina	April 24, 1778	June 25, 1778	July 21, 1778
11	New Jersey	Nov. 20, 1778	Nov. 25-26, 1778	Nov, 26, 1778
12	Delaware	Feb. 1, 1779	Feb. 16, 1779	2-22-1779 to 5-5-1779
13	Maryland	Feb. 2, 1781	Feb. 12, 1781	March 1, 1781

CHAPTER V
THE FOURTH UNITED AMERICAN REPUBLIC

THE UNITED STATES OF AMERICA
"We The People"

The start date for the *Fourth United American Republic* also eludes the test of general acceptance by the political and academic communities. After challenging Robert C. Byrd for his U.S. Senate Seat in 1994, I came together with him on his idea of marking September 17th, each year, as the anniversary of the signing of the *Constitution of 1787*. Byrd's bill was enacted by Congress with a provision requiring schools and federal agencies to set aside time to study the Constitution on or about the anniversary date. September 17th, as noted in the last chapter, marks the Philadelphia Convention's completion of the Constitution of 1787 which was curried to New York, debated by the USCA and sent to the states on September 28, 1787, unchanged by delegates. These events, however, do not mark the start of the *Fourth American United Republic*. The Constitution of 1787, which ultimately formed the current American United Republic, required ratification by nine states before the USCA would be forced to dissolve itself and implement a plan of installing the new tripartite federal government.

On September 13th, 1788, the USCA agreed, after much debate, to keep the *Constitution of 1787* United States seat of government in New York. The USCA then approved a plan to dissolve itself and implement the *Constitution of 1787*. Congress resolved on September 13th that March 4th, 1789, would be the starting date of the current and *Fourth United American Republic*:

:

Whereas the Convention assembled in Philadelphia pursuant to the resolution of Congress of the 21st of Feb., 1787 did on the 17th. of Sept of the same year report to the United States in Congress assembled a constitution for the people of the United States, whereupon Congress on the 28 of the same Sept did resolve unanimously "That the said report with the resolutions and letter accompanying the same be transmitted to the several legislatures in order to be submitted to a convention of Delegates chosen in each state by the people thereof in conformity to the resolves of the convention made and provided in that case" And whereas the constitution so reported by the Convention and by Congress transmitted to the several legislatures has been ratified in the manner therein declared to be sufficient for the establishment of the same and such ratifications duly authenticated have been received by Congress and are filed in the Office of the Secretary therefore Resolved That the first Wednesday in January next be the day for appointing Electors in the several states, which before the said day shall have ratified the said constitution; that the first Wednesday in February next be the day for the electors to assemble in their respective states and vote for a president; and that the first Wednesday in March next be the time and the present seat of Congress the place for commencing proceedings under the said constitution.[210]

On October 2nd Congress debated where to relocate Secretary Thomson's office and the nation's records. The USCA, in an arrangement to keep the capital in New York, exacted an agreement from Mayor James Duane and the New York City council to renovate completely the building they currently occupied to accommodate the new tripartite government. The extensive work that was planned required the USCA to find other quarters for Thomson, federal staff, congressional meetings, and the nation's records. The War Office and Department of Foreign Affairs had occupied six rooms at Fraunces Tavern since 1785. The initial two year lease had expired in May, 1787, but the USCA had renewed the space for another year, and had added some Treasury Offices. Incredibly, the USCA, whose republic was founded by a Congress that first caucused in a Philadelphia tavern, was considering leasing a New York tavern as the final seat of the "lame duck" unicameral government experiment. On October 2nd, 1788, the USCA resolved:

The committee consisting of Mr. [Thomas Tudor] Tucker, Mr. [John] Parker, and Mr. [Abraham] Clark to whom was referred a letter from the Mayor of the city of New York to the Delegates having reported, That it appears from the letter referred to them, that the repairs and alterations intended to be made in the buildings in which Congress at present Assemble, will render it highly inconvenient for them to continue business therein, that it will therefore be necessary to provide some other place for their accommodation, the committee having made enquiry find no place more proper for this purpose than the two Apartments now appropriated for the Office of Foreign Affairs.

---

[210] *JCC, 1774-1789*, September 13, 1789

They therefore recommend that the said Apartments be immediately prepared for the reception of Congress and the papers of the Secretary. Resolved, that Congress agree to the said report. [211]

On October 6, 1788, renovations began on the building that would be called thereafter, Federal Hall. The USCA moved their offices to Fraunces Tavern and reconvened on October 8th; on motion by Henry Lee that was seconded by John Armstrong, Congress resolved::

That considering the peculiar circumstances attending the case of Muscoe Livingston, late a Lieutenant in the navy of the United States, in the settlement of his accounts, Resolved, that the Commissioner for the marine department adjust the said account, any resolution of Congress to the contrary notwithstanding.[212]

The rest of the session was spent reviewing Governor Arthur St. Clair's letter and five enclosures from the Northwest Territory. On the 9th they assembled again and passed a resolution permitting the Board of Treasury to satisfy a United States Lottery claim providing that the beneficiaries "do give security that no further Claim on account of said Prize Ticket shall be made upon the United States by the Heirs, Executors or Administrators of the said deceased, Gail, or either of them."[213]

On October 10th, 1788, Massachusetts, Connecticut, New York, New Jersey, Pennsylvania, Virginia, North Carolina and South Carolina assembled (along with only one delegate each from New Hampshire, Rhode Island, Delaware and Maryland) in a final USCA. Only Georgia, as with the first 1774 Continental Congress, failed to send delegates. The USCA in their last official act suspended the work of the commissioners who had been appointed to settle the states' federal accounts. The USCA's last motion was made by Abraham Clark and seconded by Hugh Williamson,

That the Secretary at War be and he hereby is directed to forbear issuing warrants for bounties of land to such of the officers of the late army who have neglected to account for monies by them received as pay masters of Regiments, or for recruiting or other public service, until such officers respectively shall have settled their accounts with the commissioner of army accounts, or others legally authorized to settle the same, and have paid the balances that may be found due from them, into the treasury of the United

---

[211] *JCC, 1774-1789*, October 2, 1788
[212] *Ibid,* October 8, 1788
[213] *Ibid,* October 9, 1788

States, anything in the land ordinance passed the 9th day of July 1788 to the contrary notwithstanding. [214]

The Delegates tabled the measure, *"the question was lost"* and USCA adjourned. Despite the adjournment and several unsuccessful attempts to form more quorums, it was necessary for some delegates including President Griffin, to conduct the nation's business in New York until the new government took office on March 4th, 1789. Cyrus Griffin, John Brown, John Dawson, James Madison, and Mann Page were elected on October 31st, 1788 as Delegates to the USCA from Virginia. President Griffin wrote in November:

Be so obliging to inform the House of Delegates that I shall continue in New York to execute the important Trust with which the general Assembly is pleased to honor me. I receive this further Mark of their Confidence with gratitude and pleasure & will endeavor to answer the expectations of my Country.[215]

The USCA Journals report the final days of the *Third United American Republic* as thus:

October 13-16 fails to achieve quorum. October 21, 1788 Two states attended namely Massachusetts and South Carolina and from New Hampshire Nicholas Gilman from Connecticut Benjamin Huntington from Pennsylvania William Irvine from Maryland Benjamin Contee from Virginia Cyrus Griffin and from North Carolina Hugh Williamson. October 22-November 1, 1788 there appear attended occasionally from New Hampshire Nicholas Gilman, from Massachusetts Samuel A Otis and George Thatcher, from Rhode island Peleg Arnold, from Connecticut Benjamin Huntington and Pierpont Edwards, from New Jersey Jonathan Dayton, from Pennsylvania William Irvine, from Maryland Benjamin Contee, from Virginia Cyrus Griffin, from North Carolina Hugh Williamson, and from South Carolina Daniel Huger John Parker and Thomas Tudor Tucker. November 3, 1788 Pursuant to the Articles of the Confederation only two Gentlemen attended Benjamin Contee for Maryland and Hugh Williamson for North Carolina. November 15, 1788 Cyrus Griffin from Virginia attended; December 1, 1788 John Dawson from Virginia and; December 6, 1788 Nicholas Eveleigh from South Carolina attended; December 11, 1788 Jonathan Dayton from New Jersey attended; December 15, 1788 Thomas Tudor Tucker from South Carolina; December 30, 1788 Samuel A Otis from Massachusetts; January 1, 1789 James R. Reid from Pennsylvania, Robert Barnwell from South Carolina; January 8, 1789 Abraham Clarke from New Jersey; January 10, 1789 Trenche Coxe from Pennsylvania; January 26, 1789 Nathaniel Gorham from Massachusetts; January 29, 1789 George Thatcher from Massachusetts; February 6, 1789 David Ross from Maryland; February 12, 1789 John

---

[214] *JCC 1774-1789*. October 10, 1788
[215] *LDC 1774-1789*. Cyrus Griffin to Thomas Matthews, November 22, 1788

Gardner from Rhode island. February 18, 1789 David Gelston from New York February 19, 1789 Nicholas Gilman from New Hampshire; March 2 Philip Pell from New York.[216]

Although the start date of the *Fourth United American Republic* was set by the USCA as March 4th, 1789. The first federal bicameral congress, unlike the first federal congress, did not convene on the prescribed date set for the commencement of the new republic due to quorum challenges. It would not be until April 1st, 1789, that the U.S. House of Representatives was able to achieve a quorum. Five days later, on April 6th, the U.S. Senate achieved a quorum and elected its officers. Nevertheless, the last USCA legislated the start date of the Fourth United American Republic on March 4, 1789 and this date is the birthday of the current United States republic.

The United States presidential election of 1788–89 was the first quadrennial presidential election and was held from Monday, December 15th, 1788, to Saturday, January 10th, 1789. It remains the only election ever to take place partially in a year that is not a multiple of four. On April 6th, 1789, after reaching a quorum, the U.S. Senate tallied and certified the electoral votes from ten states, for President and Vice President.[217] The electoral votes in four states (Delaware, Maryland, Massachusetts and New Hampshire) each resulted in a tie because under the new constitution, an elector was able to vote for two Presidents. Washington, however, handily won the election with 69 electoral votes, with John Adams second at 34 votes, followed by John Jay (9 votes). Under the unamended *Constitution of 1787,* second place was automatically awarded the office of Vice President.[218]

---

[216] *JCC 1774-1789.* October 10, 1788

[217] Rhode Island and North Carolina still had not ratified the Constitution of 1787. The New York legislature could not agree on a method for choosing electors and did not participate in the first presidential election.

[218] In 1789 the electors voted only for the office of President rather than for both President and Vice President. Each elector was allowed to vote for two people for the U.S. Presidency. The person receiving the greatest number of votes became President while the second largest vote candidate became Vice President. If no candidate received a majority of votes, then the House of Representatives would choose among the five highest top candidates, with each state getting one vote. In the presidential election of 1800 Thomas Jefferson and Aaron Burr tied at 73 votes. It took the House of Representatives 36 ballots to finally choose Jefferson over Burr who became Vice President. This contentious affair resulted in the adoption of the Twelfth Amendment in 1804, which directed the electors to use separate ballots to vote for the President and Vice President. While this solved the problem at hand, it ultimately had the effect of lowering the prestige of the Vice Presidency, as the office was no longer for the leading challenger for the Presidency.

On April 16th, 1789, President-elect George Washington began his journey from Mount Vernon to New York City. The trek took seven days and his route was transformed into celebrations by citizens and officials who turned out in large numbers to receive him along the way. The towns of Alexandria, Baltimore, Wilmington, Philadelphia, Trenton and Elizabethtown were particularly enthusiastic in their efforts to honor the President-elect. Dutch Legation Secretary, Rudolph Von Dorsten, describes Washington's entrance into New York City:

President George Washington made his entry into New York on Thursday, April 23d. On the previous day a barge left this city. The barge was built expressly by the citizens of New York, and was rowed by thirteen pilots, all dressed in white. A committee of three Senators and five Representatives on behalf of Congress, and three of the first officers on behalf of New York, went to Elizabethtown in New Jersey, to welcome the President, and to await his arrival there. His Excellency was also accompanied by some well-equipped sloops and by a multitude of small craft with citizens of New Jersey and New York on board.

Once in New York Washington was received by Governor George Clinton, NYC Mayor James Duane and other officers. Another account of Washington's arrival in New York is provided by former USCA President Elias Boudinot:

We soon arrived at the Ferry Stairs, where there were many Thousands of the Citizens waiting with all, the eagerness of Expectation, to welcome excellent Patriot to that Shore, which he had regained from a Powerful Enemy by his valour & good conduct. We found the Stairs covered with Carpeting & the Rails hung with Crimson. The President being preceded by the Committee was received by the Governor & the Citizens in the most brilliant Manner. Here he was met on the wharf with by many of his old & faithful officers & fellow Patriots who had borne the Heat & Burthen of the Day with him, and who like him had experienced every reverse of Fortune with fortitude & Patience, and who now joined the universal Chorus of welcoming their great deliverer (under Providence) from all their Fears. It was with difficulty a Passage could be made by the Troops thro the pressing Crowds, who seemed to be incapable of being satisfied by Gazing at this Man of the People. You will see' the particulars of the Procession from the Wharf to the House appointed for his residence in the News Papers, the Streets were lined with the inhabitants as thick as the People could stand, and it required all the Exertions of a numerous Train of City Officers with their Staves to make a Passage for the Company. The Houses were filled with Gentlemen & Ladies the whole distance, being about half a Mile, and the windows to the highest Stories, were illuminated by the sparkling Eyes of innumerable Companies of Ladies, who seemed to vie with each other to show their Joy on this great Occasion. It was half an hour before we could finish our Commission by introducing the President for his residence as soon as this was done, notwithstanding his great Fatigue of both Body &

Mind, he had to receive all the Gentlemen & Officers to a very large amount, who wished to show their respect in the most affectionate manner...[219]

It took a full half hour for Washington to arrive at his new residence, 3 Cherry Street, located one block from the East River, near the present-day Brooklyn Bridge. It would take a full week before Congress could agree on how the formal Presidential inauguration should be conducted.

On April 30th, 1789, George Washington was escorted to the newly-renovated Federal Hall located at Wall and Nassau Street. The building, as described by historian Ron Chernow:

... came richly laden with historical associations, having hosted John Peter Zenger's trial in 1735, the Stamp Act Congress of 1765 and the Confederation Congress from 1785 to 1788. Starting in September 1788, the French engineer Pierre-Charles L'Enfant had remodeled it into Federal Hall, a suitable home for Congress. L'Enfant introduced a covered arcade at street level and a balcony surmounted by a triangular pediment on the second story. As the people's chamber, the House of Representatives was accessible to the public, situated in a high-ceilinged octagonal room on the ground floor, while the Senate met in a second-floor room on the Wall Street side, buffering it from popular pressure. From this room Washington would emerge onto the balcony to take the oath of office. In many ways, the first inauguration was a hasty, slapdash affair. As with all theatrical spectacles, rushed preparations and frantic work on the new building continued until a few days before the event. Nervous anticipation spread through the city as to whether the 200 workmen would complete the project on time. Only a few days before the inauguration, an eagle was hoisted onto the pediment, completing the building. The final effect was stately: a white building with a blue and white cupola topped by a weather vane.[220]

There was, as yet, no U.S. Chief Justice so the oath was administered by New York Chancellor Robert R. Livingston on Federal Hall's second floor balcony, overlooking a crowd assembled in the streets. Mrs. Eliza Susan Morton Quincy, wife of Josiah Quincy, provides this account of the inauguration:

I was on the roof of the first house in Broad Street ... and so near to Washington that I could almost hear him speak. The windows and roofs of the houses were crowded; and in the streets the throng was so dense, that it seemed as if one might literally walk on the heads of the people. The balcony of the hall was in full view of this assembled

---

[219] Elias Boudinot of New Jersey to Hannah Boudinot, April 24, 1789, Princeton University Library
[220] Ron Chernow, *George Washington: The Reluctant President*, Smithsonian magazine, February 2011

multitude. In the centre of it was placed a table, with a rich covering of red velvet; and upon this, on a crimson velvet cushion, lay a large and elegant Bible. ... All eyes were fixed upon the balcony; where, at the appointed hour, Washington entered, accompanied by the Chancellor of the State of New York, who was to administer the oath; by John Adams, the Vice-President; Governor Clinton; and many other distinguished men. ... His appearance was most solemn and dignified. Advancing to the front of the balcony, he laid his hand on his heart, bowed several times, and then retired to an arm-chair near the table. The populace appeared to understand that the scene had overcome him, and were at once hushed in profound silence. After a few moments, Washington arose, and came forward. Chancellor Livingston read the oath according to the form prescribed by the Constitution; and Washington repeated it, resting his hand upon the Bible. Mr. Otis, the Secretary of the Senate, then took the Bible to raise it to the lips of Washington; who stooped, and kissed the book. At this moment, a signal was given, by raising a flag upon the cupola of the Hall, for a general discharge of the artillery of the Battery. All the bells in the city rang out a peal of joy, and the assembled multitude sent forth a universal shout. The President again bowed to the people, and then retired from a scene such as the proudest monarch never enjoyed. Many entertainments were given, both public and private; and the city was illuminated in the evening.[221]

President Washington, Vice President Adams, and the members of Congress retired to the Senate Chamber. Here the President delivered the first inaugural address that was drafted by James Madison. Washington explained his disinclination to accept the presidency and highlighted his own shortcomings, including "frequent interruptions in health," that we was "unpractised in the duties of civil administration," and intellectually "inheriting inferior endowments from nature." Washington left the presidential prerogative "to recommend to your consideration, such measures as he shall judge necessary and expedient" to Congress, except for suggesting they consider amendments to the constitution that were proposed by the states' conventions.

After the inauguration, each branch of Congress went about establishing its own rules for conducting the nation's business, just as the USCA had done eight years earlier, after the implementation of the *Articles of Confederation*. The House and the Senate also established joint committees drawing up conference rules. They dealt with the logistics of communication with the President and between the two legislative bodies. There was much for everyone to do in forming this new republic, ranging from immediately raising revenues for funding the federal government to reformulating existing departments and passing laws, including the Northwest

---

[221] Eliza Susan Quincy, *Memoir of the life of Eliza S.M. Quincy*, Wilson and Son, Boston, 1861, p. 52.

Ordinance, which had been enacted under the Articles of Confederation. Three important acts would be passed establishing three executive departments under the U.S. Presidency -- after Congress rejected a U.S. Senate Committee's proposal that the president should be called "His Highness the President, Protector of the Liberties of the United States." The major 1789 legislation passed by the First Federal Bicameral Congress and signed by President Washington includes:

> On June 1st, 1789: *An Act to regulate the Time and Manner of administering certain Oaths* was the first law passed by the United States Congress and signed into law by President George Washington after the ratification of the U.S. Constitution. Parts of the law still remain on the books;

> On July 4th, 1789 *An Act for laying a Duty on Goods, Wares, and Merchandises imported into the United States* was passed to immediately establish the tariff as a regular source of revenue for the federal government and as a protection of domestic manufacture;

> July 20th., 1789 *An Act imposing Duties on Tonnage* laid out various rates of duty on the tonnage of ships and vessels entered in the United States from foreign countries;

> On July 27th, 1789 *An Act for Establishing an Executive Department, to be Denominated the Department of Foreign Affairs* was passed. John Jay, Articles of Confederation Secretary of Foreign Affairs turned down reappointment but agreed to serve as acting Secretary until a Presidential appointment was confirmed. During the enactment of this bill a debate arose as to the power of removal of the Foreign Secretary. One side contended that the power belonged to the President, by virtue of the executive powers of the Government vested in him by the constitution. The other side maintained that the power of removal should be exercised by the President, conjointly with the Senate. The important question was decided by Congress in favor of the President's power to remove the heads of all these Departments, on the ground that they are Executive Departments;

> On July 31st, 1789, *An Act to regulate the Collection of the Duties imposed by law on the tonnage of ships or vessels, and on goods, wares and merchandises imported into the United States* was passed establishing ports of entry in each of the eleven states where duties were to be collected. North Carolina and Rhode Island, who had not ratified the new constitution, were subject to the same goods' duties as were foreign countries. *Be it therefore further enacted, That all goods, wares and merchandise not of their own growth or manufacture, which shall be imported from either of the said two States of Rhode Island and Providence Plantations, or North Carolina, into any other port or place within*

the limits of the United States, as settled by the late treaty of peace, shall be subject to the like duties, seizures and forfeitures, as goods, wares or merchandise imported from any State or country without the said limits;

➤ On August 5th, 1789, *An Act for settling the Accounts between the United States and individual States* was passed appointing and paying commissioners to carry into effect the May 7th, 1787 ordinance and subsequent resolutions established by the USCA *"... for the settlement of accounts between the United States and individual States;"*

➤ On August 7th, 1789, *An Act to establish an Executive Department, to be denominated the Department of War* was passed. Former USCA Secretary of War Henry Knox was re-appointed by President Washington and confirmed by the U.S. Senate. The Department of War oversaw all military affairs until Congress created a separate Navy Department in 1798. The National Security Act, passed by Congress in 1947, designated departments for the Army, Navy, and the Air Force. A National Military Establishment, renamed the Department of Defense in 1949, administered these departments;

➤ Also on August 7th, 1789, *An Act to provide for the Government of the Territory Northwest of the river Ohio* was passed. This bill was the reenactment of the Northwest Ordinance passed by the USCA in July 1787 *"so as to adapt the same to the present Constitution of the United States."* Former USCA Governor Arthur St. Clair was re-appointed by President Washington and confirmed by the U.S. Senate;

➤ On August 20th, 1789, *An Act providing for the Expenses which may attend Negotiations or Treaties with the Indian Tribes, and the appointment of Commissioners for managing the same* was passed;

➤ On September 1st, 1789, *An Act for Registering and Clearing Vessels, Regulating the Coasting Trade, and for other purposes* was passed providing for the licensing and enrollment of vessels engaged in navigation and trade;

➤ On September 2nd, 1789, *An Act to establish the Treasury Department* was passed. The act assigns duties to the Secretary, Comptroller, Auditor, Treasurer, Register, and Assistant to the Secretary. It prohibits persons appointed under the act from engaging in specified business transactions and prescribes penalties for so doing. It also provides that if information from a person other than a public prosecutor is the basis for the conviction, that person shall receive half the fine. Alexander Hamilton was appointed Secretary of the Treasury by President Washington and was confirmed the same day by the U.S. Senate;

➤ On September 11th, 1789, *An Act for establishing the Salaries of the Executive Officers of Government, with their Assistants and Clerks* was passed;

➤ On September 15th, 1789, *An Act to provide for the safe-keeping of the Acts, Records and Seal of the United States, and for other purposes* was passed. This law changed the name of the Department of Foreign Affairs to the Department of State because certain domestic duties were assigned to the agency. These included: Receipt, publication, distribution, and preservation of the laws of the United States; Preparation, sealing, and recording of the commissions of Presidential appointees; Preparation and authentication of copies of records and authentication of copies under the Department's seal; Custody of the Great Seal of the United States; Custody of the records of the former Secretary of the Continental Congress, except for those of the Treasury and War Departments. Thomas Jefferson was appointed by President Washington September 25, 1789 and confirmed by the U.S. Senate the following day. Chief Justice John Jay served as Acting Secretary of State until Secretary Jefferson returned from France. Other domestic duties for which the Department was responsible at various times included issuance of patents on inventions, publication of the census returns, management of the mint, control of copyrights, and regulation of immigration;

➤ On September 22nd, 1789, *An Act for the temporary establishment of the Post-Office* was passed. *"That there shall be appointed a Postmaster General; his powers and salary and the compensation to the assistant or clerk and deputies which he may appoint, and the regulations of the post-office shall be the same as they last were under the resolutions and ordinances of the late Congress."* Samuel Osgood was appointed Postmaster General by President Washington on September 26th, 1789 and confirmed by the U.S. Senate the following day;

➤ Also on September 22nd, 1789, *An Act for allowing Compensation to the Members of the Senate and House of Representatives of the United States, and to the Officers of both Houses* was passed. Unlike the USCA, whose members were paid by their respective states, the congressmen were paid $6.00 a day from the new federal treasury;

➤ On September 23rd, 1789, *An Act for allowing certain Compensation to the Judges of the Supreme and other Courts, and to the Attorney General of the United States* was passed with salaries ranging from $4,000 for the Chief Justice to $800 for the Delaware Federal District Judge. The Attorney General's salary was set at $1,500 while Associate Justices of the Supreme Court were paid $3,500;

> On September 24th, 1789 *An Act for allowing a compensation to the President and Vice President of the United States* was passed with the salaries of $25,000[222] and $5,000 respectively.

> On September 24th, 1789 the *Judiciary Act* was established. The Act calls for the organization of the U.S. federal court system, which had been sketched only in general terms in the U.S. Constitution. The act established a three-part judiciary that was made up of district courts, circuit courts, and the Supreme Court. The act also outlined the structure and jurisdiction of each branch. John Jay was appointed U.S. Chief Justice and Edmond Randolph appointed Attorney General by President Washington on September 24th, 1789 and the two were confirmed by the U.S. Senate on September 26th;

> On September 29th, 1789, *An Act to regulate Processes in the Courts of the United States* was passed authorizing the courts of the United States to issue writs of execution as well as other writs;

> On September 29th, 1789, *An Act making Appropriations for the Service of the present year* was passed. Specifically the bill provided for *"a sum not exceeding two hundred and sixteen thousand dollars for defraying the expenses of the civil list, under the late and present government; a sum not exceeding one hundred and thirty-seven thousand dollars for defraying the expenses of the department of war; a sum not exceeding one hundred and ninety thousand dollars for discharging the warrants issued by the late board of treasury, and remaining unsatisfied; and a sum not exceeding ninety-six thousand dollars for paying the pensions to invalids"*;

> On September 29th, 1789, *An Act providing for the payment of the Invalid Pensioners of the United States* was passed. The act specified *"that the military pensions which have been granted and paid by the states respectively, in pursuance of the acts of the United States in Congress assembled, to the invalids who were wounded and disabled during the late war, shall be continued and paid by the United States, from the fourth day of March last, for the space of one year, under such regulations as the President of the United States may direct"*;

> On September 29th, 1789, *An Act to recognize and adapt the Constitution of the United States the establishment of the Troops raised under the Resolves of the United States in Congress assembled, and for other purposes therein mentioned* was passed. The act specified *"that the establishment contained in the resolve of the late Congress of the third day of October, one thousand seven hundred and*

---

[222] The 1789 historic standard of living value of $25,000 income or wealth is projected to be $658,000 in 2012 dollars.

eighty-seven, except as to the mode of appointing the officers, and also as is herein after provided, be, and the same is hereby recognized to be the establishment for the troops in the service of the United States;"

➢ On September 29th, 1789, *An Act to alter the Time for the Next Meeting of Congress* was passed adjourning the bi-cameral congress until January 5, 1790,

The 1790 session of the first congress was also notable. One of the most important measures that this congress faced was addressing over two hundred amendments to the U.S. Constitution that had been proposed by the states during the ratification process. After eliminating replication, the number stood at nearly 90, with most calling for a reorganization of the federal government's structure. James Madison was able to push his reluctant colleagues into considering 17 new amendments. Congress would eventually whittle these down to 12 amendments in 1790, which were sent to the states for ratification. Ten of these amendments were ratified by the states and today they are known as the Bill of Rights.

SUMMARY OF THE FOURTH UNITED AMERICAN REPUBLIC

- The Fourth United American Republic was established by the U.S. *Constitution of 1787* and began, by order of the Eighth USCA, on March 4th, 1789;

- On April 1st, 1789, the United States House of Representatives achieved its first quorum;

- On April 6th, 1789, the United States Senate achieved its first quorum and elected its officers;

- On April 30th, 1789, George Washington was inaugurated at Federal Hall as President and Commander-in-Chief of the United States of America;

- On September 25th, 1789, the First Congress of the United States proposed to the state legislatures 12 amendments to the Constitution that met arguments most frequently advanced against it;

- On November 12th, 1789 North Carolina became the 12th State to ratify the 1787 U.S. Constitution;

- On February 1st , 1790, the United States Supreme Court assembled for the first time;

- On May 29th, 1790, Rhode Island became the thirteenth State to ratify the U.S. Constitution of 1787, meeting the now-defunct Articles of Confederation requirement of unanimous approval;

- On December 15th, 1791, by three-fourths of the state legislatures, Bill of Rights Amendments 3 to 12 were ratified and today constitute the first ten amendments of the Constitution. Amendment 2 (of the original 12) concerning "varying the compensation for the services of the Senators and Representatives" was finally ratified on May 7th, 1992, as the 27th Amendment to the Constitution. The first amendment, which concerned the number of constituents for each Representative, was never ratified.[223]

THE FOURTH UNITED AMERICAN REPUBLIC
United States of America *"We The People"*
1789 Electoral Votes[224]

NEW HAMPSHIRE	Five electors appointed by state legislature on January, 7 1789 from top ten candidates elected at large by people on December 15, 1788.
George Washington	5 votes
John Adams	5 votes
MASSACHUSETTS	Voters in eight districts nominate Electors on December 18, 1788; on 7 January 7, 1789, the legislature chose one elector from the two men receiving the highest number of votes in each district and appointed two additional Electors.
George Washington	10 votes
John Adams	10 votes
CONNECTICUT	Seven Electors chosen by the state legislature on January 7, 1789.
George Washington	7 votes
John Adams	5 votes
Samuel Huntington	2 votes

---

[223] The First of the 12 amendments proposed by Congress was not ratified read: *"After the first enumeration required by the first article of the Constitution, there shall be one Representative for every thirty thousand, until the number shall amount to one hundred, after which the proportion shall be so regulated by Congress, that there shall be not less than one hundred Representatives, nor less than one Representative for every forty thousand persons, until the number of Representatives shall amount to two hundred; after which the proportion shall be so regulated by Congress, that there shall not be less than two hundred Representatives, nor more than one Representative for every fifty thousand persons."* See the last Chapter for a discussion of this measure.

[224] Papers of George Washington, Alderman Library , University of Virginia, 2012 http://gwpapers.virginia.edu/documents/presidential/electoral.html

NEW JERSEY	Seven Electors chosen by the Governor and Privy Council on January 7, 1789.
George Washington	6 votes
John Jay	5 votes
John Adams	1 vote
DELAWARE	Election of Electors by voters in three districts on January 7, 1789, certified by Privy Council on January 24, 1789.
George Washington	3 votes
John Jay	3 votes
PENNSYLVANIA	Ten Electors elected at large by voters on January 7, 1789.
George Washington	10 votes
John Adams	8 votes
John Hancock	2 votes
MARYLAND	Eight Electors chosen at large by voters on January 7-10, 1789. Two were absent on February 4 when ballots were cast for President.
George Washington	6 votes
Robert H. Harrison	6 votes
VIRGINIA	Twelve Electors chosen by voters in 12 districts on January 7, 1789. One district failed to make returns, and one elector failed to attend the balloting on February 4, 1789.
George Washington	10 votes
John Adams	5 votes
George Clinton	3 votes
John Hancock	1 vote
John Jay	1 vote
SOUTH CAROLINA	Seven Electors chosen by legislature on January 7, 1789.
George Washington	7 votes
John Rutledge	6 votes
John Hancock	1 vote
GEORGIA	Five Electors chosen by the legislature on January 7, 1789.
George Washington	5 votes
John Milton	2 votes
James Armstrong	1 vote
Edward Telfair	1 vote
Benjamin Lincoln	1 vote
TOTALS:	138 votes
George Washington	69 votes

John Adams	34 votes
John Jay	9 votes
Robert H. Harrison	6 votes
John Rutledge	6 votes
John Hancock	4 votes
George Clinton	3 votes
Samuel Huntington	2 votes
John Milton	2 votes
James Armstrong	1 vote
Edward Telfair	1 vote
Benjamin Lincoln	1 vote

Constitution of 1787 Ratification Order

	Date	State	Votes		%
			Yes	No	71.25%
1	December 7, 1787	Delaware	30	0	100
2	December 12, 1787	Pennsylvania	46	23	66.66
3	December 18, 1787	New Jersey	38	0	100
4	January 2, 1788	Georgia	26	0	100
5	January 9, 1788	Connecticut	128	40	76.1
6	February 6, 1788	Massachusetts	187	168	53.7
7	April 28, 1788	Maryland	63	11	85.13
8	May 23, 1788	South Carolina	149	73	67.11
9	June 21, 1788	New Hampshire	57	47	54.8
10	June 25, 1788	Virginia	89	79	52.02
11	July 26, 1788	New York	30	27	52.63
12	November 21, 1789	North Carolina	194	77	71.58
13	May 29, 1790	Rhode Island	34	32	51.51

The Fourth United American Republic's Seats of Government
March 4, 1789 to Present

New York City	March 3,1789 to August 12, 1790	NY City Hall
Philadelphia	December 6,1790 to May 14, 1800	Congress Hall
Washington DC	November 17, 1800 to Present	Two US Capitol Buildings,

1787 U.S. Constitution Presidents - 1789 to 2009

D- Democrat Party, F- Federalist Party, I-Independent, R-Republican Party, R -
Republican Party that Split into the National Republicans and Democrats Party 1828
& W- Whig Party*

George Washington (I)
(1789-1797)

John Adams (F)
(1797-1801)

Thomas Jefferson (R*)
(1801-1809)

James Madison (R*)
(1809-1817)

James Monroe (R*)
(1817-1825)

John Quincy Adams (R*)
(1825-1829)

Andrew Jackson (D)
(1829-1837)

Martin Van Buren (D)
(1833-1837)

William H. Harrison (W)
(1841)

John Tyler (W)
(1841-1845)

Millard Fillmore (W)
(1850-1853)

Franklin Pierce (D)
(1853-1857)

James Buchanan (D)
(1857-1861)

James K. Polk (D)
(1845-1849)

Zachary Taylor (W)
(1849-1850)

Abraham Lincoln (R)
(1861-1865)

Jefferson Davis** (D)
(1861-1865)

Andrew Johnson (R)
(1865-1869)

Ulysses S. Grant (R)
(1869-1877)

Rutherford B. Hayes (R)
(1877-1881)

James A. Garfield (R)
(1881)

Chester Arthur (R)
(1881-1885)

Grover Cleveland (D)
(1885-1889)

Benjamin Harrison (R)
(1889-1893)

Grover Cleveland (D)
(1893-1897)

William McKinley (R)
(1897-1901)

Theodore Roosevelt (R)
(1901-1909)

William H. Taft (R)
(1909-1913)

Wilson Woodrow (D)
(1913-1921)

Calvin Coolidge (R)
(1921-1929)

Herbert C. Hoover (R)
(1929-1933)

Franklin D. Roosevelt (D)
(1933-1945)

Harry S. Truman (D)
(1945-1953)

Dwight D. Eisenhower (R)
(1953-1961)

John F. Kennedy (D)
(1961-1963)

Lyndon B. Johnson (D)
(1963-1969)

Richard M. Nixon (R)
(1969-1974)

Gerald R. Ford (R)
(1973-1974)

James Earl Carter, Jr. (D)
(1977-1981)

Ronald W. Reagan (R)
(1981-1989)

George H. W. Bush (R)
(1989-1993)

William J. Clinton (D)
(1993-2001)

George W. Bush (R)
(2001-2009)

Barack H. Obama (D)
(2009-present)

**Confederate States of America

CHAPTER VI

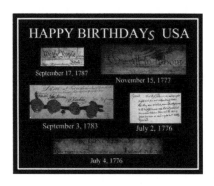

AMERICA'S FOUR UNITED REPUBLICS: WHO WAS FIRST?

WHICH UNITED COLONY OF AMERICA WAS THE FIRST STATE?

- ☐ The resolution of the 12 colonies declaring themselves as *Free and Independent States* was passed July 2ⁿᵈ, 1776. New York would not approve statehood until July 9ᵗʰ, 1776.
- ☐ There is a manuscript, however, that records the roll-call vote on July 2ⁿᵈ, 1776, on the actual "Resolution for Independency." The manuscript clearly indicates that New Hampshire was the first colony to approve independence and therefore holds the right of being the first State to officially declare itself independent from Great Britain.

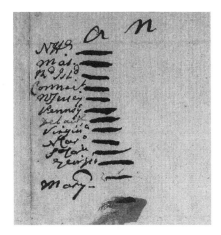

United Colonies of America roll-call vote result written on the original Continental Congress manuscript of the July 2ⁿᵈ, 1776 *"Resolution for Independency."* The roll indicates that New Hampshire was the first state to vote for independence. New York is not listed, as the delegation abstained from the vote - *Image courtesy of the Papers of the Continental Congress, 1774-1783; Records of the Continental and Confederation Congresses and the Constitutional Convention, 1774-1789, Record Group 360; National Archives.*

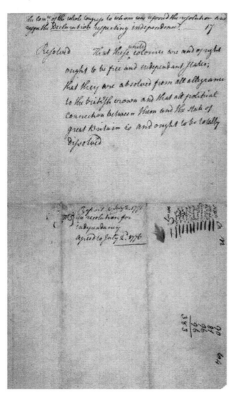

United Colonies of America Resolution For Independency with roll-call vote results written on the July 2, 1776 - Image courtesy of the Papers of the Continental Congress, 1774-1783; Records of the Continental and Confederation Congresses and the Constitutional Convention, 1774-1789, Record Group 360; National Archives

UNITED STATES OF AMERICA
Thirteen Independent States United in Congress Republic
STATE APPROVAL ORDER

United Colonies of America	Resolution For Independence	Declaration of Independence
U.S. State Order by Vote: New Hampshire, Massachusetts, Rhode Island, Connecticut, New Jersey, Pennsylvania, Delaware, Virginia, Maryland, North Carolina, South Carolina, & Georgia.	July 2, 1776	July 4, 1776
New York	July 9, 1776	July 9, 1776

- The first federal constitution, the Articles of Confederation, was passed on November 15th, 1777 in York, Pennsylvania but it required ratification by all thirteen states. Virginia was the first to ratify the Articles of Confederation on December 16th, 1777, with Maryland being the last on February 2nd, 1781. Delaware, which claims to be the First U.S. State, ratified the Articles of Confederation on February 9th, 1779.

US STATEHOOD ORDER
ARTICLES OF CONFEDERATION

	State	State Passes Ratification	Reported to Congress	Delegates Sign
1	Virginia	Dec. 16, 1777	June 25, 1778	July 9, 1778
2	South Carolina	Feb. 5, 1778	June 25, 1778	July 9, 1778
3	New York	Feb. 6, 1778	June 23, 1778	July 9, 1778
4	Rhode Island	Feb. 16, 1778	June 23, 1778	July 9, 1778
5	Georgia	Feb. 26, 1778	June 25, 1778	July 9, 1778
6	Connecticut	Feb. 27, 1778	June 23, 1778	July 9, 1778
7	New Hampshire	March 4, 1778	June 23, 1778	7-9-1778 to 8-8-1778
8	Pennsylvania	March 5, 1778	June 25, 1778	7-9-1778 to 7-9-1778
9	Massachusetts	March 10, 1778	June 23, 1778	July 9, 1778
10	North Carolina	April 24, 1778	June 25, 1778	July 21, 1778
11	New Jersey	Nov. 20, 1778	Nov. 25-26, 1778	Nov, 26, 1778
12	Delaware	Feb. 1, 1779	Feb. 16, 1779	2-22-1779 to 5-5-1779
13	Maryland	Feb. 2, 1781	Feb. 12, 1781	March 1, 1781

- The current United States constitution was passed by the Philadelphia Convention of 12 States on September 17, 1787. Delaware was the first State to ratify the current the Constitution of 1787 on December 7, 1787 with Rhode Island being the last on May 29, 1790.

UNITED STATES OF AMERICA:
WE THE PEOPLE REPUBLIC

Constitution of 1787 Ratification Order

	Date	State	Votes		%
			Yes	No	71.25%
1	December 7, 1787	Delaware	30	0	100
2	December 12, 1787	Pennsylvania	46	23	66.66
3	December 18, 1787	New Jersey	38	0	100
4	January 2, 1788	Georgia	26	0	100
5	January 9, 1788	Connecticut	128	40	76.1
6	February 6, 1788	Massachusetts	187	168	53.7
7	April 28, 1788	Maryland	63	11	85.13
8	May 23, 1788	South Carolina	149	73	67.11
9	June 21, 1788	New Hampshire	57	47	54.8
10	June 25, 1788	Virginia	89	79	52.02
11	July 26, 1788	New York	30	27	52.63
12	November 21, 1789	North Carolina	194	77	71.58
13	May 29, 1790	Rhode Island	34	32	51.51

Virginia First to Ratify
U.S. Constitution of 1777

Delaware First to Ratify
U.S. Constitution of 1787

NEW HAMPSHIRE WAS THE FIRST COLONY TO DECLARE ITS INDEPENDENCE FROM GREAT BRITAIN

Answer: New Hampshire is the *"First State"* since the "Granite State" was the first in the July 2nd, 1776, roll call to adopt independence. **Virginia** was the *"First State"* to ratify the *Articles of Confederation,* while **Delaware** was the *"First State"* to ratify the *Constitution of 1787.*

WHO WAS THE FIRST PRESIDENT OF THE CONTINENTAL CONGRESS?

- On September 5th, 1774, a convention of 11 British North American Colonies assembled in what they would later call the Continental Congress of the United Colonies of North America and elected Virginia Delegate **Peyton Randolph**, President.
- On July 2nd and 4th, 1776 a 12-state Continental Congress majority (New York abstained) passed the *Resolution of Independence* and *Declaration of Independence*, respectively, declaring the Colonies *"Free and Independent States."* Massachusetts Delegate **John Hancock** was serving as President.

Answer One: Peyton Randolph was the first President of the Continental Congress of the United Colonies. John Hancock was the first President of the Continental Congress of the United States.

CONTINENTAL CONGRESS
OF THE UNITED COLONIES PRESIDENTS
Sept. 5, 1774 to July 1, 1776

Peyton Randolph	September 5, 1774	October 22, 1774
Henry Middleton	October 22, 1774	October 26, 1774
Peyton Randolph	May 20, 1775	May 24, 1775
John Hancock	May 25, 1775	July 1, 1776

THE SECOND UNITED AMERICAN REPUBLIC
CONTINENTAL CONGRESS OF THE UNITED STATES PRESIDENTS
July 2, 1776 to February 28, 1781

John Hancock	July 2, 1776	October 29, 1777
Henry Laurens	November 1, 1777	December 9, 1778
John Jay	December 10, 1778	September 28, 1779
Samuel Huntington	September 29, 1779	February 28, 1781

COMMANDER-IN-CHIEF UNITED COLONIES & STATES OF AMERICA

George Washington	June 15, 1775	December 23, 1783

WHO WAS THE FIRST PRESIDENT OF THE UNITED STATES IN CONGRESS ASSEMBLED UNDER THE ARTICLES OF CONFEDERATION?

☐ On March 1st, 1781 the Continental Congress of the United States of America adopted the 13-State ratified *Constitution of 1777*, Articles of Confederation.

☐ The *Constitution of 1777* provided for a unicameral governing body called the "United States in Congress Assembled" (USCA).

☐ On March 2nd, 1781, the Delegates, who were duly elected by the 13 States after each one had ratified the *Articles of Confederation*, convened in Philadelphia as the United States in Congress Assembled.

☐ Connecticut's Samuel Huntington presided over the United States in Congress Assembled as its President.

Answer: Samuel Huntington was the first President of the United States in Congress Assembled under the Articles of Confederation.

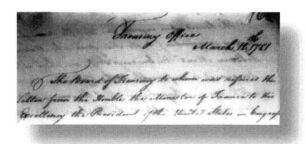

U. S. Treasury letter referring to Samuel Huntington as *His Excellency the President of the United States, in Congress Assembled -- Library of Congress image.*

PRESIDENTS OF THE UNITED STATES IN CONGRESS ASSEMBLED

Samuel Huntington	March 1, 1781	July 6, 1781
Samuel Johnston	July 10, 1781	Declined Office
Thomas McKean	July 10, 1781	November 4, 1781
John Hanson	November 5, 1781	November 3, 1782
Elias Boudinot	November 4, 1782	November 2, 1783
Thomas Mifflin	November 3, 1783	June 3, 1784
Richard Henry Lee	November 30, 1784	November 22, 1785
John Hancock	November 23, 1785	June 5, 1786
Nathaniel Gorham	June 6, 1786	November 13, 1786
Arthur St. Clair	February 2, 1787	October 29, 1787
Cyrus Griffin	January 22, 1788	January 21, 1789

WHO WAS THE FIRST PRESIDENT AND COMMANDER-IN-CHIEF OF THE UNITED STATES OF AMERICA?

- ☐ President Washington was not only the first Commander-in-Chief of the United States of America but he held that office in all four stages of the nation's development:

  - o *United Colonies of America Republic - Thirteen British Colonies United in Congress*: Elected on June 16, 1775 and serving under the Continental Congress UCA.
  - o *United States of America - Thirteen Independent States United in Congress Republic:* Serving July 2, 1776 to March 1, 1781 under the Continental Congress USA.
  - o *United States of America - A Not Quite Perpetual Union Republic:* Serving March 2, 1781 to December 23, 1783 under the United States in Congress Assembled.
  - o *United States of America - We The People Republic:* Inaugurated Commander-in-Chief and President of the United States on April 30, 1789.

Answer: George Washington was the first President and Commander in Chief of the United States.

WHO WAS THE FIRST VICE PRESIDENT OF THE UNITED STATES?

The office of Vice President and its counterpart, the President of the U.S. Senate, did not exist in the first three stages of the United States' founding. The USCA on April 15th, 1782, considered creating the office of Vice President when President John Hanson took ill, with this resolution:

A motion was then made by Mr. [Samuel] Livermore, seconded by Mr. [Elias] Boudinot, in the following words: That a Vice-president be chosen by ballot, to exercise the office of Vice-president of Congress in the absence or inability of the President, until the first day of November next; and that in case of such absence or inability, the Vice-president shall exercise all the powers of President.[225]

---

[225] *JCC, 1774-1789*, April 15, 1782.

The motion was tabled and the creation of a Vice Presidential office in 1782 was lost. Under the *Constitution of 1787's* Article II an office of Vice President, who also serves as President of the United States Senate, was established.

Answer: John Adams was the first Vice President of the United States of America and President of the U.S. Senate being duly elected by the electors of 11 States. He was sworn into office on April 21st, 1789. Although sworn into office nine days before George Washington took his office as President, Adams did not assume the duties or swear the oath to *"faithfully execute the Office of President of the United States."* Therefore, claims that John Adams was the first President of the United States under the current U.S. Constitution are false.

WHO WAS THE FIRST SPEAKER OF THE UNITED STATES HOUSE OF REPRESENTATIVES?

The House of Representatives and its Speaker's office did not exist in the first three republics of the United States' founding. Under Article I in the *Constitution of 1787* the House of Representatives was formed. The USCA resolved that the new *Constitution of 1787* government would commence on March 4th, 1789. On that date the House of Representatives Journals report:

Being the eleven States have respectively ratified the Constitution of Government of the United States, proposed by the Federal Convention, held in Philadelphia, on the 17th of September, 1787. Congress of the United States, begun and held at the city of New York, on Wednesday, the fourth of March, one thousand seven hundred and eighty-nine, pursuant to a resolution of the late Congress, made in conformity to the resolutions of the Federal Convention of the 17th September, 1787; being the first session of the Congress held under the Constitution aforesaid. On which day, the following members of the House of Representatives appeared and took their seats, to wit:

From Massachusetts: George Thatcher, Fisher Ames, George Leonard, and Elbridge Gerry. **From Connecticut:** Benjamin Huntington, Jonathan Trumbull, and Jeremiah Wadsworth. **From Pennsylvania**: Frederick Augustus Muhlenberg, Thomas Hartley, Peter Muhlenberg, and Daniel Heister. **From Virginia:** Alexander White. **From South Carolina**: Thomas Tudor Tucker. But a quorum of the whole number not being present, the House adjourned until to-morrow morning eleven o'clock.[226]

---

[226] Journals of the U.S. House of Representatives, March 4, 1789

The House of Representatives was unable to form a quorum from March 4 - April 1, 1789. On April 1st, the members elected the first Speaker of the House:

That this House will proceed to the choice of a Speaker by ballot. The House accordingly proceeded to ballot for a Speaker, and upon examining the ballots, a majority of the votes of the whole House was found in favor of Frederick Augustus Muhlenberg, one of the Representatives for the State of Pennsylvania. Whereupon, the said Frederick Augustus Muhlenberg was conducted to the chair, from whence he made his acknowledgments to the House for so distinguished an honor.[227]

Answer: Pennsylvania Representative Frederick Augustus Muhlenberg was the first Speaker of the U.S. House of Representatives.

WHO WAS THE FIRST CHIEF JUSTICE OF THE UNITED STATES?

The U.S. Supreme Court and office of Chief Justice did not exist in the first three republics of the United States' founding.

- ◘ The U.S. Continental Congress formed a Court of Appeals as prescribed in the Articles of Confederation. In 1781, upon the constitution's ratification, the USCA appointed Court of Appeals judges as defined in Article IX of the Articles of Confederation.
- ◘ There was no Supreme Court for appeals under the Articles of Confederation. These judicial matters were conducted by the USCA also according to Article IX of the Articles of Confederation. Specifically Article IX stated:

    ... The United States in Congress assembled shall also be the last resort on appeal in all disputes and differences now subsisting or that hereafter may arise between two or more States concerning boundary, jurisdiction or any other causes whatever; which authority shall always be exercised in the manner following. Whenever the legislative or executive authority or lawful agent of any State in controversy with another shall present a petition to Congress stating the matter in question and praying for a hearing, notice thereof shall be given by order of Congress to the legislative or executive authority of the other State in controversy, and a day assigned for the appearance of the parties by their lawful agents, who shall then be directed to appoint by joint consent, commissioners or judges to constitute a court for hearing ...[228]

---

[227] Ibid, April 1, 1789.
[228] *JCC, 1774-1789*, Articles of Confederation Article IX, March 1, 1781.

- ☐ It was not until after March 4th, 1789, under the *Constitution of 1787*, that a Supreme Court and the office of Chief Justice were established in the United States;
- ☐ Acting Secretary of State John Jay was appointed Chief Justice by President Washington on September 24th, 1789. Two days later, the United States Senate unanimously confirmed John Jay as Chief Justice of the United States.

Answer: The first Chief Justice of the United States of America was John Jay. He took the oath of office on October 19th, 1789.

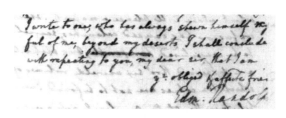

WHO WAS THE FIRST ATTORNEY GENERAL OF THE UNITED STATES?

The office of Attorney General did not exist in the first three republics of the United States' founding.

- ☐ The *Judiciary Act of 1789* was passed by the U.S. House and Senate, and signed into law on September 24th, 1789 by President George Washington.
- ☐ The Act created the Office of Attorney General.

Answer: President George Washington nominated Edmund Randolph on September 25th, 1789. Randolph was confirmed the following day by the U.S. Senate. Randolph did not learn of his appointment until early October and wrote President Washington a conditional acceptance letter on October 8th, 1789.

WHO WAS THE FIRST U.S. SECRETARY OF STATE?

The office of Secretary of State did not exist in the first three stages of the United States' founding.

- ☐ A Secretary of Congress in both Continental Congresses and the USCA did serve in the first three republics of the United States conducting domestic duties similar to those of the current U.S. Secretary of State. Charles Thomson served in this position from the formation of the Colonial Continental Congress on September 5th, 1774, until the dissolution of the United States in Congress Assembled on March 3rd, 1789.

☐ A Secretary of Foreign Affairs also served as a United States executive official under the Articles of Confederation conducting and overseeing diplomacy similar to that of the current U.S. Secretary of State.

  o The U.S. Continental Congress voted on January 10th, 1781 to establish a Department of Foreign Affairs. On August 10th, 1781, the USCA elected the first Secretary of Foreign Affairs, Robert R. Livingston;

  o Under the *Constitution of 1787*, the Act of July 27th, 1789, reestablished the Articles of Confederation's Department of Foreign Affairs as a Presidential Executive Department. The act provided that the principal officer therein should be the Secretary for the Department of Foreign Affairs. John Jay, who was the second Secretary of Foreign Affairs under the Articles of Confederation, remained in the position as Acting Secretary of Foreign Affairs under the *Constitution of 1787*.[229]

☐ On September 15th, 1789, *"An Act to provide for the safe keeping of the Acts, Records and Seal of the United States, and for other purposes"* became law with President George Washington's approval. This law changed the name of the Department of Foreign Affairs to the Department of State because domestic duties of the Secretary of the USCA were combined into the agency with its foreign affairs.

  o John Jay agreed to accept the position as Acting Secretary of State until a Presidential appointment was made, accepted and approved by the U.S. Senate;

  o John Jay was neither confirmed by the U.S. Senate nor did he take the oath of office to serve as Secretary of State but continued serving in that capacity until March 22nd, 1790;

  o On September 25th, 1789, Thomas Jefferson was appointed by George Washington as Secretary of State, confirmed by the U.S. Senate on the following day, and took office on March 22nd, 1790.

---

[229] George Washington to John Jay, Acting Secretary of Foreign Affairs, June 8, 1789. George Washington Papers,

Answer: Thomas Jefferson was the first U.S. Secretary of State, swearing the oath of office on March 22nd, 1790.

WHO WAS THE FIRST U.S. SECRETARY OF WAR?

The office of Secretary of War existed under the Articles of Confederation from 1781 until 1788 and continued under the *Constitution of 1787* from 1789 to 1947.

- ▣ On October 30th, 1781, the USCA elected Benjamin Lincoln the first Secretary of War. On March 8th, 1785, the USCA elected Henry Knox the Second Secretary of War;

- ▣ On August 7th, 1789, *An Act to establish an executive department, to be denominated The Department of War* was passed and provided that a "Secretary for the department of War to be appointed in consequence of this act." President Washington appointed Henry Knox Secretary of War on September 11th, 1789 and Knox was confirmed by the U.S. Senate the following day;

- ▣ On July 26th, 1947, President Harry Truman signed the National Security Act of 1947, which set up a unified military command known as the *National Military Establishment,* as well as creating the Central Intelligence Agency, the National Security Council, National Security Resources Board, United States Air Force (formerly the Army Air Forces) and the Joint Chiefs of Staff. The act placed the National Military Establishment under the control of a single Secretary of Defense. The Secretary of War title was changed to Secretary of the Army.

Answer: Benjamin Lincoln was the first Secretary of War elected by the USCA under the Articles of Confederation. Henry Knox was the first Secretary of War appointed and confirmed by the U.S. Senate on September 11th, 1789, under the current U.S. Constitution.

WHO WAS THE FIRST SECRETARY OF THE TREASURY?

The office of Secretary of the Treasury did not exist in the first three republics of the United States' founding.

- ▣ There was no single executive officer in charge of the U.S. Treasury until the department was reformulated by the U.S. Continental Congress shortly after they learned the 13th State, Maryland, had ratified the Articles of Confederation. On February 7th, 1781, an office of *Superintendent of Finance* was created. In a unanimous vote, Congress appointed Robert Morris on February 10th 1781: "Robert Morris, Esquire, was unanimously elected, having been previously nominated by Mr. Floyd."[230]

- Robert Morris resigned this position on November 1st, 1784, paying all the debts he contracted as Superintendent of Finance with a small surplus in the USCA Treasury. Morris was nominated and elected a United States Senator from Pennsylvania to the first Congress under the current U.S. Constitution;

- On September 2nd, 1789, *An Act to Establish the Treasury Department* was enacted under the current U.S. Constitution"

  "Be it enacted by the Senate and House of Representatives of the United States of America, in Congress assembled , that there shall be a department of Treasury, in which shall be the following officers, namely; a Secretary of the Treasury to be deemed head of the department which provided for an executive officer entitled, Secretary of the Treasury. it enacted by the Senate and House of Representatives of the United States of America, in Congress assembled , that there shall be a department of Treasury, in which shall be the following officers, namely; a Secretary of the Treasury to be deemed head of the department which provided for an executive officer entitled, Secretary of the Treasury."[231]

- On September 11th, 1789, George Washington nominated Alexander Hamilton as the first Secretary of the Treasury. On that same day the rules of the U.S. Senate were dispensed and the members confirmed the Hamilton's appointment as the first Secretary of the U.S. Treasury.

Answer: Alexander Hamilton was the first U.S. Secretary of the Treasury.

---

[230] *JCC, 1774-1789*, Tuesday February 10, 1781

[231] Laws of the United States of America, from the 4th of March, 1789, to the 4th of March, 1815, John Bioren and W. John Duane, Volume I Philadelphia, 1815 - An Act to Establish the Treasury Department, enacted September 2, 1789.

WHO WAS THE FIRST TREASURER OF THE UNITED STATES?

The office of U.S. Treasurer existed in all four stages of the United States.

▣ On July 29th, 1775, the U.S. Continental Congress *Resolved, That Michael Hillegas, and George Clymer, Esqrs. be, and they are hereby appointed, joint treasurers of the United Colonies.*[232]

▣ On May 14th, 1777, the U.S. Continental Congress enacted a resolution, in an attempt to improve United States Lottery sales and build confidence in the notes, named Michael Hillegas as the sole Treasurer of the United States;

▣ On September 1st, 1781, the USCA reformulated the U.S. Treasury and on the 19th elected Michael Hillegas as the first U.S. Treasurer [233] under the Articles of Confederation.

▣ On September 2nd, 1789 *An Act to Establish the Treasury Department* was enacted under the current U.S. Constitution. Michael Hillegas continued to serve as U.S. Treasurer after the passage of the Act until September 11th, 1789, when Samuel Meredith became the first Treasurer appointed under the current U.S. Constitution.

Answer: Michael Hillegas was the first Treasurer of the United States, serving in that capacity under all four republics of the United States Founding. On September 11th, 1789, Samuel Meredith was nominated and confirmed as the first U.S. Treasurer appointed under the current U.S. Constitution. He was, however, the second Treasurer of the United States, which is acknowledged on the U.S. Treasury website.[234] Michael Hillegas, except for Commander-in-Chief George Washington, was the only federal executive to serve in the same office during all four republics of the United States Founding.

WHO WAS THE FIRST UNITED STATES POSTMASTER GENERAL?

The office of Postmaster General was established by the Second Continental Congress, United Colonies of America, in 1775. The office still exists under the current U.S. Constitution.

---

[232] *JCC, 1774-1789*, June 29, 1775
[233] *JCC, 1774-1789*, September 19, 1781
[234]http://www.treasury.gov/about/history/Pages/edu_history_treasurers_index2.aspx

- On July 26th, 1775, the Colonial Continental Congress established the Postal Department with this resolution: "The Congress then proceeded to the election of a postmaster general for one year, and until another is appointed by a future Congress, when Benjamin Franklin, Esquire was unanimously chosen."[235] Franklin served in this role until he was appointed Peace Commissioner to France, leaving the United States in October 1776;

- On November 7th, 1776, the U.S. Continental Congress appointed Richard Bache the second Postmaster General. On January 28th, 1782, the USCA replaced Richard Bache with Ebenezer Hazard after reorganizing the department under the Articles of Confederation;[236]

- On September 22nd, 1789, *An Act for the Temporary establishment of the Post Office* was established. Samuel Osgood was appointed and confirmed by the United States Senate on September 26th, 1789.

Answer: The first Postmaster General of the United States was Benjamin Franklin, who served in this position in the first two republics of the U.S. Founding. The United States Postal Service recognizes Franklin as the first Postmaster General on their website.[237] Richard Bache, the son in law of Benjamin Franklin, served as the second Postmaster General in the *Second United American Republic* but was the first to serve under the Articles of Confederation. Samuel Osgood was the first Postmaster General to serve in the *Fourth United American Republic* under the *Constitution of 1787*.

WHO WAS THE FIRST BLACK U.S. PRESIDENT?

On a final note, I have found it necessary, due to the volume of phone calls, emails and even curious YouTube Videos, to address the fact that President John Hanson **was neither a "Moor" nor** the first black President of the United States. Barrack Hussein Obama holds that most historic honor.

In 2007 Cyril Innis Junior published an article that included a National Archives picture of a black man named John Hanson.[238] Innis also included in his paper a $2

---

[235] *JCC, 1774-1789*, July 26, 1775
[236] *JCC, 1774-1789*, January 28, 1782

[237] http://about.usps.com/who-we-are/postal-history/pmg-franklin.pdf
[238] Cyril Innis, Jr., *A Black Man, A Moor, John Hanson*, 2007, http://www.itsabouttimebpp.com/Announcements/pdf/Cyril_Innis_Jr.pdf,

bill reverse image with a Declaration of Independence signer circled, claiming that the image was that of John Hanson the "black Moor" at the July 4th signing. *YouTube* videos purporting this myth have now exceeded over 250,000 views. The following email reports the myth has gone International:

From: Kenneth Bowling   Sent: Saturday, January 05, 2013 11:34 AM
To: Stan Klos   Subject: Re: Unbelievable
Setting: Saturday morning at the Dalston Market in North London midst the Turkish, English, Pakistani, and African shoppers and the clothing, fish, and vegetable-fruit stalls. For Sale: A PHOTOGRAPH of John Hanson, the first Black president of the Continental Congress. Ken Bowling

Sixth-plate daguerreotype, ca. 1856 of John Hanson from Mr. Innis Article – *Image from the Library of Congress* [239]

John Hanson was not a 1776 Continental Congress Delegate nor a signer of the Declaration of Independence. The 1776 Delegate member Mr. Innis circles as John Hanson on the $2 bill is actually George Walton of Georgia, a slave holder. Additionally, there was no photography in 1783 (when President Hanson died) so such a daguerreotype photograph of the former President is a technological impossibility. The picture of the black "Moor," depicted by Innis, is actually a Sixth-plate daguerreotype, ca. 1856, [240] of John Hanson the 19th-century Liberian Senator from Grand Bassa County who championed the relocation of slaves and others to Liberia.

---

[239] National Archives and Records Administration, http://www.loc.gov/exhibits/ treasures/trr033.html. The form of photography known as "daguerreotype" was introduced in France in 1839. A sixth-plate daguerreotype measures 2 ¾" by 3 ¼".
[240] National Archives and Records Administration, http://www.loc.gov/exhibits/ treasures/trr033.html

What is on the Back of the Two Dollar Bill?

The back of the $2 bill has an engraving of the signing of the Declaration of Independence. In the image is a man who has dark skin and wearing a powdered wig while sitting at the table just to the left of the men standing in the center of the engraving. This dark skinned man i John Hanson in his position as president of the continental congress.

In the original painting hanging in the U.S. Capitol Rotunda, the dark skinned man does not appear!!!

The Back of the $2.00 Bill with Innis' circling the alleged "Black Moor John Hanson" [241]

Answer: The first Black President of the United States was Barack Obama and not John Hanson. Sadly, John Hanson's will bequeathed 11 slaves to his heirs in 1783.

WHAT WAS THE FIRST CAPITAL OF THE UNITED STATES OF AMERICA?

If we define "capital" as "seat of government" of the United States, the list of federal capitals and their respective buildings, or "capitols," is quite long. In keeping with the organization of the U.S. Founding into four distinct American United Republics, the following list of United Colonies and States *Seats of Government* is offered for review:

THE FIRST AMERICAN REPUBLIC'S SEATS OF GOVERNMENT
Sept. 5, 1774 to July 1, 1776

Philadelphia	Sept. 4, 1774 - Caucus Only	City Tavern
Philadelphia	Sept. 5, 1774 to Oct. 24, 1774	Carpenters' Hall
Philadelphia	May 10, 1775 to July 1, 1776	Pennsylvania State House

---

[241] Op Cit

CITY TAVERN, PHILADELPHIA
September 1, 1774 - Caucus Only

The City Tavern was located at 138 South 2nd Street, at the intersection of Second and Walnut Streets of Philadelphia, Pennsylvania. Delegate John Adams referred to the City Tavern in Philadelphia as the *"most genteel tavern in America."* It was commissioned by the Social Elite as the Merchants' Coffee House in 1773. This Federal brick structure was utilized as a Tavern until it was badly damaged by a fire in 1834. It was rebuilt to its original floor plan in the 1970's for the Bicentennial and currently functions as tavern and restaurant owned by the United States Department of Interior.

The discussions at this tavern meeting were significant as the decision was made, with 25 to 30 delegates present, that the members would wait until September 5th, for the additional delegates to arrive, before proceeding to business. Specifically it was agreed that the Delegates would meet "Monday next" at 10 am at City Tavern to discuss where to conduct their first meeting.

Silas Deane wrote to Elizabeth Deane on September 1, 1774:

The Delegates from Virginia, Maryland, the Lower Counties, & New York, are not arrived. We spent this Day in visiting Those that are in Town, & find them in high Spirits particularly the Gentlemen from the Jersies, and South Carolina. In the Evening We met to the Number of about Thirty drank a Dish of Coffee together talked over a few preliminaries, & agreed to wait for the Gentlemen not arrived untill Monday Next, before We proceeded to Business. [242]

---

[242] *LDC 1774-1789*, Silas Deane to Elizabeth Deane on September 1, 1774.

CARPENTERS' HALL, PHILADELPHIA
September 5, 1774 – October 24, 1774

Carpenters' Hall is located in Philadelphia, Pennsylvania. It was built as a four-story Georgian Colonial brick building between 1770 and 1773 by the Carpenters' Company. Designed by architect Robert Smith (1722-1777), the structure was declared a United States National Historic Landmark in 1970. The building is still utilized as a meeting place for the Carpenters' Company. It was in Carpenters' Hall that the United Colonies Continental Congress first convened and founded the First United American Republic.

As decided at City Tavern on September 1st, 1774, deputies representing eleven colonies assembled at 10 am at the tavern. According to Delegate James Duane:

The Members of the Congress met at Smith's [Sic City] Tavern. The Speaker of the Pensylvania Assembly having offerd the Congress the use of the State house; & the Carpenters the use of their Hall, It was agreed to take a View of each. We proceeded to the Carpenter's hall. Mr .Lynch proposed the Question whether as that was in all respects Suitable it ought not to be fixed upon without further Enquiry.

I observed that if the State house was equally convenient it ought to be preferred being a provincial & the Carpenter's Hall a private House. And besides as it was tenderd by the Speaker it seemed to be a piece of respect which was due to him, at least to enquire whether the State House was not equally convenient. The Question was however called for; & a great Majority fixed upon the Carpenters hall. [243]

---

[243] *LDC 1774-1789*, James Duane Diary September 5th, 1774.

PHILADELPHIA STATE HOUSE
May 10, 1775 to July 1, 1776

Pennsylvania State House is located on Chestnut Street between 5th and 6th Streets in Philadelphia. Now known as Independence Hall, this red brick building was built between 1732 and 1753 as the colonial seat for the Province of Pennsylvania. Edmund Woolley, the builder, designed the building with Andrew Hamilton in its distinctive Georgian style. Two smaller buildings were added in the construction with City Hall to the east and Congress Hall to the west. The United Colonies Continental Congress first convened here on May 10th, 1775.

THE SECOND AMERICAN REPUBLIC'S SEATS OF GOVERNMENT
July 2, 1776 to February 28, 1781

Philadelphia	July 2, 1776 to Dec. 12, 1776	Pennsylvania State House
Baltimore	Dec. 20, 1776 to Feb. 27, 1777	Henry Fite's House
Philadelphia	March 4, 1777 to Sep. 18, 1777	Pennsylvania State House
Lancaster	September 27, 1777	Lancaster Court House
York	Sept. 30, 1777 to June 27, 1778	York-town Court House
Philadelphia	July 2, 1778 to July 19, 1778*	College Hall* - PA State House
Philadelphia	July 19, 1778 to February 28, 1781	PA State House
True Dates Unknown		

PHILADELPHIA STATE HOUSE
July 2, 1776 to Dec. 12, 1776

On July 2nd, 1776, United Colonies Continental Congress delegates from 12 states declared themselves "Free and Independent" states, thus establishing the Second United American Republic. On July 4th, 1776 they issued the Declaration of Independence naming the new republic the United States of America.

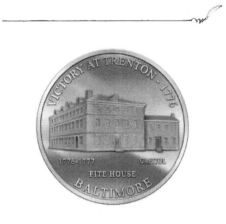

HENRY FITE HOUSE
December 20, 1776 to February 27, 1777

On Friday, December 20th, 1776, Congress convened in a spacious three-story and attic house standing on the southwest corner of Sharpe and Baltimore Streets. The house was built by Jacob Fite, and was then the farthest house west in the town. It was a *"three-story and attic brick house, of about 92 feet front on Market Street, by about 50 or 55 feet depth on the side streets, with cellar under the whole; having 14 rooms, exclusive of kitchen, wash-house and other out-buildings, including a stable for 30 horses."* It had a ten window-long room with two fireplaces and Congress signed a three-month lease for 180 pounds.

The Goddard Declaration of Independence Broadside
Image Courtesy of the Library of Congress

It was at this site that the Continental Congress issued on January 18th, 1777 the resolution to print a Declaration of Independence Broadside that included all the signers' names. Printer Mary Katherine Goddard[244] was one of the first to offer the use of her press, despite the British Crown deeming the DOI a treasonable document. Her printing, the Goddard Broadside, is where the public learned for the first time who had signed the Declaration. One of the signers of the DOI, Thomas McKean, is not listed on the Goddard broadside, signifying that he had not yet signed his name to the engrossed DOI. The Broadside was presented to the delegates at the Fite House which, in the years before it was destroyed by fire in 1862, would be known as Congress Hall. A bronze plaque is prominently displayed at the historic site.

---

[244] Mary Katherine Goddard (June 16, 1738 – August 12, 1816) was an early American publisher and the first American postmistress. She was the first to print the Declaration of Independence with the names of the signatories. She served as Baltimore's postmaster for 14 years (1775-1789).

Image Courtesy of Historic.us

PHILADELPHIA STATE HOUSE
March 4, 1777 to September 18, 1777

After General Washington's victories at Trenton and Princeton, the British re-fortified their lines in New Jersey and abandoned their plans to occupy Philadelphia. A road weary Continental Congress returned to the Pennsylvania State House on March 4th, 1777.

LANCASTER COURT HOUSE
September 27, 1777

Lancaster Court House was a 1730 brick structure, 30' x 30', with a brick pavement floor. The Court House was crowned with a small spire that had a clock of two faces, one for the south and the other for the north. The structure burnt down in 1781 and was replaced with a much larger structure in 1785 that is often depicted, incorrectly, as the Continental Congress Capitol building. Upon their arrival on September 27th, 1777, the Continental Congress convened but was forced to vacate the building the following day. The Pennsylvania officials, who had also fled Philadelphia, required the meeting space for the use of their State government business.

YORK TOWN COURT HOUSE
September 30, 1777 to June 27, 1778

York-Town Court House was constructed by William Willis in 1756 and stood in the "Centre Square" of two 80' thoroughfares. The 45' x 45' Georgian Brick Colonial Court House stood in the Center of West Market Street until 1841. In this Court House the Delegates received notice of Washington's loss at Brandywine, Burgoyne's surrender at Saratoga, Franklin's success in achieving an alliance with France and the struggles of the Continental Army in Valley Forge. Also in this building the delegates hammered out and passed the *Constitution of 1777*, better known as the Articles of Confederation. A replica of the Court House was built in 1976 by the York County Bicentennial Commission; it stands in a small colonial park at the intersection of West Market Street and the Codorus Creek.

COLLEGE HALL, PHILADELPHIA[245]
July 2, 1778 to July 19, 1778

On June 20th, 1778, the news that the British had evacuated Philadelphia on June 18th reached Congress. The city was in complete celebration with barn fires, the lighting of the courthouse and fireworks. On Wednesday June 25th the Continental Congress would vote to adjourn on the 28th and reconvene *"From this place to meet at Philadelphia, on Thursday, the second of July next."*[246]

When Franklin was told that Sir William Howe had taken Philadelphia, his answer was that it was more likely that Philadelphia had taken Sir William Howe. There can be now no question that the stay of the British army in Philadelphia in the winter and spring of 1778 was damaging to the British cause. During this occupation seven

---

[245] College Hall and Dorms, Fourth Street and Arch, Philadelphia, PA contemporary view, Circa 1780, by Pierre Eugene Du Simitiere. Original is in the Historical Society of Pennsylvania Collection.
[246] *JCC, 1774-1789*, Journals of the Continental Congress, June 25th, 1778.

hundred of the private soldiers deserted; while the conduct of the officers was marked by a luxury in singular contrast with the stern endurance of excessive hardships shown by Washington and those who served under him at Valley Forge.[247]

Water color by Charles M. Lefferts, Circa 1913

The Continental Congress was unable to form a quorum at the Philadelphia State House on July 2nd. The Journals report, *"According to adjournment, the president and a number of members met at the State House in Philadelphia on Thursday the 2d of July, and adjourned from day to day, to the present."* [248] Congress achieved a quorum on July 7th not at the State House but at the College of Philadelphia as evidenced by Joseph Bartlett's letter to John Langdon on July 13, 1778:

The Congress meets in the College Hall, as the State House was left by the enemy in a most filthy and sordid situation, as were many of the public and private buildings in the City. Some of the genteel houses were used for stables and holes cut in the parlor floors and their dung shoveled into the cellars. The country Northward of the City for several miles is one common waste, the houses burnt, the fruit trees and others cut down and carried off, fences carried away gardens and orchards destroyed. Mr. Dickenson's and Mr. Morris' fine seats all demolished-in short I could hardly find the great roads that used to pass that way. The enemy built a strong abattee with the fruit and other trees from the Delaware to Schuylkill and at about 40 or 50 rods distance along the abattue a quadrangular fort for cannon and a number of redoubts for small arms; the same on the several eminences along the Schuylkill against the City.[249]

---

[247] Jared Sparks, ed.,, *Diplomatic Correspondence of the U.S.*, Washington, D.C., 1830, p. 307
[248] *Ibid*, July 2, 1778
[249] Jordan, John W., "Sessions of the Continental Congress held in the College of Philadelphia in July, 1778," *Pennsylvania magazine of history and biography*, Volume 22. Historical Society of Pennsylvania,, p. 114

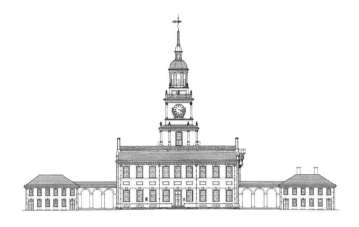

PHILADELPHIA STATE HOUSE
July 19, 1778 to February 28, 1781

Henry Laurens on July 15th wrote this to Rawlins Lowdens discussing the conditions of the Pennsylvania Statehouse and the need for Congress to utilize the College of Philadelphia for its meetings:

On that day I left York Town and arrived here the 30th-from various impediments I could not collect a sufficient number of States to form a Congress earlier than the 7th Instant; one was the offensiveness of the air in and around the State House, which the Enemy had made an Hospital and left it in a condition disgraceful to the Character of civility. Particularly they had opened a large square pit near the House, a receptacle for filth, into which they had also cast dead horses and the bodies of Men who by the mercy of death had escaped from their further cruelties. I cannot proceed to a new subject before I add a curse on their savage practices

Congress in consequence of this disappointment have been shuffling from Meeting House to College Hall the last seven days & have not performed half the business which might and ought to have been done, in a more commodious situation. [250]

---

[250] Edmund Cody Burnett, , *Letters Of Members Of The Continental Congress*, The Carnegie institution of Washington, 1926, p. 333.

By July 19th, 1778 the Pennsylvania State House was put into good repair enabling both the United States Continental Congress and the Pennsylvania Supreme Council to meet as their members mandated.

THE THIRD AMERICAN REPUBLIC'S SEATS OF GOVERNMENT
March 1, 1781 to March 3, 1789

Philadelphia	March 1, 1781 to June 21, 1783	PA State House
Princeton	June 30, 1783 to July 3, 1783*	Prospect House - Nassau Hall
Princeton	July 3, 1783 to Nov. 4, 1783	Nassau Hall
Annapolis	Nov. 26, 1783 to Aug. 19, 1784	Maryland, State House
Trenton	Nov. 1, 1784 to Dec. 24, 1784	French Arms Tavern
New York City	Jan. 11, 1785 to Nov. 13, 1788	NY City Hall
New York City	Nov. 1788 to March 3,1789	Fraunces Tavern
	True Dates Unknown	

PHILADELPHIA STATE HOUSE
March 1, 1781 to June 21, 1783

On March 1st, 1781 in the Philadelphia State House, the *"Perpetual Union,"* known as the United States of America, became a *Constitution of 1777* governmental reality. The last entry in the old Continental Congress Journals recorded a full printing of the Articles of Confederation, ending with signers John Walton, Edward Telfair, and Edward Langworthy of Georgia that began:

Articles of Confederation and perpetual Union between the states of New Hampshire, Massachusetts-bay, Rhode Island and Providence Plantations, Connecticut, New York, New Jersey, Pennsylvania, Delaware, Maryland, Virginia, North Carolina, South Carolina and Georgia." I. The Stile of this Confederacy shall be **The United States of America.**

This date marked the birth of the *Third United America Republic: The United States of America, A Not Quite Perpetual Union.*

"Prospect," Princeton, N.J., in 1779
[From the painting by Maria Templeton in possession of Mrs. Hughes Oliphant]

PROSPECT HOUSE, PRINCETON, N.J.
June 30, 1783 to July 3, 1783

Several historians maintain that the USCA first convened at Colonel George Morgan's House, named Prospect, when they first assembled in Princeton. I was unable to find any record of their assembly in the 1784 USCA Journals, delegate letters, period newspapers and magazines at Morgan's house at Princeton University.

Varnum Collins, however, makes a compelling case that the USCA did assemble at Prospect:

The evidence favoring the view that "Prospect" was the scene of the opening meetings is more compelling in its strength. Congress had come to Princeton hastily and apparently without making any effort to ascertain definitely the practical accommodations of the village. Mr. Boudinot may have had Nassau Hall in his mind as a meeting place at the outset; but when Colonel Morgan, who was well acquainted in Congress, stated in his letter of the 25th that one of his buildings contained "a better room for them to meet in" than the members could be "immediately accommodated with elsewhere." Mr. Boudinot probably accepted the offer as at least a temporary arrangement. Furthermore in the list of available accommodations issued in October by the citizens of Princeton, Colonel Morgan announces his willingness to have "the Congress Room" in his house fitted up for winter use if desired. It is difficult to explain this designation of any room at "Prospect" unless a previous occupation of it by Congress had given it a right to that title. Finally it is noted in a memorandum book of Charles Thomson, Secretary of Congress, that the sheet of paper bearing the record of the distribution of ten sets of the Journal was lost "in removing the Office from the House of Col. Morgan to the College." Unfortunately, this record is dated merely "1783;" but when half of the rooms in Nassau Hall were vacant it is altogether improbable, considering the close relation existing between the Secretary of Congress and that body itself, that he should have used Colonel Morgan's house as an office if Congress were sitting in Nassau Hall. It is easier to believe that he moved his belongings over to the college building because Congress was moving also. We may, then, take it for granted that the first three meetings (June 30th, July 1st and 2d) were held in Colonel Morgan's house and that thereafter the sessions were held in the college building, in the library room presumably, except on state occasions, when they were held in the prayer-hall. The library-room which had been stripped by the British was on the north side of the second floor over the main entrance, and was about thirty by twenty-four feet in size.[251]

Additionally, Princeton University's website on the Prospect House states:

Prospect House owes its name to the stone farmhouse first constructed on the site in the mid-18th century by Colonel George Morgan, western explorer, U.S. Agent for Indian Affairs and gentleman farmer. The superb eastern view from that farmhouse prompted Colonel Morgan to name his estate "Prospect." Morgan's estate, a popular stopping off place in Revolutionary times, was visited by such diverse groups as a delegation of Delaware Indians, 2,000 mutinous soldiers of the Pennsylvania Line and the Continental Congress. When Prospect was acquired in 1849 by John Potter, a wealthy

---

[251] Varnum Lansing Collins, , *The Continental Congress at Princeton.* The University library, 1908, pp. 57-58.

merchant from Charleston, S.C., he replaced the colonial structure with the present mansion.[252]

Accepting that the Morgan House most likely hosted the first three sessions we now turn to Princeton University's Nassau Hall, which served as the U.S. Capitol Building from July 3rd, 1783 to November 4th, 1783.

NASSAU HALL, PRINCETON, N.J.
July 3, 1783 to Nov. 4, 1783

The structure was built in 1756 at a cost of £2,900 for the College of New Jersey. Originally the brick-paved halls extended one hundred and seventy-five feet of what was the largest stone structure in the Colonies. In November, 1776, the British took possession of the building and used it as barracks and hospital but were briefly ejected by George Washington during the Battle of Princeton:

There are three flat-arched doors on the north side giving access by a flight of steps to the three separate entries (an entry refers here to the hallway on each floor running the full length of the building). At the center is a projecting section of five bays surmounted by a pediment with circular windows, and other decorations. The only ornamental feature above the cornice, is the cupola, standing somewhat higher than the twelve fireplace chimneys. Beyond these there are no features of distinction.

The simple interior design is shown in the plan, where a central corridor provided communication with the students' chambers and recitation rooms, the entrances, and the common prayer hall; and on the second floor, with the library over the central north

---

[252] Princeton University, Prospect House History,
http://www.princeton.edu/prospecthouse/history.html, March 15, 2012.

entrance. The prayer hall was two stories high, measured 32 by 40 feet, and had a balcony at the north end which could be reached from the second-story entry. Partially below ground level, though dimly lighted by windows, was the cellar, which served as kitchen, dining area (beneath the prayer hall), and storeroom. In all there were probably forty rooms for the students, not including those added later in the cellar when a moat was dug to allow additional light and air into that dungeon.[253]

For its regular sessions, the USCA met in Nassau Hall's library room, which was located over the front entrance. For official dignitary occasions, it adjourned to the chapel on the main floor. The move of the capital from Philadelphia to the College of New Jersey was a boom for the Princeton economy.

It had leaped at a bound into national importance; from a "little obscure village" it had within the week "become the capital of America." And where the "almost perfect silence" of a country hamlet was wont to reign, now nothing was "to be seen or heard but the passing and rattling of wagons, coaches and chairs." To supply the metropolitan taste of Congressmen the produce of Philadelphia markets was brought up every week, with the result that the village street now echoed to the unfamiliar "crying about of pineapples, oranges, lemons, and every luxurious article both foreign and domestic."[254]

---

[253] Henry L Savage,., ed., *Nassau Halls, 1756-1956*, Princeton: Princeton University Press,, 1956. .
[254] Collins, *op.cit.*, p. 57 references a letter of Ashbel Green, a senior in college, to his father, July 5th, 1783 cited in H. C. Alexander, *Life of J. A. Alexander* (1870), Vol. I, p. 16, as well as the *Independent Gazeteer* of November 1st, 1783.

MARYLAND STATE HOUSE
ANNAPOLIS, MD
November 26, 1783 to August 19, 1784

The building where the USCA failed to assemble initially was designed by Joseph Horatio Anderson in 1771. Its construction began in 1772 but was not completed until 1779 due to the struggle for Independence. The building is Georgian and was constructed in brick. A small portico projects out from the center of the building and is crowned by a pediment. There are two high arched windows that frame the entrance. On both floors, large rectangular windows line the facade. A cornice is topped by another pediment and the sloping roof gives way for a central octagonal drum atop which rests a dome. The large dome is topped by a balustrade balcony, another octagonal drum and a lantern. The Interior of the Dome, from floor to ceiling, is 113' with the building itself encompassing 120,900 square feet under roof. It is the oldest American State Capitol still in continuous legislative use.

In this capitol the Maryland legislature passed and Governor Lee, on February 2nd, 1781, signed into law the final state's ratification of the Articles of Confederation. The State House was also the site where Commander-in-Chief George Washington resigned his commission to USCA President Thomas Mifflin. The USCA at Annapolis would also convene enough states to ratify the *Definitive Treaty of Peace* ending the War for Independence.

FRENCH ARMS TAVERN
TRENTON, NJ
November 1, 1784 to December 24, 1784

The USCA assembled in the French Arms Tavern that was erected in 1730 as a private residence of stone and stucco. The building was two stories high, with a gabled roof that measuring 45 feet in width and 43 feet in depth plus a narrower extension in the rear. The house stood on the southwest corner of King (now Warren) Street and Second (now State) Street in Trenton, New Jersey. The rear extension on the Second Street side served as kitchen and servants' quarters. The building was owned by John Dagworthy until his death in 1756. For two years during this period, from 1740 to 1742, it was the official residence of Governor Lewis Morris. In 1760 it was sold to Samuel Henry, an iron manufacturer, who made it his residence until he leased the property to Jacob G. Bergen in 1780 for use as a tavern.

Before opening the tavern, which he named *"Thirteen Stars,"* Bergen made extensive changes in the building. He added a third story, with a gabled, dormer-windowed roof; converted two of the first-floor rooms into one room 20 feet in width and 43 feet in length, which became known as the *"Long Room;"* and set up a barroom in the basement. In 1783 the building was described as a *"Dwelling-house 45 by 43 Feet, 3 Stories, 11 Rooms, eight with Fireplaces, a Kitchen and Stabling for 12 Horses."* The Building's name later changed to the *French Arms,* celebrating France's role in the defeat of Cornwallis at Yorktown, when John Cape took over the tavern's management. Bergen returned to the tavern in 1783 and retained the French Arms name.

In 1784 a commission appointed by the New Jersey Legislature leased the tavern, which was still the largest building in town, for the use of the USCA. The Long room walls were repapered, the floors were carpeted and a platform erected in the center of the south side of the room between the two fireplaces. Thirteen new tables covered with green cloth and forty-eight new Windsor chairs were provided for the delegates.[255]

The USCA stay at Trenton was brief and most of its time was spent in appealing to the states to send delegates. John Jay, who was a strong opponent of President Richard Henry Lee, had returned as a delegate to USCA at Trenton and was not in favor of a Trenton capitol. Additionally, Jay had yet to accept the position of Secretary of Foreign Affairs. He was lobbied hard by both southern and northern delegates to accept the position. Jay hesitated because he wanted the capitol in his hometown of New York along with the right to select his owns clerks and assistants as Foreign Secretary.

On the topic of the capital, the Southern States made every effort to have the resolution mandating alternate sessions at Trenton and Annapolis repealed. On December 20th, the USCA passed a resolution that repealed the proposed two capital system and provide money for the erection of federal buildings:

---

[255] Godfrey, *The Mechanics Bank*, pp. 25-6.

Resolved, that it is inexpedient for Congress at this time to erect more than one federal town public buildings for their accommodation at more than one place. Resolved, (by nine states,) That a sum not exceeding one hundred thousand dollars be appropriated for the payment of the expense of erecting such buildings; provided always, that hotels or dwelling-houses for the members of Congress representing the different states, shall not be understood as included in the above appropriation.[256]

John Jay managed to gather enough support to relocate the capital temporarily to New York if he were to accept the position of Foreign Secretary. With this understanding, he introduced a resolution aimed at removing Trenton and Annapolis as the temporary federal capitals:

That it is expedient Congress should determine on a place, at which they will continue to sit until proper accommodations in a federal town shall be erected, and that the subsisting resolutions respecting the alternate temporary residence of Congress at Trenton and Annapolis, be repealed.[257]

Jay then resigned his seat in USCA and took the oath of office as Secretary for Foreign Affairs before Justice Isaac Smith of the New Jersey Supreme Court. The following day Foreign Affairs Under-Secretary, Henry Remsen, Jr. turned over all the department papers to John Jay. The following official dispatch, Jay's first, was sent to the French Chargé d'Affaires, Marquis de Barbé-Marbois:

Having accepted the place of Secretary for Foreign Affairs, it becomes my duty to inform you that Congress will adjourn to-morrow to meet at the City of New York on Tuesday, the 11th day of January next.[258]

Remarkably, the capital of the United States America, for the first and last time, had been moved to persuade a member of its Congress to accept an executive position in the federal government.

---

[256] Journals of the USCA, Monday, December 20, 1784
[257] Ibid, Tuesday, December 21, 1784
[258] DCC, op. cit. , p. 401

OLD NEW YORK CITY HALL
January 11, 1785 to November 13, 1788

The capitol building that housed the USCA was eighty-five years old in 1785. In January, 1698, a committee was appointed to report on the necessity of a new building for New York's governmental offices. A new structure was recommended at a site *"opposite the upper end of Broad St."* The committee contracted James Evetts and his subsequent design was presented and approved by the colonial government. To fund the construction, the old city hall, *"excluding the bell, the King's arms, and the iron-work belonging to the prison,"[259]* were sold at public auction to a merchant, John Hodman, for the sum of £920. The cage, pillory, and stocks, however, remained in front of the old building for a year afterwards while the new structure was being built. The foundation stone of the building was laid, with some ceremony, in August 1699, as evidenced by a warrant drawn for paying the expense incurred on that occasion. March 1700 records indicate the Colonial Common Council contracted with William Mumford to carve the King's, Colonial Governor Lord Bellamont's and Lieutenant-Governor, Captain Nanfan's arms *of the size of the three blank squares left in the front of the City Hall for that purpose.[260]* Moldings of stone were required to be made around each coat-of-arms, each to be cut on one stone, unless a stone sufficiently large for the King's arms could not be procured, in which case two stones might be used. The contract called for them to be completed within six months and Mumford was to receive forty-one pounds four shillings. The building, thus, was completed in late 1700 or early 1701, although the exact date is unknown.

---

[259] Willis, Samuel et al, *The Manual of the Corporation of the City of New York*. New York: Common Council, 1862, p. 538
[260] *Ibid.*

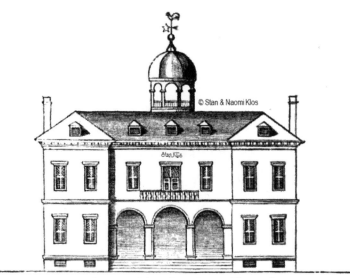

𝔉ront on 𝔚all 𝔖t. 𝔉acing 𝔅road 𝔖t.

In 1703, the cage, pillory, whipping-post, and stocks were removed from Coenties slip[261] and erected in the upper end of Broad Street, a little below the New City Hall. In 1715, Mr. Stephen Delancy, a *"liberal and wealthy merchant"*, presented the city with fifty pounds, which he had received as his salary as representative of the city in the General Assembly. He suggested, after being asked, that the funds be used to purchase of a clock, to be placed in the cupola of the City Hall. In 1716 an agreement was accordingly made with clockmaker Joseph Phillips for its construction. It was provided, that the largest wheel of the clock should be nine inches in diameter, and that there should be two dial-plates of red cedar, painted and gilt, each to be six feet square. The price paid was sixty-five pounds.

---

[261] Coenties Slip was an artificial inlet in the East River for the loading and unloading of ships that was land-filled in 1835. New York's first City Hall once stood at Coenties Alley and Pearl Street, just to the north of Coenties Slip. In is now a historic pedestrian walkway.

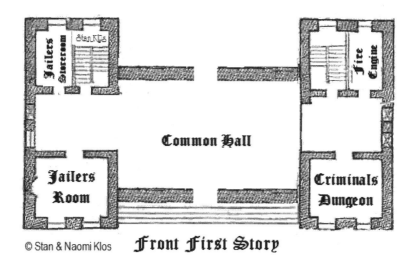

Front First Story

It was not until the year 1718 that the balcony called for in the original plans was constructed. In 1738 it was found that the cupola of this building was *"very rotten and in danger of falling."* The old cupola was dismantled and a new one of the same specification was erected in its place.

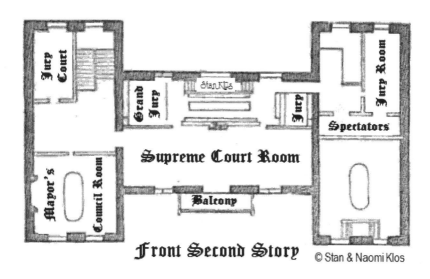

Front Second Story

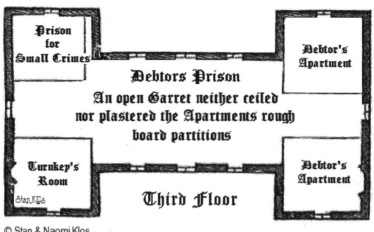

Prison
for
Small Crimes

Debtor's
Apartment

Debtors Prison
An open Garret neither ceiled
nor plastered the Apartments rough
board partitions

Turnkey's
Room

Debtor's
Apartment

Third Floor

In 1763, which was a period when improvements, both private and public, were greatly encouraged in the city, the City Hall, now 63 three years old, was altered and improved, at very considerable expense. The colonial committee of the Common Council approved a plan of *"alterations and ornaments"* to the building and to defray the computed cost of three thousand pounds, a lottery was established. Among other improvements, the building was made higher, and roofed with copper procured from England. The balcony in the front of the building was extended out to range with the two wings. A cupola of more imposing dimensions was raised upon the building, along with a bell of larger dimensions than the old one.

In January of 1785, the USCA conducted their meetings on the second floor, which was once the room of the NY Supreme Court. A room adjoining the meeting room was still occupied *"and the noise of the scholars in their recitations was so annoying as to disturb the debates. Complaint being made of this, the school was*

184

discontinued." [262] This building would be the site where both the Northwest Ordinance and the *Constitution of 1787* would be hotly debated with the former being enacted and the latter being sent on to the states, unchanged, for ratification.

FRAUNCES TAVERN,
NEW YORK CITY
October 6, 1788 to March 3, 1789

The building known as *"Fraunces Tavern"* was erected as a residence in 1719 by Stephen de Lancey, a French Huguenot. He had amassed great wealth as a merchant and built this 55' x 42' brick house on the corner of Broad and Pearl Streets in lower Manhattan Island. The house remained in Lancey's possession as a residence until the firm, Lancey, Robinson & Company, purchased it in 1759 for office and warehouse uses. Three years later the house was sold to Samuel Fraunces for £2,000.

Fraunces completely renovated the building and reopened it as a public tavern. The Queens Head Tavern became an important hostelry that he either managed or leased to others until 1776 when New York was occupied by the British and Fraunces was imprisoned.

---

[262] Willis, Samuel et al, *NYC Manual*, p. 541.

According to his own account, he "submitted to serve for some Time in the Menial Office of Cook in the Family of General Robertson [General James Robertson, British Governor of New York City, 1780-1783] without any Pay, or Perquisite whatsoever, Except the Privilege of disposing of the Remnants of the Tables which he appropriated towards the Comfort of the American Prisoners within the City." Exactly when Fraunces resumed operation of the tavern is not known, but his offer of sale on March 17, 1781, was unsuccessful.[263]

Fraunces' advertisement in the New York Royal Gazette read:

"An elegant Three Story and a Half Brick Dwelling House, situated in Great Dock Street, at the corner of Broad Street, the property of Mr. Samuel Fraunces, and for many Years distinguished as the Queen's Head Tavern; in which are nine spacious Rooms, besides five Bed-chambers, with thirteen Fire places, an excellent Garret in which are three Bed rooms well finished, an exceeding good Kitchen, and a Spring of remarkable fine Water therein; a most excellent Cellar under the whole, divided into three commodious apartments; a convenient Yard with a good Cistern and Pump, and many other conveniences too tedious to mention; the whole in extraordinary good repair,... "[264]

New York City records indicate that Fraunces was running the tavern again in 1783 and 1784. In 1785, after leasing the building to the USCA he sold the property for £1,950 to George Powers, a Brooklyn butcher. In 1788, the USCA whose Continental Congress first caucused in a Philadelphia Tavern was now considering leasing this New York Tavern as the final federal capitol building of the United States under the Articles of Confederation. On October 2nd, 1788, the USCA resolved:

The committee consisting of Mr. [Thomas Tudor] Tucker, Mr [John] Parker, and Mr [Abraham] Clark to whom was referred a letter from the Mayor of the city of New York to the Delegates having reported, That it appears from the letter referred to them, that the repairs and alterations intended to be made in the buildings in which Congress at present Assemble, will render it highly inconvenient for them to continue business therein, that it will therefore be necessary to provide some other place for their accommodation, the committee having made enquiry find no place more proper for this purpose than the two Apartments now appropriated for the Office of Foreign Affairs. They therefore recommend that the said Apartments be immediately prepared for the

---

[263] Office of the Historian, Department of State, Buildings of the Department of State, http://history.state.gov/departmenthistory/section 11.
[264] New York Royal Gazette, March 17, 1781.

reception of Congress and the papers of the Secretary. Resolved, that Congress agree to the said report. [265]

Born in a Tavern and now ending in a Tavern, the United Colonies and States governments had occupied eleven different capitol buildings in eight different cities: Philadelphia, Baltimore, Lancaster, York, Princeton, Annapolis, Trenton and New York. The federal government would return once again to Philadelphia before being permanently relocated to Washington D.C. in 1800.

THE FOURTH AMERICAN REPUBLIC'S SEATS OF GOVERNMENT
March 4, 1789 to Present

New York City	March 3,1789 to August 12, 1790	Federal Hall
Philadelphia	December 6,1790 to May 14, 1800	Congress Hall
Washington DC	November 17, 1800 to Present	Two US Capitol Buildings, White House, Supreme Court

On April 30th, 1789, George Washington was escorted to the newly-renovated Federal Hall located at Wall and Nassau Street. The newly remodeled building:

... came richly laden with historical associations, having hosted John Peter Zenger's trial in 1735, the Stamp Act Congress of 1765 and the Confederation Congress from 1785 to 1788. Starting in September 1788, the French engineer Pierre-Charles L'Enfant had remodeled it into Federal Hall, a suitable home for Congress. L'Enfant introduced a covered arcade at street level and a balcony surmounted by a triangular pediment on the second story. As the people's chamber, the House of Representatives was accessible to the public, situated in a high-ceilinged octagonal

---

[265] *Journals of the USCA*, October 2, 1788

room on the ground floor, while the Senate met in a second-floor room on the Wall Street side, buffering it from popular pressure. From this room Washington would emerge onto the balcony to take the oath of office. In many ways, the first inauguration was a hasty, slapdash affair. As with all theatrical spectacles, rushed preparations and frantic work on the new building continued until a few days before the event. Nervous anticipation spread through the city as to whether the 200 workmen would complete the project on time. Only a few days before the inauguration, an eagle was hoisted onto the pediment, completing the building. The final effect was stately: a white building with a blue and white cupola topped by a weather vane.

FEDERAL HALL

Old New York City Hall
March 4, 1789 to August 12, 1790

There was, as yet, no U.S. Chief Justice so the oath was administered by New York Chancellor Robert R. Livingston on Federal Hall's second floor balcony, overlooking a crowd assembled in the streets.

Inauguration of George Washington at Federal Hall in New York City, April 30, 1789; oil painting by Ramon de Elorriaga, c. 1899. - The Granger Collection, New York

President Washington, Vice President Adams, and the members of Congress retired to the Senate Chamber. Here the President delivered the first inaugural address that was drafted by James Madison. Washington explained his disinclination to accept the presidency and highlighted his own shortcomings, including "frequent interruptions in health," "unpractised in the duties of civil administration," and intellectually "inheriting inferior endowments from nature." Washington left the presidential prerogative "to recommend to your consideration, such measures as he shall judge necessary and expedient" to Congress except for suggesting they consider amendments to the constitution that were proposed by the states' conventions.

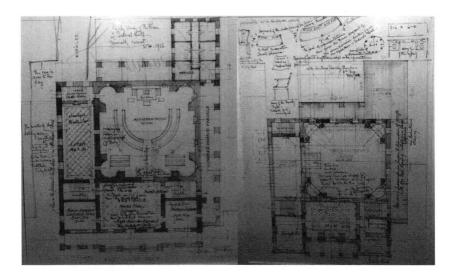

Pictures of the 1789 floorplan of Federal Hall - courtesy Historic.us

After the inauguration, each branch of Congress went about establishing its own rules for conducting the nation's business. The House and the Senate also established joint committees drawing up conference rules. They dealt with the logistics of communication with the President and between the two legislative bodies. There was much for everyone to do in forming this new republic ranging from immediately raising revenues for funding the federal government to reformulating existing departments and passing laws, including the Northwest Ordinance, that were enacted under the Articles of Confederation. Three important acts would be passed establishing three executive departments under the U.S. Presidency -- after Congress rejected a U.S. Senate Committee's proposal that the president should be called "His Highness the President, Protector of the Liberties of the United States."

CONGRESS HALL
December 6, 1790 to May 14, 1800

Chestnut St & 6th Street
Philadelphia, PA 19106
Pictures Courtesy of U.S. National Park Service

Congress Hall is located on the corner of Chestnut and 6th Streets and was originally built to serve as the Philadelphia County Courthouse. It was designed by architect Samuel Lewis and construction began in 1787 and completed in 1789. The US Congress, assembled in New York's Federal Hall, passed the *An Act for establishing the temporary and permanent seat of the Government of the United States,* which established a temporary U.S. Capital in Philadelphia from 1790 - 1800. It was signed into law by President George Washington on July 16th, 1790. The new Courthouse, consequently, served as the meeting place of the U. S. Congress from December 6, 1790 to May 14, 1800 with the House of Representatives meeting on the main floor, while the Senate assembled upstairs.

The building was tendered for the purpose of temporarily housing the federal government by the Philadelphia Commissioners. In this building President George Washington and Vice President John Adams' inaugurations occurred for their second terms. Vice President John Adams presided in the Senate while Speaker Frederick A. Muhlenberg presided over the House of Representatives. In Congress Hall, the First, Second, Third, Fourth, Fifth and Sixth US Congresses convened until the adjournment of the first session of the Sixth Congress on May 14, 1800. Sadly, the announcement was also made to Congress of former President Washington's death in this chamber.

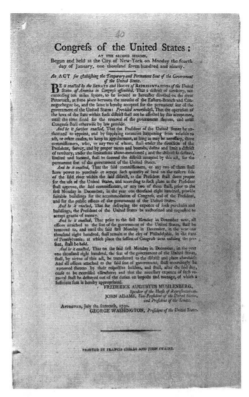

An Act for establishing the temporary and permanent seat of the Government of the United States - image from *An American Time Capsule: Three Centuries of Broadsides and Other Printed Ephemera*

Representative Henry Lee would deliver his famous oration to over 4,000 citizens, appropriating, with the modification of a word or two, John Marshall's expression that the dead hero was *" First in war, First in peace, and First in the hearts of his countrymen."*

On the morning after Christmas Day, the House convened in its chamber in Congress Hall in Philadelphia. Once assembled, the Representatives somberly proceeded to the city's German Lutheran Church to attend a memorial Joint Session for former President George Washington who had died of a throat infection on December 14 at his Mount Vernon (Virginia) home. Major General Henry Lee—Washington's military protégé and a Member of the House from Virginia in the 6th Congress (1799–1801)—delivered a spirited oration to an audience of 4,000 mourners including President John Adams and his wife, Abigail. "Where shall I begin in opening your view to a character throughout sublime?" Lee said. "Shall I speak of his warlike achievements, all springing from obedience to his country's will—all directed to his country's good?" He then traced Washington's military accomplishments in the French and Indian War and the Revolutionary War, and his service to his nation out of military uniform—culminating in eight years as the first U.S. President. Washington, Lee intoned, had been "First in war, first in peace, and first in the hearts of his countrymen." At the conclusion of the service, Members of the House returned to their chamber where they adjourned for the remainder of the day. [266]

The structure at Fifth and Chestnut streets was begun after the passage by the Assembly of the Charter of 1789. The large elegant Georgian brick building was finished in 1791 and almost immediately appropriated for the uses of the national government. On the first floor, the Speaker of the House sat in a large arm-chair, with a table before him like a toilette, covered with green cloth, fringed. The Speaker's seat was elevated about two feet and was located on the west side of the hall. The members' seats were in three rows of desks, rising one above another in the form of a semi-circle, opposite the Speaker. These writing-desks were mahogany with large armed chairs with leather liottoms. There are two fireplaces, on each side of the hall with stoves.

Congress Hall, Interior, Second Floor, Senate Chamber
Independence National Historical Park Picture

---

[266] United States House of Representatives, *"Historical Highlights: President George Washington's Memorial Service"* http://history.house.gov/HistoricalHighlight/Detail/36398?ret=True, retrieved December 27, 2014.

Theophilus Bradbury, U.S. Representative from Massachusetts, wrote his daughter on December 26th, 1795 that:

The Senate chamber is over the south end of the hall; the Vice President's chair is in an area (like the altar in a church) at the south end. The senators' seats, two rows of desks and chairs, in a semi-circle, but not raised from the floor. The floors of both halls are covered with woolen carpets. The lower room is elegant, but the [upper] chamber much more so. You ascend the stairs leading to the chamber at the north end, and pass through an entry, having committee rooms on each side; in that on the east side of the Senate chamber is a full length picture of the King of France, and in the opposite room is one of his Queen. . . . They wore presented by the King. There is a building on the cast side of the hall on Chestnut street for offices, connecting the hall with Pennsylvania state-house, in which their General Court is now sitting: this is as large a building as Congress Hall, and these buildings form the north side of the square or mall. [267]

According to the US Senate Historian's online article titled *The Senate Moves to Philadelphia*:

A specially woven Axminster carpet, featuring the Great Seal of the United States, covered the plain board floor. The chamber's thirteen windows, hung with green wooden Venetian blinds and crimson damask curtains, provided added daytime illumination, while candles placed on members' desks lit the chamber for rare late afternoon and evening sessions.

The members who inaugurated this chamber were an experienced lot. More than three-quarters had served in the Continental Congress and in state legislatures. Ten had participated in the Constitutional Convention. Nearly half were college graduates; two-thirds had some legal training.

The large back room on the second floor, known as the Common Council Chamber, is where the Supreme Court of the United States assembled in 1791. Its sessions continued to be held here until August 15th, 1800. In Congress Hall sat Chief Justices John Jay, John Rutledge and Oliver Ellsworth. The associate justices, during the ten years, were William Cushing, James Wilson, John Blair, James Iredell, Bushrod Washington, Samuel Chase, Thomas Johnson, William Paterson, and Alfred Moore.

---

[267] Ibid.

Among the historic events that took place here were the presidential inaugurations of George Washington (his second) and John Adams; the establishment of the First Bank of the United States, the Federal Mint, and the Department of the Navy; and the ratification of Jay's Treaty with England. During the 19th century, the building was used by Federal and local courts. The building, inside and out, has been restored as much as possible to the period of time when the building was the U.S. Capitol.

THE U.S. CAPITOL
November 17, 1800 to Present

The U.S. Capitol Building is located in Washington, D.C., at the eastern end of the National Mall on a plateau just under 90 feet above the level of the Potomac River. The site commands a westward view across the Capitol Reflecting Pool to the Washington Monument 1.4 miles away, and the Lincoln Memorial, 2.2 miles away.

The legislation enabling the federal capital to be permanently located in the District of Columbia was contentious. Article I, Section 8 of the Constitution (1787), which gave the Congress legislative authority over *"such District (not exceeding ten Miles square) as may, by Cession of Particular States, and the Acceptance of Congress, become the Seat of the Government of the United States..."* Treasury Secretary Alexander Hamilton was instrumental in brokering a compromise between the Southern and Northern States. The Southern States agreed that if the capital were located along the banks of the Potomac River they would permit the federal government to take on debt incurred during the American Revolutionary War.

The Architect of the U.S. Capitol writes:

> In 1788, the state of Maryland ceded to Congress "any district in this State, not exceeding ten miles square," and in 1789 the state of Virginia ceded an equivalent amount of land. In accordance with the "Residence Act" passed by Congress in 1790, President Washington in 1791 selected the area that is now the District of Columbia from the land ceded by Maryland (private landowners whose property fell within this area were compensated by a payment of £25 per acre); that ceded by Virginia was not used for the capital and was returned to Virginia in 1846. Also under the provisions of that Act, he selected three Commissioners to survey the site and oversee the design and construction of the capital city and its government buildings. The Commissioners, in turn, selected the French engineer Pierre Charles L'Enfant to plan the new city of Washington. L'Enfant's plan, which was influenced by the gardens at Versailles, arranged the city's streets and avenues in a grid overlaid with baroque diagonals; the result is a functional and aesthetic whole in which government buildings are balanced against public lawns, gardens, squares, and paths. The Capitol itself was located at the elevated east end of the Mall, on the brow of what was then called Jenkins' Hill. The site was, in L'Enfant's words, "a pedestal waiting for a monument."[268]

The legislation also included the establishment of Philadelphia as a temporary seat of government for ten years (1790-1800), until the nation's capital in Washington, D.C. would be ready. On December 19, 1960, the Capitol was declared a National Historic Landmark by the National Park Service.

U.S. Capitol circa 1861

Image Courtesy of
The Library of Congress

---

[268] Architect of the Capitol, *Capitol Campus, United States Capitol's Location, July 4, 1776,* http://www.aoc.gov/cc/capitol/capitol_location.cfm

CHAPTER VII
ARTICLE THE FIRST

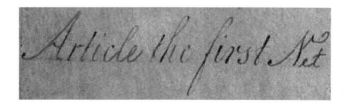

SABOTAGE OR CLERICAL ERROR

In the first edition of this book, a case was made for ratifying the *Constitution of 1787's* forgotten first amendment, *Article the First,* which remains before the States. What follows in this chapter is a retraction of that plea and an in-depth analysis of *Article the First,* based solely on primary sources. This chapter was necessary to correct certain errors in my previous edition and to examine the charge that the *Bill of Rights'* original first amendment failed ratification due to political sabotage.

CHECKS AND BALANCES

In 1787, the framers took the lessons learned over 13 years from both the state governments and three different unicameral *United American Republics* to enact a constitution peppered with "checks and balances." Most U.S. citizens know that this fundamental "check and balance" principle ensures that each branch of the government (executive, judicial, and legislative) exercises some measure of influence over the other branches. These Constitutional "checks and balances" were specifically designed to prevent any one branch from accumulating too much power while encouraging cooperation between branches as well as comprehensive debate on contentious policy issues.

What citizens do not understand, however, is that the framers of the *Constitution of 1787* and the *Bill of Rights* provided two additional checks on the federal government that were most potent but are currently defunct. In the last edition, this chapter argued that these rejected checks are primarily the reason why the states and citizens are disengaged from the federal legislative process and distrustful of Congress.

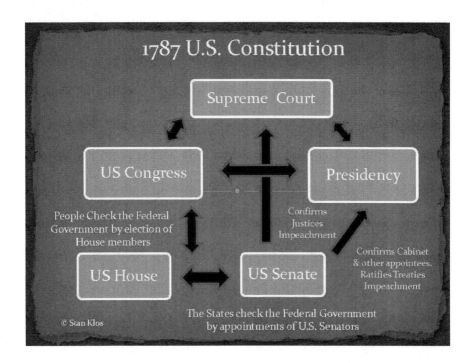

The first forgotten check on the federal government can be found in the *Constitution of 1787's Article I, Section 3* and it states: "The Senate of the United States shall be composed of two Senators from each State, chosen by the Legislature thereof for six Years; and each Senator shall have one Vote." In other words, *Article I, Section 3* required each state's legislative body, rather than its citizens, to choose its two U.S. Senators.[269] This Senate provision was the original instrument that ensured "State Rights" in the legislative, executive and judicial branches of the federal government because all presidential nominations for executive and judicial posts take effect only when confirmed by the Senate, and international treaties become law only when approved by a two-thirds vote of the Senate.[270]

From 1789 until 1913, United States Senators served, essentially, as ambassadors of the individual states to the Federal Government. Senators unequivocally represented their States' interest and took instructions directly from the legislative

---

[269] This important check of the States over the U.S. Senate was overturned by the Progressive Republicans when they voted to send the Constitution's Seventeenth Amendment to the States for ratification on May 13, 1912.

[270] *Constitution of 1787, Article II, Section 2, Clause 2.*

branch of their respective state governments. The first significant example of state power in this regard was in 1788, when Patrick Henry, as a powerful member of the Virginia House of Delegates, used his voting block to thwart James Madison's aspirations for a seat in the United States Senate. Henry then used his influence to draw-up a Virginia Congressional District that gave James Monroe the voter advantage over Madison in the House race between two future U.S. Presidents. In order to placate Patrick Henry's anti-federalist supporters, James Madison was forced to promise that, if elected, he would introduce constitutional amendments. Winning his home county of Orange 216 to 9, Madison won the election by 1,308 to 972 over James Monroe.

Madison questioned the necessity of a federal bill of rights but was forced to face the issue early in the first House session. On June 8th, 1789, he introduced in the House proposed amendments that were primarily related to civil liberties rather than the structure of the government. Henry and the antifederalists believed Madison's proposals were a far cry from the Amendments that they had proposed at the ratification convention and, on August 13th, antifederalists introduced amendments changing the structure of the federal government and protecting the rights of the states from encroachment. The debate was vibrant and Representative Madison, due to Patrick Henry's blocking of his election to the Senate, found himself the pivotal Congressman in framing what we now call the *Bill of Rights*.

Under the *Constitution of 1787 Article I, Section 3*, U.S. Senators were also actively engaged in the election of local State legislators. When Abraham Lincoln and Stephen Douglas traveled around Illinois in 1858 debating each other as they vied for a seat in the U.S. Senate, they weren't looking for votes from the citizens. Douglas, the incumbent senator and Lincoln, who had served one term in the House, were seeking votes from the State Delegates and Senators in the Illinois legislature. For 124 years, State legislators, not lobbyists,[271] worked closely with U.S. Senators in drafting bills to be introduced in Congress. U.S. Senators spent the majority of their time in the Senate actually conducting the nation's business, as opposed to today's members whose schedules are consumed with fund raising-related duties.[272]

---

[271] See discussion, below.

[272] Ryan Grim and Sabrina Siddiqui, *Call Time For Congress Shows How Fundraising Dominates Bleak Work Life*, Huffington Post, 01/08/2013 - "The amount of time that members of Congress in both parties spend fundraising is widely known to take up an obscene portion of a typical day -- whether it's "call time" spent on the phone with potential donors, or in person at fundraisers in Washington or back home. Seeing it spelled out in black and white, however, can be a jarring experience for a new member, as related by some who attended the November orientation."

The 17th Amendment's provision for direct popular vote elections, while purportedly giving "power to the people," in fact stripped the States' constitutional check over the Senate.[273]

LIMITING THE SIZE OF CONGRESSIONAL DISTRICTS INSTEAD OF THE HOUSE

The second forgotten check – a maximum citizen limit for Congressional Districts – is more multifaceted because, although loosely followed by Congress for 120 years, it was never enacted. This original people's check on the federal government was proposed by Congress on September 25th, 1789, as the first article in the *HR/Senate 12-Amendment Resolution* commonly known as the "Bill of Rights." Its first amendment, known as *Article the First*, proposed a 50,000 maximum citizen limit on Congressional Districts to ensure that the House of Representatives would be comprised of citizen-legislators who were personally known to their constituents. Today, *Article the First* remains the only amendment in the *Bill of Rights* not ratified.

In direct opposition to the spirit of *Article the First*, the 435-member limitation set on the House of Representatives was launched on August 8th, 1911, when President William H. Taft (R) signed the 62nd Congress' *Apportionment Act of 1911*, increasing House membership from 391 to 433. The act also included provisions to add two more members when New Mexico and Arizona became states. The legislation took effect on March 13th, 1913, during the 63rd Congress (1913–1915).

The bill's modest increase of Representatives from the previous census was a direct result of members raising concerns that the House was growing to an unwieldy size. Republican Representative Edgar Crumpacker of Indiana, however, who chaired the House Committee on the Census, argued just the opposite:

Members are . . . supposed to reflect the opinion and to stand for the wishes of their constituents. If we make the ratio [of persons per Representative] too large the idea of representation becomes attenuated and less definite. The personal interest of the

---

[273] The Editorial Board, *Dark Money Helped Win the Senate*, Sunday Review Editorial, New York Times, 11/8/2014 - "The next Senate was just elected on the greatest wave of secret, special-interest money ever raised in a congressional election. What are the chances that it will take action to reduce the influence of money in politics? Nil, of course."

voter in his representative becomes less important to him, and we may lose something of the vital strength of our representative form of government. [274]

For the first time after a decennial census, Congress failed to re-apportion the House in 1920. Previously, the House had reapportioned itself in a manner that expanded the representation of the early Congresses. The methods for calculating apportionment by the 1920's, however, caused the smaller rural states to lose representation to the larger urbanized states, whose population was growing. Additionally, *Article the First* had not been ratified to cap Congressional Districts at 50,000, so Congress was free to break the 120 year-old tradition: the *Constitution of 1787* called only for at least one Representative per state and no more than one Representative for every 30,000 persons. A political battle erupted between rural and urban factions resulting in no reapportionment following the 1920 Census.

It was not until the eve of the next census that Republican Majority Leader John Q. Tilson of Connecticut took the lead in developing a House reapportionment plan for the 1930's. In direct opposition to *Article the First*, Tilson led the effort to pass the *Permanent Apportionment Act of 1929*, fixing the number of Representatives at 435. The House of Representatives Historian writes:

Signed into law on June 18, 1929, the Permanent Apportionment Act capped House Membership at the level established after the 1910 Census and created a procedure for automatically reapportioning House seats after every decennial census. Republican Majority Leader John Q. Tilson of Connecticut approvingly declared that the act dispelled the "danger of failing to reapportion after each decennial census as contemplated by the Constitution." But opponents, such as William B. Bankhead of Alabama, who doubted its constitutionality, had earlier described the plan as "the abdication and surrender of the vital fundamental powers vested in the Congress of the United States by the Constitution itself." [275]

In 1941, the Democratic-controlled Congress adopted the current formula for reapportioning House seat districts, still limiting the House of Representatives to 435 members (See *54 Stat.L. 761*, November 15, 1941); the House has remained at 435,

---

[274] House of Representatives Historian, The 1911 House Reapportionment, http://history.house.gov/Historical-Highlights/1901-1950/The-1911-House-reapportionment/, retrieved online 12/26/2014
[275] House of Representatives Historian, The 1911 House Reapportionment, http://history.house.gov/Historical-Highlights/1901-1950/The-1911-House-reapportionment/, retrieved online 12/26/2014

except for a temporary increase to 437 Members from 1959 to 1961, after Alaska and Hawaii achieved statehood.

Congressional Districts are now 14 times larger than the population cap proposed under *Article the First*. Following the 2010 Census, the populations of Congressional District have soared to 710,767 citizens, and, every two years, House candidates spend millions of dollars for media sound bites designed to reach over a half-million voters whom Representatives can't possibly ever know. Having created no additional House representation for over 100 years, Congress instead has employed over 12,000 "staffers" to conduct legislative business on Capitol Hill.

To put these 12,000 staffers (almost 20 per House member) in context: Up until the 1890's, House members were allotted no paid staff because their small districts' voting population numbered less than 50,000 citizens per Representative.[276] This changed in 1893, when House members were allotted one paid staff member each. The following chart shows the growth of House staff from 1893 to 2013..

Fiscal Year	Authorized Staff [277]
1893	1 to 2
1919	2
1940	3
1945	6
1949	7
1955	8
1956	9
1961	10
1965	11
1966	12
1969	13

---

[276] United States Census Bureau, Reports and statistics from the 1890 census, Males of Voting Age table, page clxxviii.

[277] Chart is taken from a 1993 Congressional Report and shows the increase in the number of staff for each member of the House of Representatives since 1893. Before 1893 the House members paid for their own staff. Since the 1919 staff allotment of two, the House of Representatives has been fixed at 435 Representatives. For more information on House staff and salaries please read The Number of Congressional Staff Is the Real Problem by Daniel J. Mitchell

1971	15
1972	16
1973	18

Today, based on the 2010 census, the 19 paid public servants allotted for each Congressional District of 539,228 voters translates into one paid public servant per 28,380 citizens over 18. Since 1910, just before the first House Apportionment Acts were passed, House staff has grown from 500 for a 92 Million Population in 1910 to 12,200 (2,420% increase) for a 308 Million Population in 2010 (342% increase), while the number of HR members increased from 394 in 1910 to 435 (9% increase) in 2010.

In 2015, Congressional Districts now exceed a population of 725,000 citizens and inexperienced staffers, usually not from their Representative's home district, are overwhelmed by the current constituent base. According to the *Washington Times,* these 24 year old staffers are running the House of Representatives:

The most powerful nation on Earth is run largely by 24-year-olds. High turnover and lack of experience in congressional offices are leaving staffs increasingly without policy and institutional knowledge, a Washington Times analysis of a decade of House and Senate personnel records shows — leaving a vacuum that usually is filled by lobbyists. Most Senate staffers have worked in the Capitol for less than three years. For most, it is their first job ever. In House offices, one-third of staffers are in their first year, while only 1 in 3 has worked there for five years or more.

Among the aides who work on powerful committees where the nation's legislation takes shape, resumes are a little longer: Half have four years of experience. When Americans wonder why Congress can't seem to get anything done, this could be a clue. It's also a sharp difference from the average government employee: Unlike many state and federal workers with comfortable salaries, pensions and seemingly endless tenures, those in the halls of power are more likely to be inexperienced and overworked. Low pay for high-stress jobs with less-than-stellar prospects for advancement takes a toll on institutional memory and expertise.

While senators make $174,000, staff assistants and legislative correspondents — by far the most common positions in the Senate — have median pay of $30,000 and $35,000, respectively, significantly less than Senate janitors and a fairly low salary for college graduates in a city as expensive as Washington. Historical pay records were transcribed from book form by the website Legistorm.

The size of committee and members' staffs have remained the same over the past decade, and salaries have often not risen with inflation — or at all. The average legislative counsel in the House made $56,000 last year, less than in 2007. While pay for parking-lot attendants in the House increased from $26,000 to $49,000 in the past decade, pay for staff assistants, who make up the bulk of the House's workforce, rose from $26,000 to $30,000. That puts them in the bottom fifth of the region's college-educated workforce. [278]

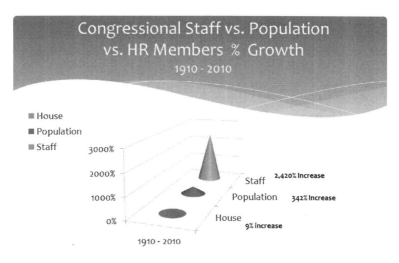

HR staff has grown from 500 for a 92 million population in 1910 to 12,200 (2,420% increase) for a 315 million population in 2010 (342% increase), while the number of HR members increased from 394 in 1910 to 435 (9% increase) in 2010. Congressional Districts now exceed 725,000 citizens.

Moreover, the combination of an inexperienced staff with elected members who spend most of their time fundraising has created a vacuum of competency that has been filled with seasoned experts paid by the money of Special Interest. National Public Radio reports that 11,000 Lobbyists are writing the House's bills:

It's taken for granted that lobbyists influence legislation. But perhaps less obvious is that they often write the actual bills — even word for word. In an example a week and a half ago, the House passed a measure that would roll back a portion of the 2010 financial reforms known as Dodd-Frank. And reports from The New York Times and Mother Jones revealed that language in the final legislation was nearly identical to language suggested by lobbyists. It's been a long-accepted truth in

---

[278] Luke Rosiak, Congressional staffers, public shortchanged by high turnover, low pay, The Washington Times - Wednesday, June 6, 2012

Washington that lobbyists write the actual laws, but that raises two questions: Why does it happen so much, and is it a bad thing?[279]

Lee Fang's "Where Have All the Lobbyists Gone?" not only provides a graphic mapping out special interest influence on Capitol Hill but provides $3.2 billion annual estimate in lobbyist spending:

On paper, the lobbying industry is quickly disappearing. In January, records indicated that for the third straight year, overall spending on lobbying decreased. Lobbyists themselves continue to deregister in droves. In 2013, the number of registered lobbyists dipped to 12,281, the lowest number on file since 2002.

But experts say that lobbying isn't dying; instead, it's simply going underground. The problem, says American University professor James Thurber, who has studied congressional lobbying for more than thirty years, is that "most of what is going on in Washington is not covered" by the lobbyist-registration system. Thurber, who is currently advising the American Bar Association's lobbying-reform task force, adds that his research suggests the true number of working lobbyists is closer to 100,000.

A loophole-ridden law, poor enforcement, the development of increasingly sophisticated strategies that enlist third-party validators and create faux-grassroots campaigns, along with an Obama administration executive order that gave many in the profession a disincentive to register—all of these forces have combined to produce a near-total collapse of the system that was designed to keep tabs on federal lobbying.

While the official figure puts the annual spending on lobbying at $3.2 billion in 2013, Thurber estimates that the industry brings in more than $9 billion a year. Other experts have made similar estimates, but no one is sure how large the industry has become. Lee Drutman, a lobbying expert at the Sunlight Foundation, says that at least twice as much is spent on lobbying as is officially reported. [280]

In summary, the failure to enact *Article the First,* the people's check on the House of Representatives, has allowed powerful Congressmen to create enormous Congressional Districts that elevate their seats to a hallowed status while rendering

---

[279] Alisa Chang, When Lobbyists Literally Write The Bill, National Public Radio, November 11, 2013

[280] Lee Fang, "Where Have All the Lobbyists Gone? On paper, the influence-peddling business is drying up. But lobbying money is flooding into Washington, DC, like never before. What's going on?" The Nation, March 10-17, 2014.

impossible a successful grass roots campaign based on ideas and issues by a working class candidate.   21st-century door-to-door campaigning is fruitless except as a public relations stunt to attract traditional media coverage or produce a viral internet opportunity. The purchase and mastery of mass media, not personal contact, is the marketing mix that ultimately persuades 540,000 eligible voters to elect and re-elect House members.

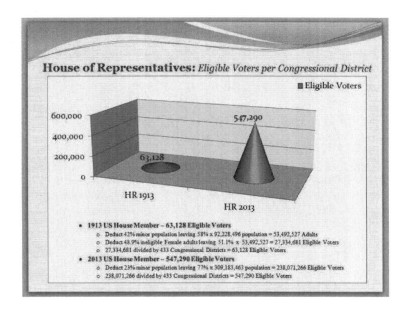

The 1789 Congress' bungling of *Article the First* has enabled powerful members of Congress to enact *House Apportionment Acts* that entrench incumbents while empowering special interests, the highly partisan two-party system, the media, and citizens of great personal wealth. These *House Apportionment Acts*, more so than any other laws, are responsible for the people losing their check on the federal government. If the citizens of the United States truly seek a mechanism to break the two-party stranglehold, end partisan politics, birth new political parties, and obliterate special interest influence over the House, then *Article the First* should be resuscitated.

WHAT HAPPENED TO THE BILL OF RIGHTS ARTICLE THE FIRST?

On September 25th, 1789, the First Bicameral Congress of the United States proposed to the state legislatures 12 amendments to the *Constitution of 1787*. This was a painstaking process because, only a year earlier, the States had proposed more than two hundred amendments during the *Constitution*'s ratification process.

When repetitious amendments are eliminated, over one hundred separate proposals can be identified. Most sought to change the structure of the federal government or the balance of power between it and the states, while others focused on protecting individual rights. [281]

The first group of amendments actually to pass were formulated by the House of Representatives (HR) on August 24th, 1789 and numbered 17 Articles. The first amendment concerned congressional apportionment and sought to limit congressional districts to a maximum size of 50,000 citizens. [282]

After the first enumeration, required by the first Article of the Constitution, there shall be one Representative for every thirty thousand, until the number shall amount to one hundred, after which the proportion shall be so regulated by Congress, that there shall be not less than one hundred Representatives, nor less than one Representative for every forty thousand persons until the number of Representatives shall amount to 200, after which the proportion shall be so regulated by Congress, that there shall not be less than two hundred Representatives, nor less than one Representative for every fifty thousand persons.

The second set of 12 approved amendments was passed by the U.S. Senate between September 4th and 9th. The Senate placed its congressional apportionment amendment as *Article the First*; it limited congressional districts to a maximum size of 60,000 citizens.

Article the First: After the first enumeration, required by the first Article of the Constitution, there shall be one Representative for every thirty thousand, until the number shall amount to one hundred, to which number one representative shall be added for every subsequent increase of forty thousand, until the representatives shall amount to two hundred, to which one representative shall be added for every subsequent increase of sixty thousand persons.

---

[281] The First Federal Congress Project, Birth of the Nation: The First Federal Congress 1789-1791, Amendments to the Constitution, http://www.gwu.edu/~ffcp/exhibit/p7/, retrieved 12/23/2014.
[282] *Journal of the First Session of the House of the Representatives:* New-York, Printed by Thomas Greenleaf, 1789, pages 103-104.

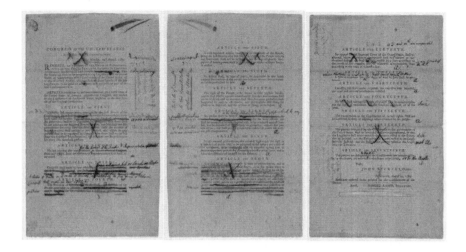

Front and Back of the proposed Amendments to the U.S. Constitution broadside as passed by the House of Representatives and on August 24th, 1789. *Images are from the National Archives of the United States.*

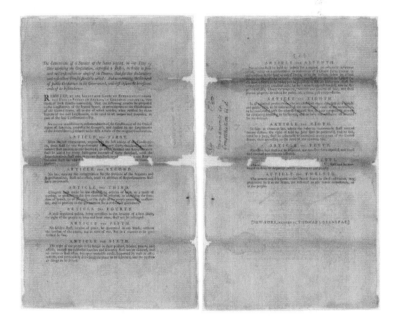

Samuel Otis, Secretary *of Senate 12-Amendment Broadside* with "ag" written in the margins of the Articles agreed to and lines through the articles that were changed by the HR-S CC. *Images courtesy: Records of the Senate in the National Archives*

The HR and Senate each elected the following members for a House–Senate Conference Committee to finalize all HR-Senate amendments "disagreed to:"

- Representatives James Madison of Virginia, Roger Sherman of Connecticut and John Vining of Delaware
- Senators: Oliver Ellsworth of Connecticut, Charles Carroll of Maryland and William Paterson of New Jersey[283]

On September 21st, 1789, a House–Senate Conference Committee (*HR-S CC*) convened to resolve the numerous differences between the two *Bill of Rights* proposals. On September 24th, 1789, the *HR-S CC* submitted their recommendations to the House of Representatives and the Senate. The original committee report, written in the hand of Senator Oliver Ellsworth, was read in the Senate by Ellsworth:

The Committees of the two Houses appointed to confer on their different votes on the Amendments proposed by the Senate to the Resolution proposing Amendments to the Constitution, and disagreed to by the House of Representatives, have had a conference, and have agreed that it will be proper for the House of Representatives to agree to the said Amendments proposed by the Senate, with an Amendment to their fifth Amendment, so that the third Article shall read as follows "Congress shall make no law respecting an establishment of Religion, or prohibiting the free exercise thereof; or abridging the freedom of Speech, or of the Press; or the right of the people peaceably to assemble and to petition the Government for a redress of grievances" And with an Amendment to the fourteenth Amendment proposed by the Senate, so that the eighth Article, as numbered in the Amendments proposed by the Senate, shall read as follows "In all criminal prosecutions, the accused shall enjoy the right to a speedy & publick trial by an impartial jury of the district wherein the crime shall have been committed, as the district shall have been previously asscertained by law, and to be informed of the nature and cause of the accusation; to be confronted with the witnesses against him; and to have compulsory process for obtaining Witnesses against him in his favour, & to have the assistance of counsel for his defence.

The Committees were also of Opinion that it would be proper for both Houses to agree to amend the first Article, by striking out the word "less" in the last line but

---

[283] John Agg, *History of Congress, exhibiting a classification of the proceedings of the Senate, and the House of Representatives, from March 4, 1789, to March 3, 1793, embracing the first term of the administration of General Washington*, Philadelphia: Lea & Blanchard 1843, page 169

one, and inserting in its place, the word "more," and accordingly recommend that the said Article be reconsidered for that purpose. [284]

This report was ordered to lie for consideration. [285]

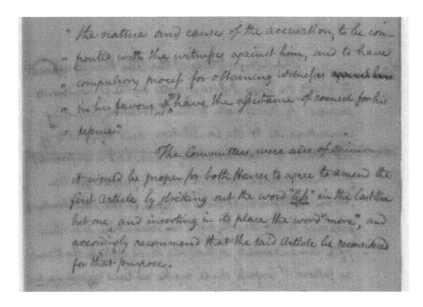

Page two of U.S. Senator Oliver Ellsworth's handwritten report of the Conference Committees recommending changes to the House version of Article the First. Images are from the Records of the Senate from the National Archives of the United States.

While the U.S. Senate attended to other matters, the House of Representatives drafted and seemingly passed a resolution adopting *HR-S CC's* recommendations and rushed it up to the Senate floor:

A Message from the House of Representatives: Mr. Beckley, their Clerk brought up the Amendments to the 'Articles to be proposed to the Legislatures of the several States, as Amendments to the Constitution of the United States;' and informed the Senate, that the

---

[284] *Conference Committee Report." Creating the Bill of Rights. Ed. Kenneth R. Bowling and Helen E. Veit. Baltimore: The Johns Hopkins University Press, 1991. 49-50. Print. manuscript source: National Archives Original Manuscript, National Archives of the United States*

[285] *Journal of the First Session of the Senate of the United States of America: Begun and Held at the City of New-York, March 4th, 1789, and in the Thirteenth Year of the Independence of the Said States, New-York*, Printed by Thomas Greenleaf, 1789, page 145.

House of Representatives had receded from their disagreement to the first, third, fifth, sixth, seventh, ninth, tenth, eleventh, fourteenth, fifteenth, seventeenth, twentieth, twenty-first, twenty-second, twenty-third, and twenty-fourth amendments, insisted on by the Senate: Provided, That the two articles which by the amendments of the Senate are now proposed to be inserted as the third and eighth articles, shall be amended to read as followeth:

Article the third. "Congress shall make no law respecting an establishment of religion, or prohibiting the free exercise thereof; or abridging the freedom of speech, or of the press; or the right of the People peaceably to assemble, and to petition the Government for a redress of grievances."

Article the eighth. "In all criminal prosecutions, the accused shall enjoy the right to a speedy and public trial, by an impartial jury of the State and district wherein the crime shall have been committed, which district shall have been previously ascertained by law, and to be informed of the nature and cause of the accusation; to be confronted with the witnesses against him; to have compulsory process for obtaining witnesses in his favor; and to have the assistance of counsel for his defence."

And provided also, That the first article be amended by striking out the word " less," in the last place of the said first article, and inserting in lieu thereof the word "more." [286]

The *HR Bill of Rights Resolution*, however, failed to incorporate the *HR-S CC* penultimate line language "in the last line but one." Instead, the House had substituted its own verbiage, "in the last place of the said first article," rendering *Article the First* dysfunctional. Despite this serious divergence from *HR-S CC's* recommendations, which no one apparently noticed, the Senate approved the *HR Bill of Rights Resolution* on September 25th, 1789.

TRANSMITTING 12-AMENDMENTS TO THE STATES

On September 24th, 1789, the House passed a resolution that ordered the proposed *Bill of Rights* to be engrossed and transmitted by President George Washington to the 11 United States, plus Rhode Island and North Carolina (even though they had not ratified the *Constitution of 1787*). The Senate approved the resolution on September 26th, 1789. The Clerk, rightly, inscribed the *Bill of Rights* according to the language of the approved *HR/Senate Bill of Rights Resolution*, even though it differed from the

---

[286] *Journal of the First Session of the Senate of the United States of America: Begun and Held at the City of New-York, March 4th, 1789, and in the Thirteenth Year of the Independence of the Said States, New-York*, Printed by Thomas Greenleaf, 1789, page 148.

HR-S CC report; this divergence ultimately doomed *Article the First* to the dustbin of failed U.S. Constitutional Amendments. According to an analysis written in 2007, the engrossed *Article the First* with its one word change was dead on arrival for the following reasons:

1. A Redundant Maximum: It imposed ... a new formula for determining the maximum size of the House. This was clearly unnecessary given that the Constitution (drafted only two years earlier) already provided the method for determining the maximum size ("shall not exceed one for every thirty Thousand"). Moreover, the new and more restrictive maximum (of one representative per 50,000) would not be activated until the total population reached 8 million, at which point a significant & discontinuous reduction in the maximum size of the House becomes imposed.

2. An Irresolvable Math Error: It incorporated an internally contradictory math error in that — for a given population range — the required maximum would be below the required minimum.

3. Failed to Maintain a Proportionate Minimum: Though the amendment proposed a proportionate minimum size as long as the total population remained below 8 million, beyond that number it effectively abandoned the need to define a minimum. This reversed the original intent of the amendment by eliminating the guidance for determining a minimum size for the House that would have been proportionally commensurate with our nation's total population. [287]

The transmittal letter reads as follows:

United States, October 2nd 1789

Sir, In pursuance of the enclosed resolution I have the honor to transmit to your Excellency a copy of the amendment proposed to be added to the Constitution of the United States. I have the honor to be, With due Consideration, Your Excellency's Most Obedient Servant,

George Washington

Image from the U.S. National Archives

---

[287] Thirty-thousand.org, *Analysis of "Article the first..."*, online publication, 2007 - http://www.thirty-thousand.org/pages/article1_analysis.htm, retrieved December 31, 2014.

Engrossed 12-Articles proposed by the 1789 Congress to amend the Constitution of 1787 that was sent to the States for ratification consideration. *Article the First* remains the only amendment, due to its dysfunctional form, not ratified by the States. *Image is from the National Archives of the United States*.

The dysfunctional *Article the First* has nevertheless since been ratified by 12 States:

Virginia on November 3, 1789; New Jersey on November 20, 1789; Maryland on December 19, 1789; North Carolina on December 22, 1789; South Carolina on January 19, 1790; New Hampshire on January 25, 1790; New York on March 27, 1790; Rhode Island on June 15, 1790; Pennsylvania on September 21, 1791; Vermont on November 3, 1791 and Kentucky on June 24, 1792.

On September 25th, 2014, the 225th birthday of the *Bill of Rights*, each of the States' Attorneys General was notified that their respective states had ratified the incorrect *Article the First* amendment to the U.S. Constitution. The response of the Attorneys General ranged from no reply to that of North Carolina, replying:

> After reviewing your materials, it appears that, if the United States House of Representatives or Senate made a mistake on approving a proposed amendment, the remedy lies with the United States Congress, not the North Carolina Assembly.[288]

There have been numerous efforts to ratify *Article the First*, as transmitted to the States, including this book's first edition. Such efforts, however, will be fruitless due to the fact that the 1789 Congress sent the dysfunctional *Article the First* to the states.[289] Furthermore, efforts to change the word "more" back to "less" in *Article the First,* which would cap Congressional Districts at 50,000 citizens, would require Congress to approve an entirely new amendment before it could be submitted to the states for ratification. Additionally, there was a recent legal challenge seeking a U.S. Federal District Court order that *Article the First* be implemented in its functional form because it was ratified by the necessary 4/5[ths] of the States on May 10th, 1790:

> *Article the First* was agreed upon and settled and was not even before the Joint Conference Committee, during the process it was noticed that there was a possible flaw in the text of "Article the First" at Line 2 (the second of the three Lines, or "Clauses"). With inclusion of the negative word "less" at Line 2, the 40,000 ratio was actually a "ceiling" ratio when in fact at Line 2 the 40,000 number was intended to be a "floor" ratio, so that once the growth or population progressed so that the Nation was at Line 2, the ratio would be between 40,000 and 50,000, but not "less" than 40,000. These were smart men, and they quickly realized that there was a simple way to correct this hard to recognize flaw so that the intent of what was actually approved would be guaranteed. All that had to be done was to exchange the new word "more" for the existing word of "less" in Line 2.

---

[288] Karen A. Blum, North Carolina Special Deputy Attorney General, typed letter signed to Stanley Klos, dated October 9, 2014
[289] *Article the First,* in its dysfunctional form, remains pending before state lawmakers because like Article the Second, which was ratified in 1992, there is no time limitation on *Article the First.* Today, with the 12 state approval, the legislatures of 28 more states could ratify *Article the First,* for the amendment to become constitutional.

Indeed, the Final Report made such a recommendation, and this is what was voted on and approved by Congress as the final form of text of "Article the First". However, thereafter some Clerk misunderstood the Final Report and did not know what a penultimate was (and apparently then incorrectly read the "Article the First" text linearly as printed in the Broadside, and not as the three "Lines" or Clauses referred to by the Joint Committee and understood by Congress) and took it upon themselves to paraphrase what they thought the Final Report meant when referring to the Final Report in the House Journal, rather than simply memorialize the verbatim text of the actual Final Report that was voted on and approved. [290]

Although I do not agree with the claim, petitioner Eugene LaVergne, Esq. correctly explains how a functional *Article the First* would have emerged in the *Bill of Rights* had the House adopted the *HR-S CC* penultimate line language "in the last line but one" verbatim in its resolution, instead of the substituting its own verbiage, "in the last place."

The *Lavergne v. John Bryson* federal case, however, was dismissed by the U.S. 3rd District Court of Appeals in 2012, which never ruled on the discrepancy between the *HR-S CC's* Final Report and the *HR/Senate Bill of Rights Resolution*.[291]

ThirtyThousand.org has a different take on the how Congress could have transmitted the dysfunctional *Article the First* to the States for ratification. They maintain *Article the First* was "effectively sabotaged":

As passed by the House, *Article the First* would have required there be at least one Representative for every 50,000 people at larger population levels. The Senate's version required one Representative for every 60,000. However, the would-be first amendment was effectively sabotaged by an ostensibly minor modification made at the last-minute by a joint House-Senate committee. In fact, this modification not only subverted the amendment's purpose, but it also introduced a mathematical defect which

---

[290] See Thomas H. LeDuc, "Connecticut and the First Ten Amendments to the Federal Constitution," S. Doc. No. 75-96, at 2-3 (1937); see also David E. Kyvig, Explicit and Authentic Acts: Amending the U.S. Constitution, 1776-1995, at 108 & n.76 (1996) (noting that "over the course of three sessions" in Connecticut, "one house or the other approved most of the amendments but the other failed to concur")

[291] Eugene Lavergne, Plaintiff-Appellant, v. John Bryson et al., Defendants-Appellees, U.S. Court Of Appeals Third Circuit, No. 12-1171: *"This is a pro se challenge to the constitutionality of longstanding aspects of the process for apportioning the House of Representatives. Plaintiff invoked the jurisdiction of the district court under 28 U.S.C.§ 2284(a). On December 16, 2011, the district court entered a final judgment dismissing plaintiff's suit. A5-A6. On January 17, 2012, plaintiff filed a timely notice of appeal from that judgment."* http://redistricting.lls.edu/files/NJ%20lavergne%2020120416%20exec.pdf

would have later rendered it inexecutable. Largely because this subtle modification was generally unnoticed initially, *Article the First* was affirmed by every state except Delaware. Had the proposed amendment not been crippled then it might have eventually been ratified (as originally worded) and, as a result, we would now have approximately 6,000 Representatives. [292]

What happened to *Article First* is a debate that has fulminated for 225 years. This sabotage charge, however, caught my attention prompting me to ask the age-old question: Who did it and why?

If *Article the First* was indeed deliberately sabotaged, we can rule out the *HR-S CC* Senate members because the committee's recommendations were read on the Senate floor by Senator Oliver Ellsworth, the report's author, and correctly entered into the minutes. The House, however, unlike the Senate, did not enter the *HR-S CC* report into its records. The House Journals record only:

> The House proceeded to consider the report of the committee of conference, on the subject-matter of the amendments, depending between the two Houses to the several articles of amendment to the Constitution of the United States, as proposed by thin House : Whereupon, Resolved, That this House doth recede from their disagreement to the first, third, fifth, sixth, seventh, ninth, tenth, eleventh, fourteenth, fifteenth, seventeenth, twentieth, twenty-first, twenty-second, twenty-third, and twenty-fourth amendments, insisted on by the Senate: ... And provided also, That the first article be amended by striking out the word " less," in the last place of the said first article, and inserting in lieu thereof the word "more." [293]

The House Journals also report that all three *HR-S CC* members voted for the bungled resolution. Therefore, any "sabotage" could only be traceable to Madison, Sherman and Vining. Additionally, *Article the First* originated as Madison's second amendment proposed on the House floor on June 8th, 1789:

> Secondly: That in article 2st. section 2, clause 3, these words be struck out, to wit, "The number of representatives shall not exceed one for every thirty thousand, but each state shall have at least one representative, and until such enumeration shall be made." And that in place thereof be inserted these words, to wit, "After the first actual enumeration, there shall be one representative for every thirty thousand, until the number amount to

---

[292] Thirty-thousand.org, *Analysis of "Article the first...",* online publication, 2007 - http://www.thirty-thousand.org/pages/article1_analysis.htm, retrieved December 31, 2014.

[293] *Journal of the First Session of the House of the Representatives: Begun and Held at the City of New-York, March 4th, 1789, and in the Thirteenth Year of the Independence of the Said States,* New-York, Printed by Thomas Greenleaf, 1789, September 24th, 1789.

after which the proportion shall be so regulated by congress, that the number shall never be less than nor more than but each state shall after the first enumeration, have at least two representatives; and prior thereto."

Larry Sabato, Professor of Political Science at the University of Virginia, offers a motive when he correctly maintains that:

Madison recognized the need for some upper ceiling on the number of House members: "A certain number [of representatives] seems to be necessary to secure the benefits of free consultation and discussion...On the other hand, the number ought at most to be kept within a certain limit, in order to avoid the confusion and intemperance of a multitude." From Madison's perspective, a 1,000-member House of Representatives, with about 300,000 constituents per representative, would seem reasonable. [294]

Therefore, Madison becomes our prime suspect because he did not want too large of a House. He was also in a position of power and if he had misgivings over capping Congressional Districts at the 50,000 citizen limit, an obscure change in a complex resolution would be a most effective way to kill the amendment quietly. Additionally, it stands to reason that only Madison could have changed the verbiage and gotten away with the sabotage:

1. The "last place of the said first article" resolution originated in the House, and thus rules out the three *HR-S CC's* Senators.
2. Had a clerk or one of the two other *HR-S CC* members constructed the dysfunctional resolution, author James Madison would surely have caught the error.
3. Only Madison, due to his ethos as a framer of the *Constitution of 1787*, could create a resolution with an error in the construction of his own amendment, and be above suspicion that chicanery was afoot.

Another factor supports Madison's role as saboteur: once it became common knowledge that *Article the First* had been submitted to the states with the wrong one word change, why didn't Madison act to have the error corrected during his eight year tenure as a powerful member of the House of Representatives? The ideal time to have repaired the dysfunctional amendment was in 1792, when the 12th State, Kentucky, ratified the dysfunctional Article, and George Washington cast the first Presidential veto, denying Congress the opportunity, based on the 1790 census, to

---

[294] Larry Sabato, *Expand the House of Representatives*, Democracy Journal of Ideas, Issue #8, Spring 2008.

create Congressional Districts below the constitutional minimum of 30,000 citizens.[295] Finally, in 1811, when the Republican Party controlled both houses of Congress and the 1810 Census apportionment created Congressional Districts at just under the 40,000 maximum prescribed in *Article the First*, why didn't now President James Madison champion his amendment? If *Thirtythousand.org* is correct and *Article the First* was effectively sabotaged by the House on September 24th 1789, then this finger points to the amendment's author, James Madison.

The members of this 1789 Congress included two future U.S. Presidents, three former Presidents of Congress, nine Declaration of Independence signers, four Articles of Confederation signers, and 15 U.S. Constitution Signers. Moreover President George Washington, Chief Justice John Jay, Secretary of State and Declaration of Independence author Thomas Jefferson, Secretary of the Treasury and U.S. Constitution signer Alexander Hamilton, Attorney General and U.S. Constitution framer Edmund Randolph, and Secretary of War Henry Knox worked behind the scenes to constitutionally cap Congressional Districts at the maximum of 60,000 or 50,000 citizens. Madison's possible sabotage aside, their debates and letters make clear that the framers of the *Bill of Rights* wanted the House of Representatives to remain answerable to people through the mechanism of small districts devoid of any undue influence by special interests. Even President James Madison, during the War of 1812 that raged 25 years after *Article the First* was proposed, worked with a House whose congressional districts did not exceed 50,000 citizens.

The 11 Amendments found in the Bill of Rights are a national treasure. Perhaps the current Congress might draw yet again upon the wisdom of the Congress of 1789, assembling a new Conference Committee to formulate a functional *Article the First* that caps Congressional districts somewhere between the 50,000 to 60,000 citizens originally proposed. With the passage of such an article, the States can recommence the national debate on whether the only amendment not ratified in the 1789 *Bill of Rights* should become the 28th Amendment to the *Constitution of 1787*.

---

[295] On 5 April, 1792, the president decided to veto the Apportionment Act of 1792 (1 Stat. 253) and returned the bill to the House of Representatives with the two objections that "there is no one proportion or divisor which, applied to the respective numbers of the States will yield the number and allotment of representatives proposed by the Bill" and that "the Bill has allotted to eight of the States, more than one [representative] for thirty thousand." Congress, after receiving Washington's veto message, the first in U.S. history, threw out the original bill and decided, on 10 April 1792, to apportion representatives at "the ratio of one for every thirty-three thousand persons in the respective States".

CHAPTER VIII
HAPPY BIRTHDAYS USA PLAY

http://www.youtube.com/watch?v=rfR3N3WuX20

Cast: Eight actors. (Note: this play was originally performed with a cast of four female (1, 3, 5, 7) and four male (2, 4, 6, 8) actors.)

<u>Four Female Actors</u>

Four actors enter holding a Betsy Ross American flag.

Actor 1: September 1st, 1774!

Actor 3: July 4th, 1776!

Actor 5: September 3rd, 1783!

Actor 7: September 17th, 1787!

All Four Actors together: Happy Birthdays USA !

(All four actors exit.)

Background Screen Shots Change: *Carpenters Hall - Independence Hall - Nassau Hall - Federal Hall*

Actor 1: September 1st, 1774: Happy Birthday USA! On this day 25 American Colonial Delegates caucused for the first time at the Philadelphia Tavern. Here Congress discussed where they should have their first meeting and who should be their first President.

The following Monday they reassembled at the Tavern and walked two blocks over to Carpenters Hall. On September 5th, 1774, the delegates formed the FIRST Continental Congress of the United Colonies of America and elected Peyton Randolph as their President. This congress would wage a war against Great Britain.

September 1st, 1774: Happy Birthday United Colonies of America. Happy Birthday USA!

Background Screen Shots Change: *Philadelphia Tavern – Carpenters Hall – Articles of Association – Peyton Randolph Medallion - George Washington Commander-in-Chief picture - Philadelphia Tavern Medallion.*

(Actor 2 enters on Actor 1's "USA," interrupting:)

Actor 2: Wait! Wait! Wait! September 1st was not the birthday of the United States -- we were still colonies. It was on July 2nd, 1776, that we declared ourselves independent from Great Britain. Richard Henry Lee, a delegate from Virginia drafted and Congress passed this resolution:

"Resolved, That these United Colonies are, and of right ought to be, free and independent States, that they are absolved from all allegiance to the British Crown, and that all political connection between them and the State of Great Britain is, and ought to be, totally dissolved."

Future President John Adams wrote his wife Abigail on that very day saying:

"The Second Day of July 1776, will be the most memorable Epocha, in the History of America. I am apt to believe that it will be celebrated, by succeeding Generations, as the great anniversary Festival. It ought to be commemorated, as the Day of Deliverance by solemn Acts of Devotion to God Almighty. It ought to be solemnized with Pomp and Parade, with Shews, Games, Sports, Guns, Bells, Bonfires and Illuminations from one End of this Continent to the other from this Time forward forever more."

July 2nd, 1776 - Happy Birthday USA!

Background Screen Shots Change: *Richard Henry Lee Medallion - Lee's resolution, John Adams and Abigail Adams pictures letter writing.*

(Actor 3 enters on Actor 2's "USA," interrupting:)

Actor 3: Hold it! Hold it! Hold it! You two are all wrong. It required all thirteen States to vote for Independence from Great Britain AND New York did not vote for Richard Henry Lee's Resolution.

It was Thomas Jefferson and his Committee of Five's "Declaration of Independence" that Congress passed on July 4th, 1776; New York made this July 4th "Declaration of Independence," not Lee's resolution, unanimous on July 9th. Everyone knows the July 4th Declaration is America's true birthday.

July 4th, 1776 - Happy Birthday USA!

Background Screen Shots Change: *Declaration of Independence – Committee of Five Picture – Thirteen State Map*

(Actor 4 enters on Actor 3's "USA," interrupting:)

Actor 4: No! No! No! - The Declaration of Independence was not a Constitution forming the United States of America. It was just 12 individual Colonies declaring their Independence using the name United States of America on July 4, 1776. New York did make it unanimous until July 9th. Today independent states or nations like France, Italy, Germany and others are doing the same name thing by calling themselves the European Union.

It wasn't until November 15th, 1777, in York Pennsylvania that the 13 independent States formed a "Perpetual Union" with a constitution called the Articles of Confederation that named the new country "the United States of America."

November 15th, 1777 - Happy Birthday to the Perpetual Union of the United States of America!

Background Screen Shots Change: *Declaration of Independence - European Union Flag, Euros, York Courthouse Medallion – Articles of Confederation.*

(Actor 5 enters on Actor 4's "USA," interrupting:)

Actor 5: Now **you** got that all wrong too! The 1777 constitution required all 13 States to ratify the new Articles of Confederation, in order to form the new sovereign nation, the United States of America. This wasn't done until the last State, Maryland finally agreed to the Articles. On March 1, 1781, after Maryland finally agreed, Congress commenced the new republic and there was a great celebration in Philadelphia. The Pennsylvania Gazette reported:

"The ratification of the constitution was immediately announced to the public by the discharge of the artillery on land, and the cannon of the shipping in the river Delaware. At two o'clock his Excellency the President of United States in Congress Assembled received on this occasion the congratulations of the Hon. the Minister of France, and of the Legislative and Executive Bodies of Pennsylvania, of the Civil and Military Officers, sundry strangers of distinction in town, and of many of the principal inhabitants.

The evening was closed by an elegant exhibition of fireworks. The Ariel frigate, commanded by the gallant John Paul Jones, fired a feu de joye, and was beautifully decorated with a variety of streamers in the day, and ornamented with a brilliant appearance of lights in the night."

March 1st, 1781: Happy Birthday USA!

Background Screen Shots Change: *Articles of Confederation – Samuel Huntington Medallion – Fireworks – Ship -*

(Actor 6 enters on Actor 5's "USA," interrupting:)

Actor 6: You all have to be kidding!

There was still a war to win in 1781. Except for France, Spain and the Dutch -- who all loathed the British for taking their land in America -- practically the entire world agreed that the so-called "United States of America" were nothing more than 13 Rebel Colonies still belonging to Great Britain.

It wasn't until September 3, 1783, when Benjamin Franklin, John Jay and John Adams negotiated the Treaty of Paris with Great Britain, that we became a free and independent nation recognized by the entire world.

September 3rd, 1783 - Happy Birthday USA!

Background Shots: *Revolutionary War shot death of Joseph Warren - Spain France Holland Map - British Empire - Treaty of Paris – spinning world globe.*

(Actor 7 enters on Actor 6's "USA," interrupting:)

Actor 7: Yeah, right - March 1st and September 3rd are our birthdays? Elias Boudinot and Samuel Huntington are the first Presidents? Pshaw!

Come on! The United States Republic really began on the day the Philadelphia Convention delegates passed our current U.S. Constitution: September 17th, 1787.

You know the "We the People" document that formed the current government of the United States? Well, everyone knows George Washington was the 1st President of the United States and it was under the 1787 constitution.

September 17th, 1787: Happy Birthday USA!

Background Screen Shots Change: *Independence Hall - Elias Boudinot -- Samuel Huntington - US Constitution of 1787 -- George Washington Gold Dollar - Betsy Ross Flag*

(Actor 8 enters on Actor 7's "USA," interrupting:)

Actor 8: What do you mean September 17th 1787? George Washington didn't take the Oath of office until 1789 and Arthur St. Clair was the President of the United States under the Articles of Confederation in 1787.

More importantly, Cyrus Griffin was the Articles of Confederation U.S. President when New Hampshire became 9th State to ratify and formally enact the new constitution on July 2nd, 1788.

July 2, 1788: Happy Birthday USA!

Background Screen Shots Change: *Washington taking the Oath of Office - Arthur St. Clair - Cyrus Griffin - New Hampshire - Great Seal by Thomson.*

(Actor 3 enters on Actor 8's "USA," interrupting:)

Actor 3: No, you are wrong; our current constitution was ratified by New Hampshire on June 28th and not July 2, 1788. Congress only *adopted* the constitution on July 2nd, so the U.S. Constitutional birthdate is June 28th, 1788, not July 2nd, 1788.

Background Screen Shots Change: *New Hampshire Coin - United States in Congress Assembled*

(Actor 7 enters after Actor 3's "2nd," interrupting:)

Actor 7: Yes, that is true but the 1788 government, while they were still meeting in Fraunces Tavern, passed a resolution dissolving the old Articles of Confederation government and started the U.S. Republic on March 4th, 1789. Happy Birthday USA!

Background Screen Shots Change: *United States in Congress Assembled*

(Actor 5 enters after Actor 8's "1789," interrupting:)

Actor 5: Wait a second! Are we saying the Continental Congress first started the United States in 1774 in a Philadelphia Tavern and the United States in Congress Assembled ended it in a New York City Tavern called Fraunces?

Background Screen Shots Change: *Philadelphia City Tavern - Fraunces Tavern*

(Actor 1 enters after Actor 5's "Fraunces")

Actor 1: That's right. The Continental Congress first caucused the government at the Philadelphia Tavern and the USA confederation government faded away in a New York Tavern. Tavern to Tavern: now that's setting the bar.

Background Screen Shots Change: *Forgotten Capitols Painting - Drinking Old Tavern Scenes.*

(Actor 4 enters after Actor 5's "bar" :)

Actor 4: I don't know about taverns or bars but the first constitution, the Articles of Confederation, required all 13 States to ratify our current constitution before the confederation was dissolved. The last State, Rhode Island, didn't ratify the Constitution until May 29th, 1790. Only then were the other States released from the Articles of Confederation constitution and "We the People" become a unified 13 State nation under the current constitution.

Happy Birthday USA - May 29th,1790 !

Background Screen Shots Change: *Articles of Confederation - Articles of Confederation article XIII - Rhode Island Quarter*

(Actors 1 through 8 start arguing, with each saying their "respective date" was the true US Birthday. Loud – gentle pushing – hugging from behind – messing up hair -- Laughter.)

Black out. Exit actors.

Background Screen Shots Change: *Happy Birthdays USA Book Cover*

_(Enter 4 actors holding a "Land of the Free Because of the Brave" Flag)

Actor 1: September 4th, 1774.

Actor 3: July 4th, 1776.

Actor 5: September 3rd, 1783.

Actor 7: September 17th, 1787.

All four together: Happy Birthdays, USA! Thank you, troops, for our Freedom.

Background Screen Shots Change: Independence Hall

APPENDIX

Webb County Heritage Museum Announces an Unprecedented Exhibition:
AMERICA'S FOUR REPUBLICS: THE MORE OR LESS UNITED STATES

The Webb County Heritage Foundation and Ms. Toni L. Ruiz will present an exhibit of rare historic documents to be displayed at the Villa Antigua® Border Heritage Museum, 810 Zaragoza Street, from January 21 – February 24, 2015. *"America's Four Republics: The More or Less United States,"* depicts America's political evolution from 1774 to 1791 and reveals four distinctly different United American Republics. To commemorate the exhibit opening, the public is invited to a Gallery Talk and Reception at the Villa Antigua® Border Heritage Museum at 6:00 pm on Wednesday, January 21st followed by a book signing.

The key storytellers of the exhibit will be more than one hundred rare and original 18th-, 19th-, and 20th-century documents, manuscripts, and letters from the United Colonies of America (1774-1776), the Thirteen Independent States United in Congress (1776-1781), the United States of America under the Articles of Confederation (1781 -1787), and We the People of the United States (1789-Present) under the 1787 U.S. Constitution and its 1789 Bill of Rights.

The priceless documents are on loan to the museum from the collection of nationally renowned author and historian, Stanley Klos who, along with Dr. Naomi Yavneh Klos of Loyola University New Orleans, led the team that assembled the exhibit. "There was no precedent when the representatives of the American colonies first convened at Carpenters Hall in Philadelphia in 1774," said Klos. "Despite their distrust of centralized authority, these revolutionaries created three distinct republics that each had significant weaknesses, but were the best that could be achieved in their moment. It took a fourth attempt, with the U.S. Constitution of 1787 supplemented by the 1789 Bill of Rights, to finally create a workable system. Our goal is to create an exhibit that familiarizes our visitors with the 15-year nation building process that ultimately created the United States of America and its evolution via the U.S. Constitution amendment process," he said.

Among the most notable exhibition highlights are: the first magazine printing of the US Constitution of 1787; an 18th Century printing of the 12 Amendments proposed by the 1789 Congress, of which ten were passed as the Bill of Rights; unique Revolutionary War and U.S. Founding letters, documents, and broadsides by George Washington, John Adams, Thomas Jefferson, Elias Boudinot, John Jay and other leaders; 19th- and 20th-Century printings, letters and documents related to U.S. Constitutional Amendments 11-27; and many other original documents from the Continental Congress, United States in Congress Assembled, U.S. Presidents, signers of the Declaration of Independence, signers of the Articles of Confederation and current U.S. Constitution.

In 1983, upon the discovery of 18th Century Philadelphia shipping records in his attic, Klos began to research and exhibit historic documents. Since then, he has amassed an impressive collection of rare documents which have headlined special exhibits at numerous universities, national historic sites, libraries, and museums. His work has also appeared in hundreds of print and digital publications including History Channel's *Brad Meltzer's Decoded, The Declaration of Independence, U.S. News & World Report* 2006 cover story, "Washington? Get In Line," and the Discovery Channel *s Unsolved History: Plots To Kill Lincoln.* Klos has authored five books: *President Who? Forgotten Founders, The Rise of the U.S. Presidency and the Forgotten Capitols, Happy Birthdays USA, Economic Home Runs,* and *America's Four Republics: The More or Less United States.*

During the month of February, Klos will also present talks and student debates at Laredo Community College, Texas A & M International University, United Independent School District, and United Day School. At the conclusion of the exhibit, Laredo Community College will host a free public lecture by Klos on Tuesday, February 24th at 6:30 pm at the Martinez Fine Arts Center on the subject of "America's Forgotten Presidents." This lecture will be a fascinating examination of the 14 men who were elected and served as our nation's Heads of State prior to the 1789 inauguration of George Washington. The talk will trace the evolution of the U.S. Presidency from the Colonial Continental Congress' unicameral government to the current Chief Executive whose role is quite distinct from the legislative and judicial branches of government. All those who attend the presentations will leave with a new appreciation for the contributions of the Presidential luminaries who preceded George Washington, the first President under the current constitution of the United States. A book signing will follow the lecture.

"People have to travel to Washington D.C. and visit the National Archives and Library of Congress to view a collection of U.S. founding documents of this caliber," explains Toni L. Ruiz, sponsor of the America's Four Republics Exhibit. "This is truly a big deal for Laredo and an incredible opportunity that I encourage everyone to take advantage of. The exhibit is important not only because the documents are national treasures, but because these primary sources tell the full story of the complex founding and continued political evolution of our great country."

Visitors can enjoy a range of new media and interactive experiences in conjunction with the "America's Four Republics" exhibit on display at the Villa Antigua® Border Heritage Museum at 810 Zaragoza St. in Laredo through February 24. Museum hours are Tuesday through Saturday from 9:00 am to 4:00 pm. Admission is $2.00. There is no admission charge on Tuesdays. For further information, contact the museum at 956-718-2727.

Library of Congress Hansonite Claims

It is essential that this Hansonite claim that the USCA of March 1st, 1781 to November 3rd, 1781, was not a true Articles of Confederation Congress be refute because it has most recently been sustained by not only by the already cited Maryland legislature, but by the Library of Congress itself. The *"Creating the United States: Road to the Constitution"* online primary source exhibit is an exceptional work by the librarians except for the fact that three primary source modules state that John Hanson was the first person to serve as President under the Articles of Confederation.

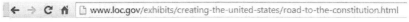

Creating the United States
Road to the Constitution

Home | Exhibition Overview | Exhibition Items | Public Programs | Learn More | Special Presentations | Acknowledgments

Sections: Creating the Declaration of Independence | Creating the United States Constitution | Creating the Bill of Rights

« Return to Creating the United States Constitution List   Next Section: Convention and Ratification »

Articles of Confederation Ratified

The Articles of Confederation and Perpetual Union was the first constitution of the United States. After more than a year of consideration, it was submitted to the states for ratification in 1777, but not enough states approved it until 1781. The Articles provided for a weak executive branch, no national power of taxation, and voting by states. On November 5, 1781, John Hanson (1715–1783) of Maryland was elected the first president under the Articles of Confederation.

A R T I C L E S
O F
CONFEDERATION
A N D
PERPETUAL UNION

[United States Continental Congress]. *Articles of Confederation and Perpetual Union Between the States of . . .* Williamsburg, Virginia: J. Dixon & W. Hunter, 1778. Rare Book and Special Collections Division, Library of Congress (048.04.00) [Digital ID# us0048_04]

Bookmark this item: http://www.loc.gov/exhibits/creating-the-united-states/road-to-the-constitution.html#obj2

Module: *Articles of Confederation Ratified* - The Articles of Confederation and Perpetual Union was the first constitution of the United States. After more than a year of consideration, it was submitted to the states for ratification in 1777, but not enough states approved it until 1781. The Articles provided for a weak executive branch, no national power of taxation, and voting by states. On November 5, 1781, John Hanson (1715–1783) of Maryland was elected the first president under the Articles of Confederation. [296]

Articles of Confederation Ratified

After Maryland's ratification established the Articles of Confederation as the first United States constitution, Thomas Rodney (1744–1811), a delegate to the Continental Congress from Delaware, recorded in his diary on March 1, 1781, that "the Completion of this grand Union & Confederation was announced by Firing thirteen Cannon on the Hill" in Philadelphia. John Hanson (1715–1783), a delegate from Maryland, was elected the first president of the confederation government.

Thomas Rodney. Diary entry, March 1, 1781. Rodney Family Papers, Manuscript Division, Library of Congress (48.00.00) [Digital ID# us0048, us0048_1, us0048_2, us0048_3, us0048_4]

Bookmark this item: http://www.loc.gov/exhibits/creating-the-united-states/road-to-the-constitution.html#obj2b

---

Module: *Articles of Confederation Ratified II* - After Maryland's ratification established the Articles of Confederation as the first United States constitution, Thomas Rodney (1744–1811), a delegate to the Continental Congress from Delaware, recorded in his diary on March 1, 1781, that "the Completion of this grand Union & Confederation was announced by Firing thirteen Cannon on the Hill" in Philadelphia. John Hanson (1715–1783), a delegate from Maryland, was elected the first president of the confederation government. [297]

---

[296] Library of Congress Exhibitions, Creating the United States: Road to the Constitution, http://www.loc.gov/exhibits/creating-the-united-states/road-to-the-constitution.html, retrieved on December 25th, 2014.
[297] Ibid.

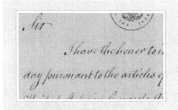
Module: *Confederation Congress Elects Its First President* - In this November 5, 1781 letter, Charles Thomson (1729-1824), secretary of the Continental Congress, informs George Washington that John Hanson (1715–1783), a delegate from Maryland, was elected the first president of Congress under the Articles of Confederation. Washington was in York, Virginia, overseeing the final details of the Cornwallis Surrender and preparing the army for their move North. Some people claim that John Hanson rather than George Washington should be considered the first president. [298]

Disseminating U.S. Founding misinformation by the State Maryland is objectionable but to have this same misinformation adopted and purported by the Library of Congress at taxpayers' expense is unequivocally intolerable.

---

[298] Ibid.

INDEX

I

Iredell, James, 123

J

Jay, John, 25, 44, 50, 92, 93, 94, 99, 102, 120, 122, 136, 138, 139, 142, 143, 149, 154, 155, 179, 180

Jefferson, Thomas, 19, 20, 32, 45, 47, 98, 106, 124, 132, 138, 155, 156

John Hanson, 7, 8, 26, 66, 68, 70, 91, **126**, 150, 151, 159, 160, 161

Black Moor, 160

Johnson, Samuel, 126

Judiciary Act, 139, 154

K

Kean, John, 107

Kennedy, John F., 27

King George III, 19, **45**, 93, 98, 100, 125

King, Rufus, 107, 115, 116, 117

Klos Yavneh Collection, 21, 25, 26, 60, 77

Knox, Henry, 137, 156

L

L'Enfant, Pierre-Charles, 134

Lafayette, Marquis de, 35

Laurens, Henry, 35, 37, 39, 40, 50, 93, 111, 149, 171

Lee, Richard Henry, 12, 25, 96, 107, 115, 116, 118, **126**, 150, 179

Library of Congress, 8, 14, 20, **27**, 37, 68, 111, 166, 195

Lincoln, Abraham

Emancipation Proclamation, 26, 27

Lincoln, Benjamin, **105**, 142, 143, 156

Livingston, Robert R., 93, 122, 134, 155

M

Madison, James, 8, 11, 12, 24, 47, 101, 107, 110, 111, 113, 115, 116, 117, 119, 120, 121, 122, 123, 124, 131, 135, 140

Madison, Dolley, 111

Maryland, 13, 18, 19, 31, 32, 34, **37**, 40, 43, 54, 55, 56, 59, 68, 69, 92, 93, 99, 101, 102, 105, 112, 120, **127**, 130, 131, 143, 146, 147, 148, 157, 172, 173, 177, 195

Annapolis, 95, 98, 101, 102, 105, 106, 172, 177, 179, 180, 187

Baltimore, 34, 50, **126**, 133, 164, 165, 166, 187

Mason, George, 121

Massachusetts, 14, 18, 19, 26, 34, **36**, 40,